Tolley
Employment
Handbook

CW00430021

Practice, procedure
and strategies for success

by
John-Paul Waite
with Barry Isted and Alan Payne

TM

Tolley
LexisNexis™

Members of the Lexis/Nexis Group worldwide

United Kingdom	LexisNexis Butterworths Tolley, a Division of Reed Elsevier (UK) Ltd, 2 Addiscombe Road, CROYDON CR9 5AF
Argentina	LexisNexis Argentina, BUENOS AIRES
Australia	LexisNexis Butterworths, CHATSWOOD, New South Wales
Austria	LexisNexis Verlag ARD Orac GmbH & Co KG, VIENNA
Canada	LexisNexis Butterworths, MARKHAM, Ontario
Chile	LexisNexis Chile Ltda, SANTIAGO DE CHILE
Czech Republic	Nakladatelstvi Orac sro, PRAGUE
France	Editions du Juris-Classeur SA PARIS
Hong Kong	LexisNexis Butterworths, HONG KONG
Hungary	Hvg Orac, BUDAPEST
India	LexisNexis Butterworths, NEW DELHI
Ireland	Butterworths (Ireland) Ltd, DUBLIN
Italy	Giuffré Editoré, MILAN
Malaysia	Malayan Law Journal Sdn Bhd, KUALA LUMPUR
New Zealand	LexisNexis Butterworths, WELLINGTON
Poland	Wydawnictwa Prawnicze PWN, WARSAW
Singapore	LexisNexis Butterworths, SINGAPORE
South Africa	Butterworths SA, DURBAN
Switzerland	Stämpfli Verlag AG, BERNE
USA	LexisNexis, DAYTON, Ohio

A CIP Catalogue record for this book is available from the British Library.

ISBN 0 754 514 889

Typeset by Wyvern 21, Bristol
Printed and bound in Great Britain by Hobbs the Printers Ltd, Totton, Hampshire

Visit Butterworths LexisNexis *direct* at www.butterworths.com

Other books from Tolley

About the Author and Co-authors

John-Paul Waite
John-Paul Waite is a practising barrister and member of the specialist employment law team at Field Court Chambers (www.FieldCourtChambers.com). He has extensive experience acting for both employers and employees in all areas of employment law. In January 2002, he was appointed to the panel of Treasury Counsel.

Barry Isted FCB, FCMI
Barry Isted is an HR consultant and company director specialising in employment law and corporate communications. An employment tribunal member since 1984, including many years on the Race Panel at London Central, he has been a director of corporate publishers Chandler Gooding since 1993.

After an early career in business journalism and film production he worked in management education, industrial relations and international HR strategy, including 11 years as personnel director of De La Rue plc. Among various former appointments and directorships he was a governor of the London Business School and president of the British Association of Communicators in Business.

Alan Payne
Alan Payne is a practising barrister and member of the specialist employment law team at 199 Strand (www.199Strand.co.uk). He has extensive experience acting for both employers and employees in the employment law field. He is fluent in French and Italian. Prior to joining the Bar in 1996, he worked abroad for a number of years as a lawyer for Heinz PLC.

Glossary

ACAS	Advisory, Conciliation and Arbitration Service
All ER	All England Law Reports
CA	Court of Appeal
CBI	Confederation of British Industry
CPR	Civil Procedure Rules
DDA	Disability Discrimination Act 1995
EAT	Employment Appeal Tribunal
ECJ	European Court of Justice
EDT	Effective date of termination
EPCA	Employment Protection (Consolidation) Act 1978
ERA	Employment Rights Act 1996
ETA	Employment Tribunals Act 1996
ETS	Employment Tribunals Service
FRU	Free Representation Unit
HL	House of Lords
ICR	Industrial Cases Reports
IRLR	Industrial Relations Law Reports
IT1	Employee's originating application, including grounds of complaint
IT3	Employer's notice of appearance, including grounds of resistance
NIRC	National Industrial Relations Court
PHD form	Preliminary Hearing Directions form (EAT)
PHR	Pre-hearing review
RRA	Race Relations Act 1976
SDA	Sex Discrimination Act 1975
TUC	Trades Union Congress
TULR(C)A	Trade Union and Labour Relations (Consolidation) Act 1992

Contents

Table of Cases

Table of Statutes

Table of Statutory Instruments

1.

Tribunals Today

Introduction [1.1]

If popularity is a test of success, employment tribunals (formerly called industrial tribunals) have passed with flying colours. The number of applications made to tribunals hear each year (currently around 112,000 of which two-thirds may be settled or withdrawn before a hearing) has surely exceeded the expectations of the legislators who created them in 1964.

At the heart of tribunals' growing popularity lie a number of factors:

- the limited circumstances in which an unsuccessful party can have a costs award made against it;

- the relative informality of proceedings;

- the lifting of the maximum cap on compensation in unfair dismissal cases, and its removal altogether in discrimination cases;

- the increased number of claims which the tribunal has jurisdiction to hear;

- the restricted avenues of appeal from a tribunal's factual findings; and

- the growing consciousness of workplace rights and obligations.

The popularity of tribunals, and the massive administrative burden which that popularity brings on the system, is a factor that parties should bear in mind when conducting their case. Chairmen are usually inundated with letters and applications from parties ranging from such matters as applications for postponement, further particulars, disclosure, preliminary hearings, pre-hearing reviews and strike outs. If a party displays an accurate knowledge of practice and procedure, and sets out its position in a clear and persuasive way, this will give them a head start when communicating with the tribunal, whether orally or in writing. This book is intended to assist in that process. It is a guide to how tribunals operate and the powers at their disposal. It is not a guide to the substantive law of employment, for which parties should consult *Tolley's Employment Handbook*.

Tribunals: the industrial jury [1.2]

Tribunals have been described by the higher courts as 'Industrial Juries' (see *Sutcliffe and anor v Big C's Marine and ors [1998] IRLR 428*). This reflects:

- Their composition (see **1.3**).

- Their knowledge and experience of the workplace – normally from the first hand experience of the two lay members, sometimes also from chairmen whose careers may have included periods in industry and commerce.

- The extensive latitude that they are afforded, provided they properly apply the law, to decide issues of fact.

Different tribunals may well take contrasting views of the same factual situation, introducing a strong element of unpredictability into their proceedings. At the same time, however, most tribunals are likely to be:

- knowledgeable about what constitutes good working practices and procedures;

- (in terms of the lay members) themselves experienced in the reality of putting such practices and procedures into effect.

The importance that tribunals attach to good practice and procedure by the employer is one of the keys to understanding the way in which they operate. The type of issues that the employer should address to meet a tribunal's concerns are covered in CHAPTER 2 – TROUBLE AHEAD?

Composition of tribunals [1.3]

A full tribunal consists of a chairman and two lay members. The chairman must be a solicitor or barrister of not less than seven years standing who is appointed by the Lord Chancellor. The two lay members are drawn from each side of industry. One is nominated by an employers' organisation (usually the CBI) and the other by an employees' organisation (usually the TUC).

The role of the chairman [1.4]

The role of the chairman is to preside over (or chair) proceedings. This means that, during the course of a hearing, he will:

- be the person (other than where the witnesses are asked questions by the lay members) who speaks to the parties;

- introduce the parties to the tribunal at the outset of the case;

- actively manage the hearing to ensure that it is conducted in accordance with the rules of natural justice;

- if a decision of the tribunal is given orally, deliver that decision;

- draft the written reasons of the tribunal;

- advise the lay members of the tribunal on the law, although a decision on a legal issue remains one for the tribunal as a whole.

In a three-person tribunal, the chairman's vote carries no greater weight than that of either of the lay members.

The role of the lay members [1.5]

The lay members will usually not speak during a hearing other than to ask questions of witnesses upon completion of their evidence. The lay members' role is not confined to deciding issues of fact. Whilst, on matters of law, they may be reluctant to depart from guidance they are given by the chairman, sometimes their practical knowledge will be relevant in deciding such issues. This is demonstrated most vividly by the fact that appeals from employment tribunals are heard by the Employment Appeal Tribunal (EAT), which is *solely* concerned with issues of law, but which still consists of a lawyer and two lay members. A former President of that tribunal, Mr Justice Wood, remarked that lay members 'sit not as assessors but as full members of the court...'.

Does the tribunal need to be unanimous? [1.6]

The answer to this question is 'no.' A 2:1 majority decision is sufficient. Where there is a majority decision, the written reasons for the decision, drafted by the chairman, will set out both the majority and the minority view. This requires the chairman, in drafting his decision, to accurately reflect both his own view and the view of the member/s with whom he is in disagreement.

Chairman sitting alone [1.7]

The vast majority of claims which a tribunal has jurisdiction to hear must be determined by a three-person tribunal. A chairman may, however, sit alone in a number of situations, including to:

- give directions under *rule 4* of the *Employment Tribunals (Constitution and Rules of Procedure) Regulations 2001 (SI 2001/1171)* and conduct a directions hearing;

- conduct a preliminary hearing under *rule 6*;
- conduct a pre-hearing review under *rule 7*;
- consider whether to strike out a claim under *rule 15(2)(c) (d)* or *(e)*;
- consider whether to grant an extension of time under *rule 17*;

In addition, there are a number of specific claims which can actually be determined by a chairman (see *section 4(2)* and *(3)* of the *Employment Tribunals Act 1996 (ETA 1996)*). These do not include unfair dismissal or discrimination cases.

The chairman's power to sit alone is discretionary. In exercising that discretion, he must consider whether the assistance of lay members is required. Under the current rules, a chairman will seek to give effect to the overriding objective in deciding this issue. As stated above, there are a number of legal issues where the input of lay members might be of assistance. The EAT has held that its assistance is necessary in disputes over whether a person is an employee and a decision, in a discrimination case, as to whether to extend time under just and equitable principles (see *Sutcliffe*).

Two-member tribunals [1.8]

A two-member tribunal is only permitted to sit with the agreement of both parties. The need for a two-member tribunal usually arises when one of the lay members either falls ill or is otherwise indisposed. Both parties have an absolute right to object and insist upon three members hearing the case. A decision to proceed without obtaining such consent will render the decision liable to be set aside upon appeal (*Quenchers Ltd v McShane EAT 514/92*). Where a two-member tribunal sits, and each is in disagreement, the chairman will carry the casting vote. In other words, a two-member tribunal gives considerably more power to the chairman.

The rules under which tribunals operate [1.9]

Unlike the civil courts, tribunals are 'creatures of statute'. This means that they were created by an act of Parliament, and that all the powers they have derive from legislation (whether acts of Parliament or statutory instruments). The current act (superseding previous acts) under which the tribunals derive their power is the *ETA 1996*. The introduction to that Act reads as follows:

> 'The Secretary of State may by regulations make provision for the establishment of tribunals to be known as employment tribunals (*ETA 1996, s 1(1)*).'

Within those words can be seen the key importance of regulations in tribunal proceedings. The Act, apart from dealing with the composition of tribunals and issues of jurisdiction, simply highlights the various areas in which regulations can be made. It is the regulations themselves that govern how tribunals operate. The current regulations in place are the *Employment Tribunals (Constitution and Rules of Procedure) Regulations 2001.* Most of the relevant rules of procedure are contained in *Schedule 1* to those regulations, although there are a number of important provisions (including the overriding objective) contained in the main body of the regulations. **Reference to 'the rules' in this book means the rules contained in *Schedule 1* of the 2001 Regulations.**

The overriding objective [1.10]

Regulation 10 of the 2001 Regulations requires the tribunal to give effect to the overriding objective when exercising any of its powers under the regulations. This is a provision which came into effect for the first time with the 2001 Regulations, and which is sufficiently important to justify a chapter of its own in this book (see CHAPTER 9 – FAIRNESS: THE OVERRIDING OBJECTIVE). The overriding objective will be a familiar concept to those experienced in the civil courts. It provides a consistent set of principles to which the tribunal must seek to give effect when exercising all of its procedural powers. The overriding objective of the rules is to enable tribunals to deal with cases justly. 'Dealing with the case justly' is stated in *regulation 10(2)* to include the following principles:

- by ensuring the parties are on an equal footing;

- saving expense;

- dealing with cases in ways proportionate to the complexity of the issues;

- ensuring that the case is dealt with fairly and expeditiously.

In relation to procedural case law *predating* the overriding objective, the tribunals may continue to have regard to it, but their first task is to give effect to the overriding objective. If they decide that the previous case law is inconsistent with the overriding objective, the latter must take precedence. This is because the previous case law was decided without reference to the overriding objective (see **1.14**). Overall, the introduction of the overriding objective is a welcome innovation in tribunal proceedings, increasing their comprehensibility and accessibility.

Claims a tribunal can hear [1.11]

The *types* of claim a tribunal has the power (or 'jurisdiction') to hear are *not* set out in the 2001 Regulations or the *ETA 1996*. They are contained in a number of other statutes that create the right to pursue that claim in the first place. So, the right at law not to be unfairly dismissed is contained in *section 94* of the *Employment Rights Act 1996* (*ERA 1996*), whilst the right to bring a claim of unfair dismissal to a tribunal is contained in *section 111* of the same Act. Similarly, the prohibition against sex discrimination (in an employment context) is contained in *section 6* of the *Sex Discrimination Act 1975* (with the definition of discrimination in *section 1* of that Act), whilst *section 63* of the Act provides for the right to complain of sex discrimination to an employment tribunal. Parties should note that tribunals now have jurisdiction to hear certain matters which were previously the sole domain of the civil courts. Notable amongst them are claims for breach of contract arising from or being outstanding upon the termination of the employment of the employee. The right to bring the case to a tribunal, however, is still created by statute, in this case the *ETA 1996, s 3* and the *Employment Tribunals Extension of Jurisdiction (England and Wales) Order 1994 (SI 1994/1623)*.

Most people associate tribunals with claims for unfair dismissal and discrimination, matters that still dominate their workload. There are, however, numerous others that a tribunal can determine.

A full list of the ever increasing number of claims that a tribunal in England and Wales has jurisdiction to consider are contained in APPENDIX I: CLAIMS A TRIBUNAL CAN HEAR. For ease of reference, the table also sets out:

- the length of employment an employee is required to have before they are entitled to bring a specific claim ('the qualifying period'); and

- the time limits within which a claim needs to be brought before the tribunal.

The tribunal's discretion to extend the prescribed time limits, referred to only briefly in footnotes, is discussed in more depth in CHAPTER 6 – TIME LIMITS.

Since tribunals derive their jurisdiction (or power to hear a claim) entirely from statute, they have no powers other than those conferred on them by Parliament. In practical terms, this means that, unless a statutory provision specifically permits a claim to be brought before a tribunal, a tribunal simply has no power to hear the matter. Even where a tribunal has discretion as to whether or not it can hear a case, the criteria that it must apply in reaching its decision will be provided for by statute or rules. Tribunals, in fact, have no inherent or residual jurisdiction.

Any decision of a tribunal acting outside its jurisdiction is null and void, irrespective of whether or not lack of jurisdiction was raised as an issue during the proceedings. So, for example, where, due to lack of available space, a tribunal held a hearing in a room marked 'private' and with a door that could not be opened from the outside, the Court of Appeal held that the tribunal had no jurisdiction to hear the case (*Storer v British Gas Plc (IDS Brief 659) [2000] ICR 603*). The Court of Appeal was of the view that since the rules require any hearing to take place in public (except in a number of limited circumstances, none of which were applicable on the facts of this case), the tribunal had no jurisdiction to hold a hearing in private. The case was therefore sent back to be reheard in public.

Jurisdiction to hear contractual claims [1.12]

Since the mid 1990s tribunals have had jurisdiction to hear a breach of contract claim if it arises or is outstanding on the termination of employment (see the *Employment Tribunals Extension of Jurisdiction (England and Wales) Order 1994*). However, only certain breaches of contract can be dealt with by the tribunal (claims relating to intellectual property rights are, for example, specifically excluded). It is important to note that tribunals do not have jurisdiction to hear breach of contract claims where the claim was lodged prior to the termination of an employee's contract (*Capek v Lincolnshire (Brief 664) [2000] ICR 878*).

Territorial jurisdiction [1.13]

Pursuant to *regulation 11(5)* of the 2001 Regulations, which came into effect on 16 July 2001, tribunals only have jurisdiction to hear cases where:

- the respondent or one of the respondents resides or carries on business in England or Wales; or

- had the remedy been by way of action in the county court, the cause of action would have arisen wholly or partly in England or Wales; or

- the proceedings are to determine a question which has been referred to the tribunal by a court in England or Wales.

For the purposes of these regulations a company is considered to 'reside' in England or Wales where:

- it has a registered office in either region (*Odeco (UK) Inc v Peacham [1979] ICR 823, EAT –* where a company had its operational base outside of England but its registered office in London, as confirmed by the records at Companies House, was held to reside in the UK. NB – a list of all companies with registered offices in England is held at Companies House); or

- where it can be established that a company 'carries on business' in England or Wales.

A recent example of where a tribunal accepted jurisdiction on the basis that a company carried on business in England, was a claim involving cabin personnel, who flew to and from England, but who were employed by a US airline. The tribunal accepted jurisdiction notwithstanding that the US companies registered office was abroad.

The status of case law in tribunal proceedings [1.14]

A tribunal's place in the court hierarchy can be summarised as follows:

Employment tribunals > Employment Appeal Tribunal > Court of Appeal > House of Lords > European Court of Justice.

Each court in this chain is bound by the decision of the court/s above it. Where there is a conflict between the decision of a lower and higher court, the decision of the latter always takes precedence. Thus a tribunal is bound to follow a decision of the Court of Appeal who in turn must follow a decision of the House of Lords. Where there is a conflict between the decision of the EAT and a higher court, for example the Court of Appeal, the latter takes precedence. Where two decisions in the same court (whether EAT, Court of Appeal or House of Lords) conflict with each other, tribunals have a choice as to which one to follow. Note, however, that the EAT, Court of Appeal and House of Lords will strive to avoid such conflicts occurring.

In an employment context, case law is predominately concerned with interpreting and construing legislation in circumstances where there is doubt as to what it means. So, for example, there is an enormous volume of case law that interprets the unfair dismissal provisions contained in *section 94* of the *ERA 1996*. Tribunals are bound by this case law. Note, however, that Parliament is entitled to introduce new legislation reversing, revising or superseding that interpretation. Thus the overriding objective in the new procedural rules takes precedence over decisions made before it came into effect. There are also areas, for example in relation to the requirements of natural justice, where the rules are silent, and the parties will have to look to case law to extract the relevant principles.

How to obtain and search for relevant case law [1.15]

For those who are not qualified lawyers, this can be a daunting process. A sensible first port of call is to obtain a relevant textbook. So, for practice and procedure, this book can be used as a starting point, pointing the reader in the direction of relevant statutes and cases. On the substantive law, a reader might have regard to *Tolley's Employment Handbook*. The textbooks will give appropriate references for the authority relied upon. Where for, example, a reference to a case is given as *[1979] IRLR 415*, this refers to the *Industrial Relations Law Reports*, 1979, page 415. A list of the relevant abbreviations will be given, usually at the beginning of the book. To obtain any piece of legislation, one of the simplest means, if the reader has Internet access, is to access the HMSO website (www.hmso.gov.uk). With case law, there are two choices: either to buy the relevant reports, usually at considerable expense, or to access them via a public library or other relevant source. It may be that a local service, such as a Citizens Advice Bureau, or ACAS, will be able to advise on how to obtain such material (see **CHAPTER 3 – GETTING ADVICE**). In referring to authorities in the tribunal, parties can reasonably expect the tribunal to have relevant statutory authorities available to them. In terms of cases, it is good practice to have copies of authorities for each member of the tribunal and the other side. If this is not possible, the tribunal should at least be given the name and reference for the authority.

The nature of tribunal proceedings today

Public or private? [1.16]

The vast majority of tribunal proceedings are required to be held in public. The exceptions are dealt with in **CHAPTER 23 – PRIVATE HEARINGS AND RESTRICTED REPORTING ORDERS**. This means that any member of the public can observe a tribunal hearing taking place, and indeed doing so is one of the best means of becoming familiar with proceedings. There is no restriction, other than in the limited circumstances described in **CHAPTER 23**, upon proceedings being reported, and there is frequently at least one reporter at a particular centre obtaining details of the cases being heard.

Formal or informal? [1.17]

The absence of wigs and gowns, the fact that everyone is seated at all times and the right of any person to appear (either on behalf of themselves or someone else) in tribunal proceedings all contribute to an atmosphere of informality. In other respects, however, tribunals are quite like civil courts. Hearings follow a similar structure (see **CHAPTER 20 – HEARING I: ORDER OF PROCEEDINGS**), with members of the tribunal asking testing questions of witnesses, and chairmen sometimes stopping parties (or their representatives) in the course of final submissions in order to deal with specific points.

Rule 11(1) requires the tribunal to, so far as it appears appropriate, seek to avoid formality in its proceedings. It further states that tribunals are not bound by the formal rules of evidence which apply to civil courts (for an explanation of the tribunal's approach to evidence, see CHAPTER 21 – HEARING II: THE CONDUCT OF PROCEEDINGS BY THE TRIBUNAL).

Tribunals strive to avoid an intimidating atmosphere and will generally assist unrepresented parties in understanding the law. At the same time, they have a wide range of procedural powers which parties must comply with. Further, they are not allowed to let informality undermine the principles of natural justice, such as giving each party a sufficient opportunity to prepare for the case it has to meet and to put its case (see CHAPTER 21).

Checklist – tribunals today

- If possible, go and observe tribunal proceedings taking place; they are open to the public and it is an invaluable way of getting familiar with how they operate.

- Recognise the importance of good practice and procedure in the workplace in most tribunal proceedings (see CHAPTER 2).

- Research the substantive law in the area in which the claim is brought.

- Consider whether there are any pre-claim requests for information which can be obtained from the other side (see CHAPTER 5 – PRE-CLAIM REQUESTS FOR INFORMATION).

- Have regard to whether the tribunal has jurisdiction to hear the type of claim in question (see).

- Consider whether there are any other jurisdictional requirements (e g twelve months' qualifying service in most non-discriminatory unfair dismissal claims).

- Keep in mind the short time limits for bringing claims (see CHAPTER 6 and APPENDIX I).

cont'd

- Think about the directions which the tribunal has the power to make before the full hearing (see CHAPTER 13 – DIRECTIONS AND DIRECTIONS HEARINGS).

- Prepare thoroughly for the full hearing.

- Familiarise yourself with how the full hearing will be conducted (see CHAPTER 20).

2.
Trouble Ahead?

Introduction [2.1]

This is a book predominately about tactics and procedures once an application to a tribunal has been made. It remains the case, however, that many disputes are won or lost before that stage. This chapter looks at some of the causes of employment disputes and at the basic steps which employers need to take to avoid successful claims. Employees should also have regard to this chapter to give an indication of the types of concerns that will be prominent in a tribunal's mind.

Origins of employment disputes [2.2]

For employees and employers alike, certain environments provide fertile ground for individual employment disputes. For example, where:

- internal procedures for dealing with grievances and disciplinary matters are non-existent, out of date and/or not clearly understood and applied by all members of staff;

- equal opportunities policies are either not in place or have been introduced without the necessary training or communication;

- accountabilities, job responsibilities and reporting lines are indistinct;

- contracts of employment, record keeping, payment systems and personnel administration in general are inadequate;

- individual employees or groups of employees have levels of absenteeism or poor timekeeping which far exceed the average of their colleagues;

- working conditions and facilities, including the tools provided, evoke widely felt discontent;

- decisions, attitudes and actions have led staff to lose trust and confidence in their managers;

- comments and attitudes are exhibited by management and staff which may be perceived as discriminatory.

In any company (but especially in one with the environmental defects described above) certain changes may trigger an employment dispute. It is particularly important that, if the employer intends to carry out such changes, it first ensures that the procedures are in place which adequately protect them from employment claims.

Events which may trigger a dispute include:

- management changes which, while designed to improve the company's efficiency, also introduce a new style, culture and standards;

- major structural changes arising from relocation, downsizing/ expansion, new processes and products and transfers of ownership;

- changes in working practices, options for flexibility, hours and payment scales;

- well publicised, if sometimes misreported, changes in the law (eg the working time regulations and minimum wage).

The foundations of success: strong practices and procedures [2.3]

For the employer, effective practices and procedures provide the armour necessary to successfully defend claims. For the employee, finding gaps in that armour will be the most likely route to success.

In the vast majority of unfair dismissal cases, the most direct issue for the tribunal will not be 'what did the employee do', but rather 'how did the employer respond?' and, in this, it will be both the quality of the employer's procedures and how it carried them out in practice which will be of fundamental importance. In cases of discrimination, the effectiveness of an internal grievance procedure will often be central.

Employers should ensure that, as an absolute minimum, they have procedures in place which deal with the following, all of which are covered by the ACAS Codes of Practice (see **2.4**):

- A grievance procedure: setting out a workable and accessible system whereby employees can complain about any aspect of their work and have that complaint investigated with appropriate action taken.

- A disciplinary procedure: setting out, as fully as possible, what is regarded as misconduct and gross misconduct and the procedures for dealing with each. A separate procedure should be adopted in relation to sickness.

- An equal opportunities policy which is communicated to all staff and is demonstrably taken seriously by the employer, for example through basic training and an effective grievance procedure.

The above is not an exhaustive list. For example, many employers will need to develop procedures relating to redundancy and relocation.

Considerations of good management practice aside, however, current and impending legislation will underline the requirement for proper disciplinary and grievance procedures, which the new *Employment Act 2002* will make compulsory. It is unlikely that these provisions in the Act will, due to their controversial impact on small employers, come in to force until late 2003. Details of the important new changes can be found in CHAPTER 29 – NEW DEVELOPMENTS: THE EMPLOYMENT ACT 2002. There is, at the time of publication, an ongoing consultation with representatives of business and employees. Those concerned about when the new provisions come into effect, and the final form which they are to take, would be advised to contact the Department of Trade and Industry, who have an office providing telephone advice to callers (Enquiry Unit tel: 020 7215 5000).

Formulating effective procedures: the Codes of Practice [2.4]

All employers, large and small, should have regard to the ACAS Code of Practice on 'Disciplinary Practice and Procedures in Employment'. Tribunals are required by law to take account of this code of practice in a relevant case, although technically the Code is not binding upon them. What does this mean in practice? In essence, the Code is the *benchmark* against which a tribunal will judge whether an employer has adopted a fair procedure. ACAS is also able to offer active advice to employers and their representatives on drawing up and implementing procedures, a facility which should be made use of (see CHAPTER 3 – GETTING ADVICE for contact details). For equal opportunities, a code of practice is published by the Equal Opportunities Commission, who are also able to offer advice. In relation to disability discrimination, a code is published by the Department for Education and Employment. Both codes are required to be taken in to account by tribunals in a relevant case. Contact details for obtaining the codes can be found in CHAPTER 3. For those acting for employees, the contents of the codes may provide useful ammunition when asserting that the employer has failed to adopt a fair procedure.

Do's and Don'ts

Do:

- Have regard to the model disciplinary and grievance procedures scheduled to the *Employment Act 2002* (and replicated in CHAPTER 29) which are likely to become compulsory at law.

- Set out clearly who the decision makers are and any rights of appeal.

- Enable employees to be informed at an early stage about problems with their performance and give them an opportunity to improve (not applicable to gross misconduct cases), with the offering of support if appropriate.

- In disciplinary cases, give employees advance notice of disciplinary charges and sufficient time and information to answer the case they have to meet.

- Provide for the carrying out of a thorough investigation, preferably by someone other than the decision maker (except with regard to grievances by employees, where both functions are often carried out by the same person).

- Require the decision maker to take account of all relevant considerations before making their decision, and if necessary postpone the decision pending further enquiries.

- Provide for disciplinary hearings to be conducted in accordance with principles of natural justice – for example the decision maker should be impartial and the employee given an opportunity to put their case and be accompanied.

- Require the decision maker not only to state what the decision is, but the reasons for that decision.

- Require accurate minutes of hearings to be kept, provided to the employee and signed by all parties.

- Adopt procedures which are clear, are not over elaborate, and are fully understood by those who apply it and use it.

Don't:

- Introduce a procedure without giving management thorough training in how to implement it.

- Fail to provide copies of procedures to all employee.

- Write a procedure without having reference to the relevant ACAS Code of Practice.

The role of evidence and note taking [2.5]

What appear at the time to be routine meetings and appraisals with staff can turn out at a later date to be important evidence in a dispute. Effective contemporaneous record taking greatly assists in proving to a tribunal that the employer's version of what took place at a particular meeting is accurate. Generally speaking, tribunals are more likely to expect employers (particularly large employers) to keep records of important meetings and events. Failure to do so could lead to that employer's version of events not being accepted.

Legal advisors will be familiar with the process of attendance notes, whereby they record interviews with clients. Employers should be encouraged to do the same thing by making brief notes of all discussions with employees relating to matters affecting their work and performance, together with any observations the employer may have. The amount of detail will vary. As a rule of thumb, the greater the element of controversy, the greater the need for detail.

Do's and Don'ts

Do:

- Ensure that handwritten or contemporaneous notes are timed, dated and retained in their original form.

- Make notes not just of meetings which took place, but of any decisions taken and the reasons for that decision.

- Wherever possible use a person not involved in the dispute (e g a secretary) to take minutes of important meetings and hearings.

- Submit minutes of disciplinary hearings to the employee who attended, asking them to comment within a specified period if they dispute the accuracy.

- Retain working diaries and appointments for some time after the end of the working year.

Don't:

- Make biased, self-serving or one-sided records – tribunals will spot it.

Note taking by employees [2.6]

Employees who feel that an issue has the potential to develop into a dispute should be encouraged to make full records themselves of meetings. Often, such entries can be made in a diary. In general, tribunals will be impressed by an employee who keeps a thorough diary of important events, even though the onus for record keeping is firmly placed on the employer.

What to do when your procedures are non-existent [2.7]

Despite the existence of employment tribunals for four decades, there are still a sizeable number of employers who have few, if any, relevant procedures in place for dealing with such matters as grievance and discipline. Such circumstances should not necessarily lead to despair on the part of the person advising them, who should bear the following in mind:

- If no formal procedures are in place, the essential requirement remains that the employer acts fairly and in accordance with the principles of natural justice.

- It is possible to carry out a fair procedure in a particular case even if the employer does not have formal written procedures. In deciding what procedure to adopt, employers should have regard both to the relevant ACAS code of conduct and the do's and don'ts box above.

- The type of standards applicable will vary enormously according to the size of the organisation concerned.

- Minor procedural flaws will frequently be overlooked by tribunals – overall fairness is their primary concern.

- If there is no formal grievance procedure, keep in mind the importance of taking complaints by employees seriously, investigating them promptly and keeping the employee informed.

- The importance of the employer's procedures will vary according to the type of claim. In unfair dismissal and most discrimination cases they are likely to be central.

Following the procedures which are in place [2.8]

There is little point in having a grievance procedure unless it is properly implemented. A number of employers fall into the error of having procedures (whether grievance or disciplinary) which lie 'on file', and

17

which are not properly understood or implemented. Such an approach can, in some circumstances, be worse than having no procedure at all. In an unfair dismissal case, an employer who fails to follow an important part of its own procedure will have difficulty in persuading the tribunal that the dismissal is fair. Likewise, failure to follow a grievance procedure can itself be a ground for constructive dismissal.

Tactics

- Tribunals are likely to penalise employers who fail to adopt fair procedures or properly carry out their own procedures.

- Use and consult ACAS in the development and implementation of procedures.

- Make notes of key events and meetings as they occur.

- Keep proper records of pay and attendance.

- Think through the legal implications of major structural change before carrying it out.

- If in doubt about the legality of a proposed measure, take advice.

- Remember that the key to dispute avoidance is strong and open communication between management and employees.

3.

Getting Advice

Introduction [3.1]

Three questions may spring to mind when it comes to the seeking of advice and representation. Do I need it? Where can I get it? How much will it cost? This chapter looks at the options both in terms of seeking general advice and securing representation in tribunal proceedings.

Do I really need advice? [3.2]

Employment tribunals are *intended* to be a forum which is accessible to parties (both employers and employees) representing themselves. Indeed, the *Employment Tribunals (Constitution and Rules of Procedure) Regulations 2001 (SI 2001/1171)* require tribunals to adjudicate on cases in such a way that (as far as possible) the parties are placed on an equal footing. This means that if one side has a professional representative, the tribunal will strive to ensure that the other side is not put at a disadvantage. Nevertheless, employment law is a growing and ever more complex area, with a large body of case law. Despite the fact that costs are generally not recoverable by the successful party, many feel that they need the reassurance and security of professional representation and advice (which can sometimes be available without charge). Unrepresented parties are now in the minority.

Even if a decision is made not to engage a representative at the hearing, it is important to be as well informed as possible when approaching tribunal proceedings. There are a number of organisations, listed below, which can provide free, general advice. It can be advantageous, both for employers and employees, to seek dispassionate advice at an early stage as to prospects of success. It is usually necessary to instruct a solicitor, barrister, consultant or Citizens Advice Bureau (CAB) to obtain an opinion specific to your case as the organisations offering general advice will usually not do so. This *may* end up saving costs.

Emotions tend to run high in employment disputes. The hard truth is that the tribunal is required to decide the case according to the law, not according to an individual's perception of justice. In an unfair dismissal case, for example, the tribunal is not permitted to ask 'what would it have done in that situation?' It must confine itself to such issues as the procedure adopted by the employer (the soundness of which is an area ripe for seeking advice upon) and whether dismissal fell within 'the range of reasonable responses' available to that employer. It may be that a potentially fair dismissal is rendered unfair by the procedure adopted. Or it may be that an employee who is outstanding and appreciated in certain areas has been fairly dismissed for the particular reason relied upon by the employer. For both employers and employees, it is important to listen to well-informed advice, which may be unpalatable in nature. Tribunal proceedings can be very demanding and it is best to embark upon them with a realistic view.

When should advice be sought? [3.3]

Advice/representation can be sought at any stage, from before a claim is brought to issues at the conclusion of proceedings, for example in relation to appeal or enforcement of awards. A representative does not have to be retained from the beginning to the end of a case. It is important to remember, however, that the advisor or representative needs to be given sufficient time to carry out the task entrusted to them. It is often sensible to obtain advice at an early stage to avoid bringing a misconceived claim or adopting an unsustainable position.

When seeking representation at a full hearing, the earlier a representative is instructed the better. As this book demonstrates, there are often a number of essential preliminary matters relating to the preparation of the case for full hearing, for example preparation of statements and evidence, disclosure of documents, seeking of directions etc. Instructing a representative from the outset of a case has the advantage of enabling that person to develop a coherent strategy for their presentation before the tribunal. It is also important to keep in mind time limits. So, if an employee is contemplating bringing a claim but needs advice, the earlier they seek it the better since they have just three months to bring a claim.

From whom should advice be sought? [3.4]

This depends upon individual requirements, such as the complexity of the case, and resources. HR managers may seek advice from ACAS, their professional or trade associations, employment law consultants, solicitors or barristers. Individual employees may approach ACAS, a CAB, an advice centre, a solicitor or barrister or their trade union. Solicitors will generally seek advice either from other practitioners in their firm or from counsel. There are also a number of lay employment advisors and it is always possible that knowledgeable friends, such as HR specialists or others who have previously been involved in employment cases, may be able to assist – even if only to the extent of advising where to go next. Finally, all parties should be aware of the benefits of seeking general advice from the organisations below.

Organisations offering free general advice

ACAS [3.5]

ACAS (contact details below) is a publicly funded, free advisory and information service open to employers, employees and their representatives (it also has a well-known conciliation role discussed elsewhere). It does not provide a representation service. It is an experienced organisation which offers general advice on employment law matters. Its advisors are unlikely to be qualified lawyers. Crucially, ACAS will also advise on the setting up of procedures and on other means of resolving disputes in the workplace. As stated in CHAPTER 1 – TRIBUNALS TODAY, tribunals are required (in relevant cases) to have regard to the ACAS codes of practice in deciding whether a fair procedure has been adopted, a fact which underlines the organisation's importance.

ACAS not only publishes codes of practice in areas such as disciplinary procedures, it also provides extensive advice to employers and employees prior to an application being made. There are telephone helplines and an informative website, with guides and information published on line (see **3.17**). Recently, Equality Direct (the organisation providing advice to employers on equality issues) and the Race Relations Employment Advisory Service have both joined ACAS, greatly strengthening the equal opportunities service that ACAS is able to offer.

A word of warning: ACAS is a general advisor, not a representative. You cannot 'retain' it to act on your behalf. It will not look at documentation personal to your case or carry out a thorough investigation in to the circumstances. It is effectively a question and answer service open to employers and employees, giving general advice to both sides. For this reason, if a member of ACAS gives wrong advice, it is difficult to sue it or hold it to account. ACAS, as its name suggests, also has a strong conciliation and mediation role, an issue which will be addressed in detail in CHAPTER 4 – OPTIONS FOR AVOIDING TRIBUNALS.

Equal Opportunities Commission (EOC) [3.6]

The EOC (contact details below) offers free, general advice to employees and employers in the field of discrimination, for example in relation to such matters as lodging questionnaires. It is an organisation set up to combat discrimination. The EOC does not usually provide a representation service. As with ACAS, it can advise on such matters as the formulation and implementation of equal opportunities policies in the workplace.

Commission for Racial Equality (CRE) [3.7]

As with the EOC, the Commission (contact details below) offers general advice to employers and employees in the area of race discrimination. It also publishes an excellent code of practice for the handling by employers of race related grievances which, if followed, will generally strengthen the employer's position in tribunal. The CRE also provides a discretionary representation service.

Disability Rights Commission (DRC) [3.8]

This is the equivalent organisation to the CRE acting in the field of disability discrimination. Contact details can be found below.

Organisations offering advice and representation

Citizens Advice Bureaux and Law Centres [3.9]

CABs and Law Centres (contact details below) are a free service open to employees and small employers. It is possible to retain them to act as a representative in employment disputes, though whether they have staff or volunteers available to do so will vary. In some cases, they may not be able to assist beyond an early stage in the proceedings.

CABs and Law Centres retain both paid staff and volunteers who have a basic training in employment law. These may, or may not, have a professional legal qualification. Some also utilise barristers and solicitors, who are either employed by them, or, more usually, provide their time as volunteers. Two organisations used by CABs and Law Centres are the Free Representation Unit (FRU) and the Bar Pro Bono Unit. FRU provide trainee and newly qualified lawyers for free. The Bar Pro Bono Unit may be able to offer a more experienced barrister. Both organisations are designed for people who lack the means to afford representation, but can only provide representation subject to availability of a lawyer willing to take on the case. If your priority is to receive the advice and/or representation of a professional lawyer through a CAB or Law Centre, the best option is to speak to the particular centre concerned and see what it can offer.

Solicitors [3.10]

Solicitors are professional lawyers regulated by the Law Society (contact details below) who offer both advice and representation (see **3.13–3.16**). The Law Society (for address and website see **3.18**) provides a list of solicitors who hold themselves out as specialising in employment law in particular geographical areas. It is often useful to take further steps to ascertain the quality of a firm or individual. This can be done by word of mouth or by asking the solicitor questions about the extent of their experience in the area. The specialist associations, for example Employment Lawyers Association or Employment Law Bar Association, do not publish a list of their members for use by the public.

Barristers [3.11]

The Bar provides a specialist advocacy and advisory service. Generally speaking, it is not possible to approach a barrister direct – you must first retain a solicitor, who then instructs counsel. Barristers are instructed for a number of reasons, for example to appear as advocate at the hearing, to provide an independent view on the prospects of success in a case or to give advice on a particular issue.

There is a growing list of organisations and associations who are permitted to instruct barristers direct under a scheme entitled 'Bar Direct'. For further details of how this can be done contact the General Council of the Bar (see contact details below).

Employment law consultants [3.12]

Unlike the civil courts, there is no requirement for a person to be a professional lawyer in order to represent a person in an employment tribunal. Various individuals and consultancy firms offer advice and/or representation services to both individuals and smaller employers. Some advertise their services in professional journals, local papers and on websites.

The consultant may, or may not, have a legal qualification. Since both the range and the quality of consultants' advice show considerable variation, it may be helpful to 'ask around' for recommendations based on personal knowledge. Whilst there are a number of good consultants with specialist expertise (including some who are not qualified lawyers), it should be noted that, unlike solicitors and barristers, they are not (unless they happen to be qualified lawyers) required to be members of a body regulating their activities. In effect, there is nothing to prevent anyone holding themselves out as an employment law consultant. It is important, therefore, to enquire as to experience and qualifications before instructing a consultant. Many consultants provide free initial consultations. In view of the fact that consultants do not have to belong to professional body, great care should be taken when agreeing terms of payment, including carefully reading any conditional fee agreement (see **3.13–3.16**).

How much will it cost? [3.13]

CABs, Law centres, ACAS, the EOC, CRE, DRC and FRU are free.

Solicitors and barristers [3.14]

Rates vary enormously from firm to firm and barrister to barrister. The amount charged will usually be dependent upon such matters as: (a) degree of experience; (b) the extent of specialisation in the area; (c) standing in the profession; and (d) importance of the case (this usually, though not always, relates to the amount of money at stake). Neither the Law Society nor the Bar Council publishes guidance figures on appropriate levels of fees. *Chambers UK Guide to the Legal Profession,* available at a number of public libraries, includes a survey of typical charge out rates for solicitors and barristers.

Note: with barristers there is usually a significant difference between their fees for advisory work (which can often be lower than that of a solicitor of equivalent experience) and their fee for appearing as an advocate in tribunal – to which there is normally a premium attached, known as the 'brief fee'. Seeking preliminary written advice from counsel can often be a cost-effective way, both for the solicitor and lay client, of proceeding in the case.

Fees should be discussed and agreed with the solicitor from the outset. It may be that the solicitor will offer an initial free consultation, although this is less likely with the more sizeable firms.

A number of firms require, if the case is not to be done on a conditional fee basis (see **3.15**), payment on account from the client before they start work.

No win, no fee [3.15]

Some solicitors (and barristers) and employment law consultants accept work on a conditional fee basis. This means that the client pays nothing unless successful in the case. On the face of it, this is an attractive option, and indeed is often the only means by which many people, predominately employees, can obtain legal representation in tribunals. What is the drawback? Whilst, if you lose, you pay nothing, if you win the lawyer is entitled to an enhanced payment of up to twice his normal fee. In employment tribunals each side usually pays their own costs – so, if you are an employee, the legal fees will be taken out of the compensation you receive.

How does it work? The client enters in to a conditional fee agreement (CFA) with the solicitor. In the agreement, the solicitor will state their normal hourly rate and then indicate the uplift (up to a maximum of 100%) which will be applied to that rate in the event of success. The extent of the uplift will normally be dictated by that solicitor's opinion as to the prospects of success. If, for example, the prospects are only 50%, the uplift will frequently be 100% on his normal fee. The agreement will also usually specify that, if the case settles, the solicitor will recover his fees for the work done at the enhanced rate. It is also likely to contain provisions for payment to the solicitor where the client refuses to take his advice to accept a reasonable settlement from the other side, and provisions for insurance. Where a barrister is engaged, a separate CFA will be concluded between the barrister, the solicitor and the client.

CFAs with employment law consultants [3.16]

The type of agreement will vary in individual cases and should be read with care.

Do's and Don'ts

Do:

- Ask about the qualifications and experience of a proposed representative.

- Ensure that terms and conditions of payment (including conditional fees) are agreed beforehand.

- Decide whether you want preliminary advice or representation to the conclusion of a case, and ensure that what is agreed is recorded.

- Try, if at all possible, to seek the advice of a person who specialises in employment law.

- Balance the costs of seeking advice (if there are any) against what is at stake in the particular dispute.

cont'd

- If you disagree, or do not understand advice, challenge it and ask further questions.

- Use ACAS for general advice on what tribunals regard as good practice in the workplace and take thorough notes of the advice you receive.

- Instruct a representative if you feel you do not have: (a) the expertise to do the case yourself; or (b) the time to give it the attention it needs.

- Remember, if you are representing yourself, do not be intimidated by the opposition, or be afraid to seek the tribunal's assistance – tribunals are intended to be open to non-lawyers.

- Always give a representative the full story, so that they can properly assess the strength of the case against you.

- Remember that the costs of running a case are not only financial – time and, possibly, emotional stress also come into the equation.

Don't:

- Use an unqualified representative unless you are satisfied as to their experience and expertise.

- Ignore clear advice given to you by a representative.

- Launch a case purely for vindictiveness or just to get your day in court.

Useful addresses

ACAS   **[3.17]**
Website: www.ACAS.org

Head Office
- Brandon House
  180 Borough High Street
  London
  SE1 1LW

London, Eastern and Southern
- Ross House
  Kempson Way

Suffolk Business Park
Bury St Edmonds
Suffolk
IP32 7AR

- Clifton House
  83–117 Euston Road
  London
  NW1 2RB

- Suites 3–5, Business Centre
  1–7 Commercial Road
  Paddock Wood
  Kent
  TN12 6EN

- Westminster House
  Fleet Road
  Fleet
  Hants
  GU51 3QL

Midlands

- Anderson House
  Clinton Avenue
  Nottingham
  NG5 1AW

- Warwick House
  6 Highfield Road
  Edgbaston
  Birmingham
  B15 3ED

North West

- Commercial Union House
  2–10 Albert Square
  Manchester
  M60 8AD

- Pavilion 1
  The Matchworks
  Speke Road
  Speke
  Liverpool
  L19 2PH

Northern

- Commerce House
  St Alban's Place
  Leeds
  LS2 8HH

- Cross House
  Westgate Road
  Newcastle upon Tyne
  NE1 4XX

Scotland

- Franborough House
  123–157 Bothwell Street
  Glasgow
  G2 7JR

South West

- Regent House
  27a Regent Street
  Clifton
  Bristol
  BS8 4HR

Wales

- 3 Purbeck House
  Lambourne Crescent
  Llanishen
  Cardiff
  CF14 5GJ

Telephone helplines

Birmingham	(0121) 456 5856
Bristol	(0117) 946 9500
Cardiff	(029) 2076 1126
Fleet, Hampshire	(01252) 811868
Glasgow	(0141) 204 2677
Leeds	(0113) 243 1371
Liverpool	(0151) 427 8881
London	(020) 7396 5100
Manchester	(0161) 833 8585
Newcastle upon Tyne	(0191) 261 2191
Nottingham	(0115) 969 3355

The Law Society [3.18]

Website: www.lawsociety.org.uk
Address:
* The Law Society's Hall
  113 Chancery Lane
  London
  WC2A 1PL
Tel: + 44 20 7242 1222
Fax: + 44 20 7831 0344
DX: 56 Lond/Chancery Ln
Email: info.services@lawsociety.org.uk

Records Centre/Information Services

Records on all solicitors and firms, including searching for a solicitor online.
Website: www.solicitors-online.com
Tel: 0870 606 2555

Office for the Supervision of Solicitors

Dealing with complaints and regulation.
Website: www.oss.lawsociety.org.uk
Public advice line – tel: 0845 608 6565

The Bar Council [3.19]

Website (*including searching for a barrister online*): www.barcouncil.org.uk

Main Office
* 3 Bedford Row
  London
  WC1R 4DB
Tel: 020 7242 0082

Complaints Department
* Northumberland House
  3rd Floor
  303–306 High Holborn
  London
  WC1V 7JZ
Tel: 020 7440 4000

Equal Opportunities Commission [3.20]

Website: www.eoc.org.uk
Address:
* Arndale House

Arndale Centre
Manchester
M4 3EQ
Tel: 0845 601 5901
Fax: 0161 838 173
Email: info@eoc.org.uk

Commission for Racial Equality [3.21]

Website: www.CRE.gov.uk

Head Office
* CRE
  Elliot House
  10–12 Allington Street
  London
  SW1E 5EH
Tel: 020 7828 7022
Fax: 020 7630 7605
Email: info@cre.gov.uk

Disability Rights Commission [3.22]

Website: www.drc.org.uk
Address:
* DRC Helpline
  Freepost MID 02164
  Stratford-upon-Avon
  CV37 9HY
Tel: 08457 622 633
Fax: 08457 778 878
Textphone: 08457 622 644
Email: ddahelp@stra.sitel.co.uk

National Association of Citizens Advice Bureaux [3.23]

Website: www.nacab.org.uk
Address:
* Myddleton House
  115–123 Pentonville Road
  London
  N1 9LZ
Tel: 020 7833 2181
Fax: 020 7833 4371

Free Representation Unit [3.24]

Website: www.org.uk
Address:
* Fourth Floor
  Peer House
  8–14 Verulam Street
  London
  WC1X 8LZ
Tel: 020 7831 0692

Law Centres Federation [3.25]

Website: www.lawcentres.org.uk
Address:
* Duchess House
  18–19 Warren Street
  London
  WC1P 5DP
Tel: 020 7387 8570
Fax: 020 7387 8368

4.

Options for Avoiding Tribunals

Introduction [4.1]

Proceeding to tribunal can be risky for all concerned. This chapter looks at the alternatives.

Drawing up compromise agreements [4.2]

Compromise agreements are an attractive option to many employers. Upon or after termination of the contract of employment, the employee signs an agreement with the employer stating that they will not pursue a statutory claim before a tribunal. Be warned: there are strict formalities governing the formation of compromise agreements that must be complied with. These, and the consequences of non-compliance, are examined in detail in CHAPTER 18 – SETTLEMENT OF CLAIMS.

Effective internal grievance procedures [4.3]

These enable employees who are dissatisfied with any aspect of their employment to make a complaint, which is dealt with according to a pre-determined procedure (see CHAPTER 2 – TROUBLE AHEAD). Grievance procedures can be utilised by the employee either before or after the making of a tribunal claim while the employment relationship is continuing.

Where an effective grievance procedure is available to the employee it may, depending on the circumstances, harm their case if they do not use it, particularly in cases of discrimination, harassment and victimisation. From the employer's perspective, a fair and thorough investigation of the grievance may resolve the dispute or strengthen the company's position at full hearing. In cases of possible constructive dismissal, it is a relatively common course for the employee to use the grievance procedure, but make it clear that this is being done 'without prejudice' to their right to treat themselves as constructively dismissed. This is designed to deal with any argument that the employee has waived the breach of contract.

Time limits [4.4]

Where grievances are raised, regard should be paid by the employee to the statutory time limits for making the relevant claim (see CHAPTER 6 – TIME LIMITS). This can be particularly relevant in discrimination cases, where time starts to run from the date of the discriminatory act. A common precaution, if there is a danger of the time limit expiring, is for the employee to make a 'protective claim' to guarantee that they will not be deprived of the right to take their case to a tribunal. In discrimination cases, tribunals have somewhat more latitude to extend time limits. Where the cause of the delay is the operation of the grievance procedure, they may do so, depending on the facts of the case.

Where a claim to the tribunal is made prior to determination of the grievance [4.5]

The acts constituting the complaint should be set out in the normal way and, at the end of the IT1 (see CHAPTER 7 – MAKING A CLAIM), it is good practice to assert (if at that stage it has been decided to use the grievance procedure) that the matters forming the basis of the complaint are or will be the subject of a formal grievance which is yet to be determined. If completing the IT3 (see CHAPTER 8 – THE EMPLOYER'S RESPONSE) for the employer, the best policy is to assert that the employer makes 'no admissions' in respect of the allegations made, but is currently considering them under its grievance procedure, and reserves the right to amend the IT3 when that procedure is complete. A tribunal will frequently agree to postpone the normal timetable in order for the grievance to be determined.

Running internal appeals against dismissal [4.6]

In cases of dismissal, it is highly desirable for the employer to offer an effective internal appeal. This should be chaired by either a senior manager within the employer organisation (preferably one who did not have direct involvement in the events which led to the dismissal) or a nominated person outside the organisation (or, where available, a non-executive director) who is brought in to determine such appeals. In addition to increasing the fairness of the process, an appeal also provides important, and sometimes essential, protection for the employer. First, the decision can be reviewed from a different perspective and at a more senior level. Second, a fair appeal may remedy procedural defects at the disciplinary hearing. The type of appeal procedure adopted is likely to depend upon the size and resources of the employer. The starting point should be the ACAS Code of Practice (see **4.9).**

Employees must keep in mind the time limits for bringing an unfair dismissal claim. A tribunal will normally not extend the three-month time limit for bringing a claim if the delay is caused by proceeding with an internal appeal (*Times Newspaper Ltd v O'Regan [1977] IRLR 101*) (see CHAPTER 6). Ordinarily, where an internal appeal is successful, the employee is reinstated with continuity of employment preserved. Where the appeal is unsuccessful, the effective date of termination is the date of dismissal, not the date of the appeal hearing. The best course in these circumstances is to make a claim for unfair dismissal within the three-month time period, notifying the tribunal at the end of the IT1 of the outstanding appeal. Employers are usually advised to adopt the 'no admissions' course outlined above.

Negotiations without prejudice [4.7]

Negotiations between the parties can take place at any time before or after the issue of a claim. Negotiations after the application has been lodged are discussed in CHAPTER 18 – SETTLEMENT OF CLAIM. A word of caution: consideration should be given in all claims that are either pending or contemplated to the conducting of negotiations on a 'without prejudice' basis. That is on the understanding that everything that is discussed will remain confidential and will not detract from the right to proceed with a claim. Where written communications are concerned, letters should be headed 'without prejudice'. Where a meeting takes place, it should be agreed between the parties (preferably in writing) that the discussions will be on a 'without prejudice' basis. If no claim is, at that stage, contemplated, then it is not possible to enter in to 'without prejudice' discussions.

Where an employer is in doubt about whether a claim is contemplated, it will have to make up its mind whether to clarify the issue with the employee. Sometimes this will have an inflammatory effect, although usually only where the employment relationship is continuing.

Examples of pre-claim negotiations include:

- in a disability discrimination case that turns on the duty to make reasonable adjustments, both parties may think it worthwhile to discuss a practical resolution;

- where there has been a dismissal, negotiations might take place to discuss a payment or other form of consideration in return for the employee agreeing not to make a tribunal claim, or, less commonly, to consideration of reinstatement of the employee;

- in a case of threatened constructive dismissal, the employee or their representative may write to the employer giving them a period of, say, seven days to negotiate and/or respond to their particular concerns 'without prejudice to their right to treat themselves as unfairly dismissed.' Due regard should be had in such circumstances to the need to act promptly.

Agreements following negotiations [4.8]

Parties will have to decide whether to enshrine an agreement into a formal compromise agreement (see **4.2**). If they do not, the agreement will not prevent the employee from pursuing a tribunal claim, but may be relied upon by the other party in seeking to argue that it would not be just and equitable for the tribunal to make an award of compensation.

ACAS Arbitration Scheme [4.9]

In unfair dismissal cases, there is now a complete alternative to taking a claim to an employment tribunal, namely the ACAS Arbitration Scheme. The purpose of the scheme is to provide a forum for deciding employment disputes which is faster, less legalistic and more informal than employment tribunals. If a party is considering using the scheme, a copy of the scheme and the guide can be obtained from ACAS (see CHAPTER 3 – GETTING ADVICE for contact details).

Employment tribunals have regard to a vast body of case law and statute. The new arbitration scheme sweeps this aside, requiring arbitrators quite simply to 'have regard to general principles of good conduct in employment relations, instead of applying legal tests or rules' (ACAS Arbitration Scheme, para 12). The ACAS Codes of Practice are expressly cited as examples of good conduct which arbitrators might wish to take in to account. Opportunities for appeal are minimal – only if there is a 'serious irregularity' can a party appeal, or if their rights under the *Human Rights Act 1998* have been breached. Other features of arbitration include the following:

- there must be both a written agreement (complying with the requirements for compromise agreements) between the parties whereby they agree to submit the dispute to arbitration and a formal waiver of tribunal rights signed by both parties;

- the arbitration process is set in motion by the parties submitting a copy of the agreement and waiver forms to the ACAS arbitration section within six weeks of the agreement being signed;

- parties are required to submit a written statement of case and documents upon which they intend to rely to the arbitrator and the other side at least 14 days prior to the hearing. If this is not complied with, a party may not adduce a statement/document at the hearing without the permission of the arbitrator;

- in complex cases or cases where disagreement over such matters as disclosure is likely, the arbitrator may hold a preliminary hearing to resolve such matters and/or give appropriate directions for full hearing;

- the arbitrator has no power to *order* disclosure of documents or the attendance of witnesses. They can give directions to that effect and may, where appropriate, draw an adverse inference if there is an unreasonable refusal to comply with a direction or request from the other party;

- no cross-examination of witnesses is allowed during the hearing: all questioning will be carried out by the arbitrator, although a party may suggest questions which can be asked;

- the hearing will be informal and will be led by the arbitrator;

- the scheme encourages a proactive fact finding exercise by the arbitrator, as opposed to an adversarial process between the parties;

- formal rules of evidence do not apply, but the arbitrator is obliged to act fairly and impartially, and give both parties an opportunity to present their case (ACAS Arbitration Scheme, para 48);

- a party can be represented at arbitration;

- the hearing usually lasts half a day;

- the hearing is strictly private and confidential;

- there is no provision for the arbitrator to make a costs award.

Situations where arbitration should not be used include:

- where there is a complex issue of law;

- where there is an issue as to jurisdiction, e g whether the claim is out of time or whether the employee has been employed continuously for twelve months. In these circumstances, the arbitrator will assume that they have jurisdiction to hear any claim. Employers be warned.

It is suggested that arbitration may not be appropriate in cases involving multiple or complex issues, large amounts of documentation and/or large numbers of witnesses.

Advantages and disadvantages of arbitration   **[4.10]**

Advantages:

- Greater accessibility and comprehensibility for unqualified parties and their representatives.

- Greater speed in the hearing a likely reduction in the time taken to settle.

- Less intimidating and formal.

- Probably less time consuming and expensive to prepare for.

- Potentially useful in cases where there is not a large amount of documentation and the issues are straightforward.

- Useful if the parties want proceedings to be confidential.

Disadvantages:

- Concluding an agreement to go to arbitration could, itself, be time-consuming.

- Arbitration may be arbitrary and unpredictable – case law is intended to promote consistency in decision making and arbitrators are not bound by it.

- No opportunity to cross-examine the other side's witnesses.

- Heavily restricted rights of appeal.

- No right to obtain orders of disclosure of documents from the other side or other interlocutory orders, such as further particulars of the other side's case.

- Less stringent standards of disclosure and pleading means parties may be taken by surprise on the day and have less opportunity to meet the other side's case.

- Tribunals already have regard to the codes of practice, with which case law is generally consistent.

Overall, it is too early to say whether arbitration will prove to be simply a more unpredictable and less thorough version of tribunal proceedings or will present an attractive, fast and accessible alternative.

Do's and Don'ts for avoiding tribunals

Do:

- Consider whether there is a way of amicably resolving a dispute.

- Make use of grievance procedures.

- Offer effective and fair internal appeals against dismissal.

- Have regard to time limits for making claims.

- Comply with the requirements for compromise agreements.

- Develop strong grievance procedures and use them.

- Consider whether negotiations should be conducted on a without prejudice or open basis.

- Look at the option of an early without prejudice round table negotiations.

- Consider arbitration.

Don't:

- Conclude that negotiations are incompatible with making/ defending a claim; the two can and do frequently go hand in hand.

- Forget about time limits whilst conducting negotiations.

- Make a decision about arbitration without obtaining a full copy of the scheme and guide from ACAS.

- Use arbitration if there is an issue as to time limits, continuity of employment or any other jurisdictional issue.

5.
Pre-claim Requests for Information

Introduction [5.1]

Pre-claim correspondence has the following advantages:

- it enables each party to gain an understanding of the other's case;

- it may facilitate settlement at an early stage, avoiding the time, expense and anxiety of proceeding to tribunal;

- in the case of exceptionally weak claims or defences, it may be adduced at the conclusion of proceedings as evidence of the losing party's unreasonableness in bringing, contesting or proceeding with the claim.

Employee's letter before claim [5.2]

The stronger and more persuasive the letter, the more likely it is to have the desired effect on the employer. The contents should be accurate, particularly in open correspondence (i e correspondence not involving the settling or compromise of the claim), as the letter may be used as evidence in any subsequent proceedings. There is nothing to prevent the employee writing an open letter whereby they set out their case, and accompanying this with a without prejudice letter giving proposals for settlement. The advantage of this is that the open letter goes 'on the record', and can be evidence of a consistent position adopted by the employee throughout the dispute.

The letter before claim should:

- Be headed 'Letter before claim'.

- Where containing an offer to settle, be headed 'without prejudice'.

- Identify the type of claim/s that the employee intends to bring.

- Set out, in outline form, the factual basis of the claim.

- State (in without prejudice letters) what is required from the employer (i e level of compensation or other remedy) in order for the claim not to proceed, giving the basis of any calculation.

- Give (in without prejudice correspondence) the employer a deadline for responding.

- State the name of the intended respondent in the action.

Example of letter before claim

[Without prejudice save as to costs (see below)].

Dear [...]

We act for Bill Smith who intends to bring proceedings against Jones and Co for unfair dismissal.

The circumstances of his dismissal were as follows: Mr Smith was, on 5 March 2002, invited to attend the office of Steve Martin, the managing director. He was informed that, due to 'a few cash flow problems', the company would be making him redundant, and that his last day of work would be 8 March 2002. He was further informed that he would receive pay in lieu of one month's notice, together with his statutory redundancy pay.

His dismissal was plainly unfair for the following reasons:

(a)   a true redundancy situation did not exist; and

(b)   in any event, an unfair procedure was carried out, including a total absence of consultation, fair selection criteria or attempts to find our client alternative work.

In relation to (a), our client will assert during tribunal proceedings that he was told, a week before his dismissal, that he 'would have to improve or the company would get rid of him'. There is compelling evidence that this was a disguised capability dismissal. He will further rely upon the fact that another person is currently performing his job on similar pay.

[The following paragraph can, if desired, be contained in a separate without prejudice letter, with the paragraphs above forming part of an open letter.]

cont'd

We ask you to pay our client the sum of £22,000 within 21 days, or we will commence proceedings on his behalf in an employment tribunal. This sum is calculated on the basis of six months' loss of earnings, which is the period our client reasonably estimates will be necessary to find alternative work of a similar level. We urge you to recognise that this figure may well increase if the case is brought to tribunal and our client has failed, by that stage, to secure alternative work.

We look forward to hearing from you.

Responding to the letter before claim [5.3]

If the letter before claim contains an offer of settlement, the response to that will be without prejudice, and not for disclosure to the tribunal. The extent to which the employer is able to provide a detailed response to the allegations made will vary from case to case. A strong and persuasive reply may have the effect of deterring the employee from proceeding, or inducing them to settle. Such letters should generally include:

• a response to the legal points raised by the employee;

• a response to the factual assertions made by the employee;

• where appropriate, a request for further information from the employee, for example in relation to any new position that they have taken up, or as to how their loss is calculated;

• a response (in a without prejudice letter) to any financial offer of the employee, either accepting it, rejecting it or making a counter offer.

Where the employee has sent an open letter setting out their claim, in which no offer of settlement is made, the employer should respond in kind, since both may then be evidence in tribunal proceedings.

Example of response

Thank you for your letter of [...]. Your client was dismissed on [...] by reason of redundancy. The version of events recited in your letter is inaccurate and misleading, in particular the implication in your letter that your client was unaware of any redundancy situation

cont'd

41

existing until the date of his dismissal and your assertion that a genuine redundancy situation did not exist.

Your client was employed as a sales officer in the West Midlands region. At a meeting on [...] the company decided that, in order to reduce overheads, it would cease to operate in that area. Two days later, your client was informed of this decision. His response was: 'well, sales have not been that great so as long as I get a decent package I don't really mind'. He was offered, at this meeting, the position of junior sales officer in the South East with no loss of pay. He declined this offer for personal reasons. He made no suggestions as to suitable alternative positions.

On [...], the board of the company decided that, in view of your client's rejection of the offer which had been made to him, there was no alternative but to make him redundant since there were no other positions which he could occupy in the organisation. Your client was informed of this fact at a meeting on [...] and in writing on [...]. He received his contractual notice period and his statutory redundancy pay. In the circumstances, he was fairly dismissed by reason of redundancy and any claim against the company will be strenuously defended. If, which is denied, there is held to be any procedural flaw, the company will assert that it is inevitable that the dismissal would have taken place in any event, and that your client's loss is nil.

Use of questionnaires in discrimination cases   [5.4]

Questionnaires can be a useful tool for applicants in discrimination cases. Essentially, they provide the applicant, within the proscribed format of the questionnaire, with the opportunity to ask questions of the employer, at an early stage, with a view to establishing whether they have been discriminated against. This is an additional facility in discrimination cases which can be used in conjuction with obtaining disclosure from the employer after proceedings have begun (see **CHAPTER 12 – DISCLOSURE**). The questionnaire and answers stand as evidence in the case. Employees are required to state the basis upon which they consider they may have been discriminated against, and the requests for information should be restricted to these issues. There is rarely direct evidence of discrimination, which places the onus on the applicant to seek evidence upon which the tribunal could draw an inference of discrimination. Questionnaires should assist both in this process and in deciding whether to bring a claim for unlawful discrimination. It can be served either before making a claim, or within 21 days of doing so, but in any event must be served within three months of the discriminatory act complained of.

The questionnaires (whether for race, sex or disability) come in a form prescribed by the Secretary of State. The questionnaires for sex discrimination can be found in APPENDIX II – QUESTIONNAIRE AND RESPONSE (SD 74).

The race questionnaire (RR65) can be found on the Commission for Racial Equality website (www.cre.gov.uk).The disability questionnaire can be found in booklet *DL56 – The Disability Discrimination Act 1995: The Questions Procedure* on the Disability Rights Commission website (www.drc-gb.org).

Each form provides scope for the employee to add additional questions themselves. Frequently, an employee will ask questions relating to such matters as:

- the qualifications of the successful candidate for a job;

- the reasons for that other candidate's selection;

- the gender or racial composition of the workforce or those with disabilities;

- an analysis of how such groups have been treated by the company in specific factual situations, for example promotion or dismissal;

- equal opportunities training carried out by the employer.

Remember that there is no 'rule' as to which questions should be answered, provided they are relevant and not oppressive in the extent of information they seek from the respondent. The applicant should think carefully about what questions are most likely to assist them. In a given case, there may well be a number of questions specific to the particular circumstances of the applicant that should be answered. For example: 'is it accepted that I was told on [...] by [...] that I was almost certain to be promoted to the job in question.' Employees are strongly advised to seek the assistance of one of the following organisations, who are able to advise in the drafting of questionnaires: The Disability Rights Commission, The Commission for Racial Equality and the Equal Opportunities Commission (see CHAPTER 3 – GETTING ADVICE). All of those organisations have websites with excellent guides on the type of questions which it is permissible to ask in questionnaires.

Responding to the questionnaire [5.5]

Employers are advised to take the questionnaire seriously since their answers will stand as evidence in the case. Although they are not obliged to respond, if the tribunal concludes that they have failed to do so deliberately and unreasonably, it will consider drawing an inference of discrimination from that fact. An employer will usually be justified in refusing to provide information if a request is irrelevant to the alleged act of discrimination or if the query is oppressive. An example of both might be where a request is made for the details of all applications for employment made to the company in the last ten years. Where an employer refuses to provide information it should include, in the form, the basis upon which it is doing so in order to protect its position. An alternative, prior to completing the form, is to write to the employee asking the relevance of the request. Simply leaving the section blank is very inadvisable.

As with the questionnaires themselves, there is a prescribed form for responding. These can be found in **APPENDIX II**. The questionnaire need not purely benefit the employee. It can also give the employer a crucial insight into the case of the employee and allow it to formulate a response.

Do's and Don'ts

Do:

- Decide whether pre-claim correspondence should be with or without prejudice – all offers to settle claims (and responses to such offers) automatically fall in to the latter category and are not for disclosure to the court, save in relation to the issue of costs.

- Consider making use of a questionnaire in discrimination cases.

- Use pre-claim correspondence as a means of facilitating settlement.

Don't:

- Allow pre-claim correspondence or questionnaires to take precedence over complying with time limits for bringing a claim.

- In open correspondence, make factual assertions which you later go back on.

6.
Time Limits

Introduction [6.1]

In general, tribunals only have the jurisdiction (i e power) to hear claims that are brought within the relevant statutory time limits. Whilst time limits cannot be waived (either by the tribunal or the parties), tribunals do have the power, in most cases, to extend the time limit if certain criteria are met. Each statute that provides for the right to bring a claim also sets out the circumstances in which a tribunal has the power to extend time; the so called 'escape clauses'. Where a statute is silent on the matter, a tribunal has no power to extend time. From an employer's perspective, it is important to bear in mind that claims can be knocked out at a preliminary hearing, *without consideration* of the substantive complaint, merely by establishing that proceedings are out of time.

This chapter looks at the process both of ascertaining whether a claim is in time and, if not, the criteria for extending time contained in the escape clauses.

Time limits for presentation of claims: the five-stage test [6.2]

A tribunal, when considering whether it has jurisdiction to hear a claim, will:

- establish whether there is a time limit applicable to a claim;

- identify the event upon which the claim is based and from which time, for the purposes of the limitation period, begins to run ('the trigger event');

- calculate the time that has elapsed between the event and the presentation of the claim ('the period');

- accept that it has jurisdiction where the period is less than or equal to the time limit prescribed by statute or rule; and

- where the period exceeds the time limit, go on to consider whether, applying the relevant criteria, the time limit can and should be extended.

A tribunal will consider these issues in strict chronological order and will first determine whether a claim is 'in time' before going on to consider whether, having regard to all the surrounding circumstances, time ought to be extended. Each of these steps will be considered below.

Stage one: does a time limit apply? [6.3]

The time limits applicable to the claims that the tribunal has jurisdiction to hear are set out in APPENDIX I – CLAIMS A TRIBUNAL CAN HEAR.

Stage two: identifying the trigger event [6.4]

All the statutory provisions that create the right to bring a claim, refer to a particular event, or 'trigger' that starts time running for the purposes of presenting a claim to the tribunal. For obvious reasons, different 'trigger' events apply to different claims.

Unfair/wrongful dismissal claims [6.5]

In general, a claim for unfair dismissal must be presented to the tribunal 'before the end of the three months beginning with the effective date of termination' (EDT) (*Employment Rights Act 1996 (ERA 1996), s 111)*). The 'trigger' date, from which time starts to run, is therefore the EDT.

Section 97(1) of the *ERA 1996* states that the EDT:

'(a)   in relation to an employee whose contract of employment is terminated by notice, whether given by the employer or employee, means the date on which the notice expires;

(b)   in relation to an employee whose contract of employment is terminated without notice, means the date upon which termination takes effect; and

(c)   in relation to an employee who is employed under a contract for a fixed term which expires without being renewed under the same contract, means the date on which the terms expires.'

Where an employee is dismissed *with* notice, the EDT is the date on which the notice expires, irrespective of whether the employee was actually required to work during the notice period. When calculating the EDT it is important to bear in mind that where an employee is given notice of termination, that the notice period runs from the day after receipt and not from the day on which notice was given (*West v Kneels*

Ltd [1986] IRLR 430). So if an employee is given one month's notice, the month starts to run from the day after they receive the notice.

On the other hand, where an employee is summarily dismissed, or dismissed *without* notice and given pay in lieu of notice to compensate them for the immediate dismissal, the EDT is the date of dismissal.

In practice, the difference between these two options can often result in an employee having an extra month to bring a claim before the tribunal (i e the four-week notice period). It is important, therefore, to consider with care the basis of dismissal and to ensure that the letter of dismissal clearly sets out the option that is chosen.

Where proceedings are issued either before notice of termination has been served, or prior to the date of dismissal, a tribunal has no jurisdiction to hear a claim for unfair dismissal. So, for example, where an employee issued proceedings upon being told that their fixed-term contract would not be renewed, but before the contract expired, their application was held to be premature and hence outside the jurisdiction of the tribunal (*Throsby v Imperial College of Science and Technology [1978] ICR 357*).

By way of exception to this general rule, *section 111(3)* of the *ERA 1996* permits a tribunal to hear claims that are presented during an employee's notice period (i e prior to the EDT but after notice of termination has been given). This exception applies also to claims for constructive dismissal where an employee, having given notice, issues a claim prior to the expiry of the notice period.

In claims for wrongful dismissal, which are essentially claims by employees seeking compensation for dismissal in a manner contrary to their contractual terms of employment, the 'trigger' date is also the EDT. There is no requirement for an employee to have worked for twelve months before bringing a wrongful dismissal claim.

Discrimination claims [6.6]

In claims involving discrimination, whether due to sex, race or disability, the relevant statutes state that 'a tribunal shall not consider a complaint...unless it is presented to the tribunal before the end of the period of three months beginning when the act complained of was done' (*Sex Discrimination Act 1975 (SDA 1975), s 76(1), Race Relations Act 1976 (RRA 1976), s 68, Disability Discrimination Act 1995 (DDA 1995), Sch 3 para 3*). In general, therefore, time starts to run from the date that the act complained of occurred.

Where, however, the act complained of is an employer's refusal to accept a grievance, time will only start to run from the date that the employee is notified of the refusal (*Aniagwu v London Borough of Hackney [1999] IRLR 303, EAT*). On the other hand, where the complaint arises from a dismissal with notice, time will begin to run from the date that the employment is terminated, and not from the date where notice was given (*British Gas Services Ltd v McCaull [2001] IRLR 60*).

Where the act of discrimination consists of an alleged failure to offer employment or promotion, time begins to run from the date of 'the decision upon it' (*SDA 1975, s 76(6)(c), RRA 1976, s 68(7)(c)*). It is submitted that this is likely to be interpreted as meaning that time starts to run from the date that any decision is communicated to an employee and not the date when the employer hypothetically came to the decision.

Certainly time only starts to run from the date when an employer is in a position to implement a decision. This was confirmed in *Swithland Motors plc v Clarke [1994] ICR 231*, a case concerning a prospective purchaser of a business who decided, prior to purchasing the business, that certain employees would be dismissed in the event that the purchase was successful. The tribunal held that time only began to run from the date that the purchaser was in a position to implement their decision, which in practical terms meant that time began to run from the day after they had purchased the business and told the employee that she was dismissed.

The Court of Appeal in *Rhys-Harper v Relaxion Group plc [2001] IRLR 460* gave a clear indication that the provisions of the three discrimination statutes are, wherever possible, to be interpreted in the same way.

By way of exception to the general rule that time starts to run from the date of the act complained of, all three discrimination statutes (*SDA 1975, s 76(6), RRA 1996, s 68(7), DDA 1995, Sch 3 para 3*. See also *Employment Protection (Consolidation) Act 1978), s 46 (3)(a)* which provides that discrimination against a person on account of raising a health and safety issue is actionable within three months of the last act where that act is part of a series of acts) provide that:

(a) where a contract includes a term that is unlawfully discriminatory, time does not begin to run as long as the unlawful term of the contract remains in force and the employee remains employed under that contract;

(b) where a discriminatory act extends over a period of time, time will only start to run from the end of the period (the end of the period is either treated as the end of employment – see *SDA 1975, s 76(6)(b)* and *RRA 1976, s 68(7)(b)* or the end of the act, whichever occurs first).

In relation to (b), an act will be treated as extending over a period of time in circumstances where it forms part of a discriminatory pattern of events, practice or policy. Thus, for example, where an employer operated a policy under which only men were eligible for a mortgage subsidy, the refusal to grant a female employee a subsidy was held to be a discriminatory act that continued throughout the lifetime of the policy. Since the policy was still operating when the applicant resigned, she was therefore entitled to bring a sex discrimination claim within three months of the date of her resignation, despite the fact that the act complained of (i e the refusal of her application for a mortgage subsidy) had taken place five months earlier (*Calder v James Finlay Corpn Ltd (1982) [1989] ICR 157*. See also *Barclays Bank plc v Kapur [1991] ICR 208 HL* where the applicants were allowed to bring their claims 17 years after joining the pension schemes).

Another example of a continuing discriminatory act is where an employer, having given assurances to an employee who has complained of discriminatory abuse, then fails to satisfactorily implement those assurances (*Littlewoods Organisations plc v Traynor [1993] IRLR 154, EAT*). In these circumstances, the act will extend until satisfactory remedial action has been taken.

It is important to distinguish between a continuing discriminatory 'act' and an act that has continuing discriminatory 'consequences'. In this context, it is critical to differentiate between a single act, such as a failure to promote, and a general regime that has a continuing discriminatory effect. The mere fact that a person continues to experience the discriminatory consequences of a decision will not justify extending the time limit. Only where the act itself is continuing will time be extended. A practical example of this distinction can be found in *Sougrin v Haringey Health Authority [1992] ICR 650,* a claim involving a nurse who alleged that her failure to be promoted at an internal appeal was due to racial discrimination. The Court of Appeal rejected her argument that the loss of pay she suffered as a result of not being promoted amounted to a continuing act of discrimination. In their view, the loss of pay was an inevitable consequence of the decision not to promote her, and that the time for bringing her claim started to run from the date that she lost her internal appeal; namely five months before she presented her claim to the tribunal.

Although, in the *Rhys-Harper* case, the Court of Appeal ruled that the three discrimination statutes should be interpreted in the same way, there remain a number of irreconcilable tribunal decisions. In particular, there is some confusion as to whether, with respect to claims under the *DDA 1995* and the *RRA 1976*, time can begin to run from the date of constructive dismissal. The difficulty arises because of Parliament's decision, in 1986, to amend only the *SDA 1975* to include the notion of 'constructive' dismissal. As a result, the Employment Appeal Tribunal (EAT), in *Metropolitan Police Commissioner v Harley [2001] IRLR 263*, held that since Parliament had specifically chosen to amend only the *SDA 1975*, the *DDA 1995* could not be said to cover constructive dismissal. Consequently, claims under the DDA *1995* had to be brought within three months of the last act of discrimination and not within three months from the date of resignation.

On the other hand, in *Derby Specialist Fabrication Ltd v Burton [2001] IRLR 69*, a different division of the EAT took the contrary view, holding that a claim under the *RRA 1976* could include constructive dismissal, notwithstanding the lack of statutory amendment, and that therefore a claim for racial discrimination made within three months of the date of resignation was 'in time'.

Until the Court of Appeal clarifies the position, it would be sensible for an employee to ensure that any disability or race discrimination claim is presented to the tribunal within three months of the act complained of.

Lastly, by way of exception to the general limitation period, it is important to remember that there is no time limit applicable to complaints that either a contractual term or a rule or collective agreement is discriminatory under the *Sex Discrimination Act 1986*.

Redundancy claims [6.7]

The general rule is that any claim for redundancy must be made within six months of the 'relevant date'. *Section 164(1)* of the *ERA 1996* defines the various ways that an employee can make a claim for redundancy, and confirms that an application will be in time where, within six months of the relevant date one of the following occurs:

- a redundancy payment is agreed and paid;

- the employee has made a claim, in writing, to the employer for such a payment;

- a question as to the employee's entitlement to, or amount of, the payment has been referred to a tribunal;

- a claim for unfair dismissal has been presented to the tribunal.

Rather uniquely, therefore, employees are permitted to present a claim for redundancy payment either to the employer or the tribunal. So long as this occurs within six months of the relevant date, the claim will be 'in time'. The relevant date, which is taken into account when calculating the limitation period is defined in *section 145* of the *ERA 1996* as follows:

- where a contract of employment is terminated without notice, the relevant date is the day that the termination takes effect;

- where a contract of employment is terminated with notice, the relevant date is the day that notice expires;

- where a contract of employment is for a fixed term, the relevant date is the last day of the fixed term.

Historically, where an employee presented a claim before the relevant date, a tribunal was thought not to have jurisdiction to hear the complaint (*Pritchard-Rhodes Ltd v Boon and Milton [1979] IRLR 19*). With the subsequent change in the law relating to unfair dismissal so as to allow claims for unfair dismissal to be brought within the notice period (*ERA 1996, s 111*), it is likely that a tribunal would now accept jurisdiction to hear a claim for redundancy presented during the notice period.

Tribunals are given a special discretionary power to extend time for a further six months in circumstances where it considers it just and equitable that an employee should receive a redundancy payment (*ERA 1996, s 164(2)*). This discretion may not be exercised, however, where a redundancy payment was agreed and paid within the first six months (i e the first category of *s 164(1)* above).

There are two exceptions to the time limit generally applicable to claims for redundancy. First, where a civil servant or Crown employee refers a question to a tribunal concerning their entitlement to the equivalent of redundancy pay (*ERA 1996, s 177*), the normal six-month limitation period does not apply. Instead, such a reference must be made within the ordinary contractual limitation period of six years (*Greenwich Health Authority v Skinner [1989] IRL 239 EAT*).

Second, where the Secretary to State has failed to make a redundancy payment on behalf of an insolvent employer (*ERA 1996, s 166*), an employee may, under *section 170* of the *ERA 1996*, refer this issue to a tribunal. No time limit is prescribed for this type of reference.

Equal pay claims [6.8]

A claim for breach of the equality clause (the equality clause, which is implied into every contract of employment, seeks to ensure that the totality of the terms and conditions of employment for a woman are no less favourable than for a man) must be referred to a tribunal either whilst an employment contract is in existence, or within six months of the contract terminating (*Equal Pay Act 1970 (EPA 1970), s 2(4)* – the six-month time limit has been confirmed by the EAT in *Preston v Wolverhampton Healthcare NHS Trust [1996] IRLR 484*). It is important to note that a tribunal has no discretionary power to extend this time limit.

Unauthorised deduction of wages [6.9]

A claim for unauthorised deduction of wages time must be presented to a tribunal within three months, beginning with the date of alleged failure to pay any sum owed to an employee under their terms of employment. In a similar manner to discrimination claims, where it can be established that there was a *series* of unlawful deductions, time will begin to run from the date of the last failure to pay the employee.

Contract claims [6.10]

Claims for breach of contract must be presented to a tribunal within three months beginning with the EDT (claims for breach of contract are brought under the *Employment Tribunal Extension of Jurisdiction Order 1994*). It is important to remember that tribunals can only hear breach of contract claims that are brought *after* the termination of employment. A tribunal simply has no jurisdiction to hear a claim for breach of contract, where the complaint is made during the currency of a worker's employment (*Capek v Lincolnshire County Council [2000] IRLR 590*).

Failure to provide written particulars [6.11]

Every employer is required to provide his employees with a written statement of particulars of employment and an itemised pay statement (*ERA 1996, s 1(1)* and *s 8*). An employee who wishes to bring a claim alleging that these statutory requirements have not been complied with may do so at any time during their employment or within three months of the termination of the contract of employment.

Stage three: calculating time

Presenting a claim [6.12]

Having identified the 'trigger event' a tribunal will then go on to determine whether the claim has been presented to the tribunal within the prescribed statutory time limit (there are exceptions to this general rule; for example claims for redundancy (where the complaint can be made to the employer)).

For the purposes of the *Employment Tribunals (Constitution and Rules of Procedure) Regulations 2001 (SI 2001/1171)*, a claim is validly presented on the day that it is physically delivered to the appropriate tribunal. In practical terms this means that an originating application can be served by post, fax or hand delivered. It is crucial to bear in mind that 'presentation' of a claim occurs on the day that the originating application is *received* by the tribunal and *not* on the date when it was posted to the tribunal.

Confirmation of receipt of the originating application should *always* be obtained so as to safeguard against the risk that the application has been lost or delayed in the post or not received as a result of transmission problems with the fax. A party should not delay in seeking confirmation. A tribunal will have little sympathy for an applicant who, having sent their originating application and not received confirmation of receipt, delays unreasonably in verifying that it has arrived (*Camden and Islington Community Services NHS Trust v Kennedy [1996] IRLR 381*).

Calculating time [6.13]

In carrying out the calculation, any reference in a statute or rule to a month or months is taken to mean 'calendar' month(s) (*Interpretation Act 1978, Sch 1*), and any reference to a specific date is deemed to include the whole 24-hour period. Consequently, so long as a claim is presented before midnight of the last day of the statutory time limit, the claim is deemed to have been presented 'in time'.

Where a statute indicates that time runs *beginning with* a particular event, the statutory period for bringing the claim *includes* the date when this event occurred (see *Pruden v Cunard Ellerman Ltd [1993] IRLR 317* for a full summary of the rules for calculating time).

Examples

Example 1: In a claim for unfair dismissal, the three-month period, within which to bring a claim, 'begins' to run from the EDT. If the EDT is 22 March, a claim for unfair dismissal will need to be presented to the tribunal before midnight on 21 June.

From the example given, it can be seen that where statute requires an act to be done *within* a specified period, a simple way to calculate the period is to start from the day before the trigger date (in that case the day before the EDT – 21 March) and to go forwards the requisite

cont'd

---

number of months (with unfair dismissal claims three months – to 21 June).

Where the time limit for bringing a claim begins to run '*of, from or after*' a particular date, the statutory period for bring the claim *excludes* that date.

Example 2: In a claim for equal pay the six-month limitation period begins to run from the date a person terminates their employment. So, for example, an employee who left his job on 6 January will have until 6 July to present a claim to a tribunal.

Where, having calculated the period of time, there is no corresponding date in the appropriate month, the limitation period is deemed to expire on the last day of that month.

Example 3: Where the EDT is 1 September, the three-month time limit should expire on midnight of 31 November. However, since November only has 30 days, the time limit will, in fact, expire on the last day of the month; namely 30 November.

This rule can give rise to some rather strange results. For example, whether the EDT is 1 December or 30 November, the limitation period will expire on the same day; namely midnight of 28 February (or 29 February in a leap year).

When considering whether or not a claim is 'in time' tribunals are strict in their application of the three-month limitation period. The fact, for example, that the last day for presenting a claim falls on a Saturday, Sunday or Bank Holiday does not affect the date when the limitation period expires. This was confirmed in *Swainston v Hetton Victory Club Limited [1983] 1 ALL ER 1179,* where the Court of Appeal rejected the applicant's submission that, although the time limit expired on Sunday 6 December, the fact that his claim had been presented to the tribunal on the next working day, namely Monday 7 December, meant that it was presented 'in time' (but see the decision in *Ford v Stakis Hotels and Inns Ltd [1988] IRLR 46NB* where a time limit expires on a weekend/bank holiday *and* the tribunal has no letterbox or other means of receiving communication during weekends/bank holidays, the time limit will be automatically extended until the next working day).

Similarly, in calculating the limitation period a tribunal will not make allowances for any anomalies that arise due to way that months are calculated. So, for example, in a claim where the EDT was 30 April and the complaint was presented one day of out of time, on 30 July, the EAT rejected the applicant's submission that the claim was in time since, had the EDT been one day later (i e 1 May), the time limit would not have expired until 31 July (*University of Cambridge v Murray [1993] ICR 460, EAT*).

Stage four: is the claim in time? [6.14]

If the answer to this question is yes, then the claim is in time and no extension need be applied for. If the answer is no, then see stage five below.

Stage five: extending the time limit

Jurisdiction [6.15]

A tribunal has no jurisdiction to hear a claim that is brought outside the relevant statutory time limit (see *Grimes v Sutton London Borough Council [1973] ICR 240*). This means that parties cannot simply agree to have a case heard where the claim has been presented out of time. Similarly, as with all jurisdictional issues, a tribunal has an obligation to satisfy itself that a claim has been presented in time, irrespective of whether the point is taken by either party. This is a continuing obligation and the issue of whether or not a claim has been brought within time can be raised at any point during proceedings (*Rogers v Bodfari (Transport) Ltd [1973] IRLR 172* – any decision of a tribunal on a claim brought outside a time limit may be challenged on the basis that the tribunal lacked jurisdiction, irrespective of whether this was argued before the tribunal. In this case, having made a finding that the dismissal was unfair, the claim was adjourned to consider compensation. At the adjourned hearing, time limits were raised for the first time and the tribunal felt compelled to dismiss the complaint).

In most cases, however, a tribunal has a statutory discretion to extend time and thereby hear a claim. The relatively few claims where a tribunal has no power to extend time and can therefore never hear an 'out of time' claim include:

- claims under the *EPA 1970*;

- claims for time off work with pay for a safety representative under *section 80* of the *Health and Safety at Work Act 1974*;

- appeals against non-discrimination notice under *section 68* of the *SDA 1975*, or *section 59* of the *RRA 1976*;

- applications for compensation where a tribunal has made a declaration of unjustifiable disciplining of trade union members under *section 67(3)* of the *Trade Union and Labour Relations (Consolidation) Act 1992 (TULR(C)A 1992)*;

- applications concerning the failure to comply with an order of the tribunal requiring the employer to pay emoluments under *section 87(6)* of the *TULR(C)A 1992*;

- applications for interim relief under *section 128* of the *ERA 1996*, or pending determination of a complaint of unfair dismissal under *section 161(2)* of the *TULR(C)A 1992* (the time limit for bringing a claim for interim relief is extremely restrictive – an employee may only bring a claim either prior to the EDT or within seven days of the EDT);

- applications for compensation where a tribunal has made a declaration of exclusion or expulsion from a trade union under *section 176(3)* of the *TULR(C)A 1992*;

- appeals against an enforcement notice or penalty notice under *section 19(4)* and *22(1) of the National Minimum Wage Act 1998* respectively;

- appeals against a non-discrimination notice under *section 10(1)* of the *Disability Rights Commission Act 1999*.

In all other cases, a tribunal retains a statutory discretion to consider extending time. The criteria applicable to the exercise of this discretion are considered below.

Extending the time limits [6.16]

Where an applicant has failed to present a claim within the relevant time limit, they may seek to persuade the tribunal to extend time under one of the so-called 'escape clauses'. The criteria that a tribunal is required to consider, when deciding whether or not to extend time, will vary from claim to claim. In practice, however, there are effectively two types of 'escape clause' that apply to the vast majority of claims.

The first, and most common clause, allows a tribunal to consider a claim that has been presented:

'within such further period as [it] considers reasonable in a case where it is satisfied that it was *not reasonably practicable* for the complaint to be presented before the end of that period of three months'. This formula is used in unfair dismissal cases – *ERA 1996, s 111(2)(b))*.'

The second clause that applies to discrimination claims (whether due to race, sex or disability) and redundancy claims, enables a tribunal to extend where 'it considers it *just and equitable* to do so in all the circumstances'.

(1) 'Not reasonably practicable' [6.17]

The burden of proving that it was not reasonably practicable to present a claim 'in time' rests squarely with the employee.

In the case of *Wall's Meat Co Ltd v Khan [1979] ICR 52 (CA)*, the Court of Appeal provided useful guidance of what is meant by 'reasonably practicable':

> 'The performance of an act, in this case the presentation of a complaint, is not reasonably practicable if there is some impediment which reasonably prevents, or interferes with, or inhibits such performance. The impediment may be physical, for instance illness of the complainant or a postal strike; or the impediment may be mental, namely the state of mind of the complainant in the form of ignorance of, or mistaken belief with regard to essential matters'.

In order to fully understand this test it is necessary to appreciate that it incorporates two distinct considerations; namely one of 'reasonableness' and one of 'practicability'. Both have to be satisfied before a tribunal will consider extending time. An employee will therefore have to provide evidence:

- as to the matters that rendered it impracticable to present the complaint in time; and

- that establishes that these matters were themselves reasonable, having regard to all the surrounding circumstances.

Consequently, even if it is accepted that an employee was, for example, ignorant of their legal rights, and that therefore it was not practicable for them to have brought the claim in time, a tribunal will go on to consider whether ignorance was, in all the circumstances, 'reasonable'. This will involve an assessment of the employee's explanation of their ignorance and, in particular, whether or not they had access to legal advice, what steps were taken to find out about their rights and whether they were misled or deceived.

The 'reasonableness' test is objective. A tribunal is therefore entitled to refuse to extend time where it considers that an employee ought to have known or been aware of their rights. For obvious reasons a tribunal is more likely to reach such a conclusion when faced with an intelligent well-educated employee who could have reasonably been expected to have investigated their rights within the time limit.

Bearing in mind the increasing public awareness of unfair dismissal, and employment rights generally, it is becoming ever more difficult for an employee to establish that ignorance of rights is reasonable. It is certainly arguable that, even where an employee has only a general idea as to the availability of a remedy, it would be reasonable to expect them not to delay in making suitable enquiries.

When considering factors that may have physically prevented the employee from presenting their claim, a tribunal will tend to attach greater weight to impediments that arose in the closing stages of the limitation period (*Schultz v Esso Petroleum Ltd [1999] 3 All ER 338*). So, for example, an employee who was physically incapacitated in the last month of the limitation period is more likely to succeed in having time extended than one who was ill for only the first month. The reason for this is that it will be more difficult for the latter to justify his subsequent failure to present the claim in the two months that remained.

Other common reasons justifying delay [6.18]

Error of advisor. The extent to which an employee can rely on an error of their advisor, to demonstrate that it was not reasonably practicable for the claim to have been presented in time, remains somewhat unclear. It would appear that where an employee is misled by an advisor who has been engaged to assist with the case, for example a solicitor, employment advisor or Citizens Advice Bureau, the employee will not be able to rely on the escape clause (*London International College v Sen [1993] IRLR CA* – although in this case the court held that, despite the wrong advice given by the solicitor, the substantial cause of the late application was the incorrect advice given by a tribunal employee, and the applicant should therefore benefit from the escape clause). Certainly, the failure by a skilled advisor to take adequate steps to ensure that the claim is or has been received in time will not, by itself, amount to an acceptable reason justifying the extension of time.

Where, on the other hand, an employee is misled by the advice of someone that they have not retained or engaged, for example a tribunal employee, they are entitled to rely on the escape clause, subject of course to establishing that reliance on the advice and subsequent actions were 'reasonable' (*Jean Sorelle ltd v Rybak [1991] IRLR 153*).

The rationale underlying this distinction appears to be that an advisor who is engaged to assist in a case is potentially liable for any incorrect advice, and it is he and not the employer who should compensate the employee for any loss suffered as a result of this advice.

Where an employee has received incorrect advice from more than one source, a tribunal will attempt to identify the advice that was the substantial cause of the late application. So, for example, in the case of *London International College v Sen [1993] IRLR 3339 CA*, where an employee received incorrect advice both from a solicitor and the tribunal, the Court of Appeal took the view that since the substantial cause of the late application was the 'reasonable' reliance on the incorrect advice given by the tribunal, the employee should benefit from the escape clause despite the fact that he had had access to skilled advice.

Delay caused by internal appeal/other proceedings: Where the sole reason for an employee having delayed presenting their complaint is the fact that they had an ongoing appeal under the employer's internal dispute procedure, this is unlikely, by itself, to justify extending time under the escape clause. As indicated above, where a decision is taken to dismiss an employee time begins to run from the effective date of termination and not from the date of any decision taken during an internal appeal brought against a dismissal.

Similarly, the fact that an employee delays presenting a complaint until after other proceedings (whether civil or criminal) have been determined is unlikely to satisfy the criteria. In *Palmer v Southend-on-Sea Borough Council [1984] IRLR 119*, two employees who had been convicted of stealing petrol and dismissed were told that if their criminal convictions were overturned, the Council might reconsider their dismissal. The convictions were overturned but the Council refused to reinstate the employees. The time limit for challenging the original dismissal had expired and the Court of Appeal refused to extend time on the basis that it had been reasonably practicable to present the complaint in time.

By way of exception to this general rule, a tribunal may be willing to extend time where the employee delays presenting a claim to the tribunal, pending the decision of an internal appeal, at the specific request of the employer (*Owen v Crown House Engineering Ltd [1973] IRLR 233, NIRC*).

Ignorance of material facts: Where, as a result of the late discovery of a fact or facts that enable a claim to be made, an application is presented out of time, tribunals have been willing to apply the 'escape clause'. In determining whether or not the late discovery of a fact justifies extending the time limit, a tribunal will apply a three-stage test, conveniently laid out in the case of *Machine Tool Industry Research Association v Simpson*

[1988] IRLR 212. Under this test an employee is required to establish that:

- it was reasonable for them not to be aware of the factual basis upon which they could bring an application to the tribunal during the limitation period;

- the knowledge gained has, in the circumstances, been reasonably gained by them, and is either crucial, fundamental or important to their change of belief and realisation that they have reasonable grounds for bringing a claim (it is important to note that there is no requirement for the employee to establish the truth of the new fact(s), only the reasonableness of a belief in it – *Marley (UK) Ltd v Anderson [1996] affd IRLR 163 CA*; and

- the acquisition of knowledge is, in any event, crucial to their decision to bring the claim.

In practice, this justification is often raised in cases involving redundancy dismissals. In *Machine Tool Industry Research Association v Simpson,* for example, an employee who, after being made redundant, became aware that another employee had been re-engaged to carry out a substantially similar job, decided to bring a claim for unfair dismissal. The Court of Appeal accepted that it was only after she discovered that another employee had been re-engaged did she become suspicious as to the 'real' reason for her dismissal, and that since this occurred after the expiry of the three-month time limit, the escape clause ought to be operated in her favour.

As with all applications for an extension of time it remains incumbent on an employee to act with all due speed once they become aware of their right to make a claim. This is neatly illustrated by the decision in *James W Cook (Wivenhoe) Ltd v Tipper [1990] IRLR 386,* a case where eight shipyard workers were made redundant but at the same time given assurances that they would be re-engaged when work picked up. In relying on this assurance, they did not bring a claim for unfair dismissal. When, after the time limit had expired, the shipyard was closed down, the workers realised that there had never been an intention of keeping it open and sought to bring a claim for unfair dismissal. The Court of Appeal accepted that time should be extended, but held that only the employees who had presented a complaint within two weeks of the closure should benefit from the 'escape clause'.

Postal delay: Historically, where it could be established that the failure to present a complaint in time arose as a result of an unforeseen delay in the postal services, this was normally considered to be an acceptable reason for extending time (*Dedman v British Building and Engineering Appliances*

Ltd [1974] 1 ALL ER 520). Any extension of time was of course subject to the employee and/or their advisor establishing that they had a reasonable expectation that the originating application would arrive in time.

The burden of proof is on the employee. In the past, this burden was relatively light since tribunals were generally willing to accept that a person who posted their application by first class post had a reasonable expectation that it would arrive the next day. Consequently, the mere fact that an employee waited until the penultimate day of the limitation period to post their application was rarely, of itself, considered 'unreasonable'.

In more recent decisions, however, tribunals recognising the increasing unreliability of the postal service, have indicated that less tolerance should be should be shown to those who wait until the penultimate day before posting their complaints (*St Basil's Centre v McCrossan [1991] IRLR 455* – 'mere evidence of expectation of delivery of a first class post may not, in the future, provide an adequate explanation'). In *McCrossan* it was suggested that the 1985 *Practice Direction* referred to in that case, relating to the delivery of documents in the High Court, offered useful guidance as to what amounted to a reasonable expectation. Under the provisions of these directions, first class post is deemed to arrive on the second working day after posting, whereas second class post is deemed to arrive on the fourth working day.

When considering whether to extend to time a tribunal will pay particular attention to the reason for the delay in presenting the application. So, for example in *McCrossan,* a case where an originating application was dictated on a Friday, but was only typed and posted on the following Tuesday (the penultimate day of the limitation period), the EAT gave a clear indication that, in future, this sort of delay might well be considered 'unreasonable'.

Where, on the other hand, an application has been lost in the post, a tribunal is only likely to extend time where it is satisfied that the employee and/or their advisor have taken all reasonable steps to check that it has been received in time. This test requires an employee to make appropriate enquiries at or near the time when a reply from the tribunal ought reasonably to have been received (*Camden & Islington Community Services NHS Trust v Kennedy [1996] IRLR 381).* The fact that an employee cannot simply rely on the presumption that 'what is posted will be delivered' is highlighted by the case of *Capital Foods Retail Ltd v Corrigan [1993] IRLR 430.* In this case, although it was accepted that the application had been posted five weeks prior to the expiry of the limitation period, the EAT refused to extend time because, in their view, the solicitors had acted 'unreasonably' by not taking any steps to check that application had been received until three months after the limitation period had expired.

Time limits applicable to the escape clause: Where a tribunal accepts that it was not reasonably practicable for an employee to have presented their claim in time, it must then consider whether the claim was in fact presented within a reasonable time thereafter. Only where it is satisfied that the employee has acted with all reasonable speed after the impediment that was preventing the presentation of the claim had been removed, will a tribunal extend time to the date that the claim was actually presented.

There is no general rule as to what constitutes a 'reasonable time' (*Marley (UK) Ltd v Anderson* – the decision by a tribunal to treat a four-week delay as inherently unreasonable, without looking at the surrounding circumstances, was wrong in law). Whether the delay in presenting the claim was reasonable will depend on the particular circumstances of each case.

(2) Just and equitable [6.19]

Under this second 'escape clause', which applies only in cases of sex, race and disability discrimination (*SDA 1975, s 76(1), RRA 1976, s 68(1) and DDA 1995, Sch 3 para 3(1)*) tribunals may grant an extension of time 'if in all the circumstances of the case, it considers that it is just and equitable to do so'. This is a far less restrictive test than the 'not reasonably practicable' formula and gives tribunals a significantly wider discretion to extend time.

Practical examples where time has been extended, in circumstances where it would not have been extended under the 'not reasonably practicable' test, include where:

- an employee delayed in presenting a claim in reliance on incorrect legal advice (*Hawkins v Ball and Barclays Bank plc [1996] IRLR 258*);

- an employee delayed presenting a complaint pending an internal appeal (*Aniagwu v London Borough of Hackney [1999] IRLR 303, EAT*); and

- a judicial decision clarifies the law so as to give an employee a new right (*Biggs v Somerset County Council [1996] IRLR 203*).

These examples are provided merely by way of illustration and should not be construed as indicative of a general rule. Whether or not it is just and equitable to extend time will depend on the particular facts of each case. So, for example, where contrary to union advice an employee delayed presenting a complaint pending an internal appeal, a tribunal refused to extend time.

Under the just and equitable test, a tribunal is required to consider the prejudice that both parties will suffer as a result of allowing or refusing to extend time. With this in mind, a tribunal will endeavour to ascertain the extent to which each party has contributed to the delay.

In deciding whether an employee should benefit from the 'escape clause' a tribunal will pay particular attention to the following:

- the length and reasons for any delay;

- the extent to which the delay may have affected the reliability or availability of the evidence;

- any steps taken by employee to ascertain the factual position and/or their legal rights (including obtaining suitable legal advice);

- the speed with which the employee acted once they became aware that they were able to make a claim; and

- the extent to which the employer contributed to the delay.

In *Hutchison v Westward Television Ltd [1977] IRLR 69,* the EAT confirmed that 'circumstances of the case' referred to the facts relevant to the application to extend time and not the merits of the substantive claim.

Claims under EC Law [6.20]

Claims based on either:

- a directly applicable provision of the *Treaty of Rome* (e g *Art 141 – equal pay*); or

- a directly effective European Council Directive (e g *Equal Pay Directive*) *75/117/EEC;*

are not subject to any specific time limits, whether under EC or UK domestic legislation. The European Court of Justice (ECJ) has ruled on numerous occasions that time limits for the enforcement of EC rights are a procedural matter to be determined by the national legislation of Member States. This is subject to the proviso that any such time limits are not less favourable than those applicable to similar domestic actions and do not render virtually impossible the exercise of the EC right/law

(*Emott v Minister for Social Welfare and A-G: C-208/90 [1993] ICR 8;
Fisscher v Voorhuis Hengelo BV: C-128/93, [1995] ICR635; Preston v
Wolverhampton Healthcare NHS Trust (No2) [2001] ICR 217* – where, after
a reference to the ECJ, the House of Lords held that the six-month time
limit under the *EPA 1970* was not less favourable than/would render
impossible the exercise of EC rights/law).

Tribunals do not have jurisdiction to hear claims from private sector
employees based solely on EC law. As the Court of Appeal held in *Biggs
v Somerset County Council [1996] 2 ALL ER 734* (see also *Barber v
Staffordshire County Council [1996] 2 ALL ER 748)*, EC law may only be
relied on before a tribunal, so as to displace a provision of domestic
legislation which is considered incompatible with a directly effective
article or directive. As a result of this decision, it is clear that a private
sector employee may only bring proceedings before a tribunal *under
existing UK legislation*. This in turn means that, even where a private sector
employee wishes to rely on EC law, any proceedings will still be subject
to the time limits applicable to the statutory claim that they choose to
bring before the tribunal.

The position is somewhat different for state employees (eg civil servants)
who may bring a claim based on a directly effective directive, even where
the directive has not yet been implemented/fully intergrated into national
legislation. The time limit for bringing these claims starts to run from the
date that the directive is fully implemented into national law (*Emmot v
Minister for Social Welfare and A-G: 208/90 [1991] IRLR 387* – see also
Biggs where the CA held that this principle only applied to directives that
required implementation). This means that proceedings may be issued
years after the circumstances or events upon which the claim is based took
place.

The Court of Appeal's decision in *Biggs* has effectively barred
retrospective proceedings based on new interpretations of EC law, for
claims where the statutory test for extending the time limit is whether 'it
was reasonably practicable to have brought the claim in time'. In that
case, the applicant, relying on a subsequent House of Lords decision in
R v Secretary of State, ex p EOC [1994] 1 ALL ER 910, sought to bring
a retrospective claim for unfair dismissal 18 years after she was dismissed.
She submitted that, as a result of the decision in *ex p EOC*, it was now
clear that the exclusion of part-time workers from the right to claim unfair
dismissal was discriminatory, and that she should be entitled to bring a
claim for unfair dismissal within three months of the date of that decision.
The Court of Appeal rejected her argument that prior to the decision in
ex p EOC, it had not 'been reasonably practicable' to bring the claim due
to the uncertainty that existed as to the state of the law. In its view, it had
been open to the applicant to have lodged a claim in 1976 and raised the

arguments at that stage. It therefore refused to treat her application as in time.

In relation to statutory claims where an extension of time can be granted on 'just and equitable' grounds, however, there would appear to remain far greater scope for bringing retrospective proceedings based on new interpretative decisions of EC law. In the case of *DPP v Marshall [1998] ICR 518,* for example, the EAT allowed a transsexual to bring a claim under the *SDA 1975,* within three months of the ECJ decision that gender reassignment fell within the ambit of the *Equal Treatment Directive (76/207/EEC) (P v S C-13/94 [1996] ICR 795),* although this was some three years after the cause of action arose.

Do's and Don'ts for applicants

Do:

- Send documents by recorded delivery.

- Keep contemporaneous notes of conversations identifying the date and the names of parties.

- Be proactive and take reasonable steps to ensure that documents have been received by the tribunal.

- Take reasonable steps to obtain advice as soon as you think that you might have a claim.

- Present an originating application outlining the facts that you feel may give rise to a claim where the limitation period is about to expire.

- Present the claim promptly after becoming aware of the facts/right to make a claim.

- Identify the act complained of and the relevant time limit for bringing a claim.

Don't:

- Wait until the penultimate day of the limitation period for presenting a claim, if you do, hand deliver the claim and obtain a receipt.

- Delay in confirming receipt of documents, making applications or enquiries.

cont'd

- Delay in making a claim merely because there is an internal appeal pending or due to ongoing negotiations to settle.

- Underestimate the difficulty of obtaining an extension of time.

Do's for respondents

Do:

- Seek clarification where there is doubt as to when the act complained of occurred.

- Give all parties (including the tribunal) as much written notice as possible of the reasons why you consider the claim to be out of time.

- Seek guidance at an early stage from the tribunal as to whether it is appropriate to determine, as a preliminary issue, the question of whether the claim is in time.

- Prepare for a hearing on time limits with the appropriate legal test in mind – 'reasonably practicable' or 'just and equitable'.

- Remember that time limits can be raised at any stage during proceedings, even at a remedies hearing or during an appeal.

Pre-action checklist [6.21]

For the applicant

Have you:

- Engaged in any appropriate pre-action communication, such as (in discrimination cases) serving a questionnaire or a letter before claim aimed at achieving what you want through settlement? (see CHAPTER 3)

- Identified the correct name of the respondent (it is useful to clarify this is pre-claim correspondence)?

- Confirmed that the claim is one which the tribunal has jurisdiction to hear?

- Had regard to time limits? (see CHAPTER 6)

- Considered taking advice (including in discrimination cases) from the Equal Opportunities Commission, Commission for Racial Equality or Disability Rights Commission? (see CHAPTER 3)

For the respondent

Have you:

- Appraised the strength of your case, including a review of any relevant documentation, such as internal memos, correspondence and notes of disciplinary hearings?

- Engaged in pre-claim correspondence with a view to forming a valid compromise agreement? (see CHAPTER 18 – SETTLEMENT OF CLAIMS)

- Had regard to whether the potential claim is in time (see APPENDIX I and this chapter) or whether there is any other possible challenge on grounds of jurisdiction?

- Considered whether it is necessary to seek specialist advice/secure representation for a hearing? (see CHAPTER 3)

Stages leading to full hearing checklist [6.22]

- What information should be included in the originating application and notice of appearance? (see CHAPTER 7 – MAKING A CLAIM and CHAPTER 8 – THE EMPLOYER'S RESPONSE)

- Have the issues been properly defined, or is there a need for a request for further information? (see CHAPTER 11 – POST CLAIM REQUESTS FOR FURTHER INFORMATION)

- Is there are any basis for requesting a preliminary hearing (see CHAPTER 15 – PRELIMINARY HEARINGS) or a pre-hearing review? (see CHAPTER 14 – PRE-EMPTIVE STRIKES)

- Is there documentation which should be requested from the other side (see CHAPTER 12 – DISCLOSURE) or from a third party? (see CHAPTER 16 – WITNESS ORDERS AND ORDERS FOR THE PRODUCTION OF DOCUMENTS)

- If the chairman has not already directed that one take place, should you request a directions hearing (see CHAPTER 13 – DIRECTIONS AND DIRECTIONS HEARINGS) in order to make an applications, or is it better to make the applications separately in writing? (see CHAPTER 13 and CHAPTER 7)

- What witnesses do you need – is a witness order likely to be necessary? (see CHAPTER 16)

- Is your case prepared for full hearing? (see CHAPTER 19 – PREPARING FOR THE FULL HEARING)

- Has a settlement of the claim been explored? (see CHAPTER 18)

7.

Making a Claim – the Originating Claim (IT1)

Introduction [7.1]

The originating application is the document, completed by the applicant, which has the effect of launching tribunal proceedings. It is usually made on a form entitled 'IT1' which can be obtained not only from employment tribunals (see CHAPTER 10 – COMMUNICATING WITH THE TRIBUNAL), but also the majority of advice centres, Citizens Advice Bureau, job centres and ACAS.

The IT1 sets out:

- what the claim is for (e g unfair dismissal, sex discrimination etc);

- the essential facts upon which the claim is based; and

- basic information about the applicant's employment, such as pay and length of service.

An effectively drafted IT1 helps create a positive first impression on both the tribunal and the respondent.

The IT1 has eleven different sections, all of which need to be completed. This chapter concentrates predominately on section 11 where the applicant is required to set out the grounds of complaint. A sample grounds can be found in APPENDIX V – CASE STUDY, which should be read in conjunction with the following notes.

Completing the originating application [7.2]

- *Box 1*: Type of complaint. Provide details here of what the claim is for, e g unfair dismissal, sex discrimination, disability discrimination. If there is more than one claim include them in numbered form, such as (1) Unfair Dismissal (2) Sex discrimination (3) Unlawful deductions from wages.

- *Box 2*: Applicant's details.

- *Box 3*: Representative's details. Once these are entered, the representative, as opposed to the applicant, will receive all relevant correspondence from the tribunal.

- *Box 4*: Dates of employment. These provide the applicant's version of when the employment began and terminated. In the majority of cases this will not be in dispute. The date of termination will be either the last day of the applicant's notice period (if they worked out that notice) or, if not, the last day they actually worked. In certain cases, such as constructive dismissal, the date of termination may be in dispute, and the date included in this box will therefore be of additional significance. With unfair dismissal, the dates included will be used by the tribunal as the basis for calculating the basic and compensatory award in the event of the applicant being successful.

- *Box 5*: Details of the employer. The details given about the employer will be used by the tribunal to contact the respondent to inform them of the application. Usually there will only be one respondent, namely the employer. However, this will not always be so. For example, in discrimination cases it is possible to pursue both the individual employee who committed the act of discrimination and their employer. Another example is in certain transfer of undertakings cases. Where there is more than one respondent, they should be listed in (1), (2), (3) order.

- *Box 6*: Connection with the respondent. It is usual in this box to include the applicant's title, e g sales manager. In certain cases, the applicant will not be an employee, for example in cases of discriminatory selection for jobs or certain other types of claim, eg under the *Working Time Regulations 1998 (SI 1998/1833)*. In such cases the nature of the relationship should be explained, such as 'applicant for job'.

- *Box 7*: Normal basic hours. Usually this refers to the minimum hours that the employee is contractually required to work.

- *Box 8*: Details of earnings. This is the basis upon which compensation is calculated by the tribunal. There is a box for insertion of the basic wage/salary (i e gross pay), a box for the insertion of the 'average take home' pay and a further box for inclusion of bonuses and benefits. Where a person's pay fluctuates, the standard practice is to give the average figure from the last twelve weeks of employment.

- *Box 9*: Date of action complained of other than dismissal. This box should be completed in conjunction with box 11, details of complaint. It requires, in non-dismissal cases, the date of the act complained of. In certain cases there will be a number of different dates upon which the applicant relies; in others the complaint may be built upon a continuing course of conduct over a period of time. In such instances, the details required are best included in box 11, details of complaint, and the words 'see section 11' added.

- *Box 10*: Remedy sought in unfair dismissal cases. The choice here is between reinstatement, re-engagement or compensation. It is common for chairmen of tribunals to clarify the remedy which is sought at the beginning of a case.

Box 11: grounds of complaint [7.3]

This is where the applicant sets out the basic facts which form the essential elements of their claim. This section is all about achieving a balance between giving sufficient, but not excessive, information about the essential elements of the claim.

Advantages of effectively drafted grounds of complaint [7.4]

- It will be the first impression that the respondent and the tribunal receive of the claim.

- Giving sufficient, but not excessive, information about the claim may prevent an application for further information (see CHAPTER 11 – POST-CLAIM REQUEST FOR FURTHER INFORMATION).

- Failure to mention something fundamental could have serious consequences if the applicant seeks to rely on that fact at the full hearing. For example, if at the hearing it is mentioned for the first time that a particular individual has discriminated against the applicant, the tribunal might either postpone the hearing to give the respondent an opportunity to prepare its response, making a costs award against the applicant or even preventing them from relying on that fact at all.

Drafting the grounds of complaint [7.5]

Many applicants (or their advisors) agonise about how much detail to include in their grounds. The purpose of the IT1 is to set out the essential elements of the claim. A good rule of thumb is to ask 'what information should be included to enable the tribunal to understand the issues in the case and the respondent to understand the case it has to meet?' Approaching the issue that way helps prevent an application for further information from the respondent.

Do's and Don'ts when drafting the grounds of complaint

Do:

- State what the claim is for (e g unfair dismissal, sex discrimination etc).

- Include the essential facts that prove that the conduct of the respondent is unlawful.

- Structure those facts around the legal test that the tribunal will apply in deciding whether the respondent has acted unlawfully.

Don't:

- Include detailed explanations as to how the applicant will prove the above.

- Include detailed legal arguments.

In order to achieve this, the applicant you will need to have a good basic knowledge of the area of employment law in which the claim arises. The following example illustrates the above points. It may also be helpful to look at the example of an IT1 (in a specific factual context) in **APPENDIX III: APPLICATION TO AN EMPLOYMENT TRIBUNAL (IT1)**.

Example

1. *Background*: The applicant's claim is for unfair dismissal. The applicant was employed by the respondent as a sales manager from 1996–2001. In December 2001, the applicant was given notice by the respondent. The reason given by the respondent was redundancy.

2. *Grounds of complaint*: The applicant contends that his dismissal was unfair for the following reasons:

    2.1. The expressed reason for dismissal, redundancy, was not the real reason. The applicant will contend that the real reason was capability and that his dismissal for that reason was unfair. In so asserting, the applicant will rely upon the fact that the issue of redundancy was raised at the same meeting on 4 December 2001 at which the applicant

cont'd

was informed that he had failed to meet his performance targets etc.

2.2. If, which is denied, redundancy was the reason for the applicant's dismissal, the applicant will contend that the respondent acted unreasonably in all the circumstances in treating this as the reason for dismissal. In so asserting, the applicant will rely, *inter alia*, upon the following:

(a) The requirement of the company for a person to carry out the type of work undertaken by the applicant had not ceased or diminished. After the applicant was dismissed, a Mr X was employed to perform the tasks the applicant had been carrying out during the last two years of his employment.

(b) The respondent failed to carry out a fair procedure by:

(i) failing to consult with the applicant over his redundancy (include basic facts in support);

(ii) failing to adopt fair selection criteria (include basic facts in support); and

(iii) failing to make any, or any sufficient, attempts to find alternative work for the applicant within the respondent's organisation (include basic facts in support).

The example structures the factual basis of the applicant's claim around the law of unfair dismissal, namely:

• what was the reason for the dismissal?

• was it a potentially fair reason (not an issue in this particular case)? and

• did the respondent act reasonably in treating it as a reason to dismiss the applicant (including the adoption of a fair procedure)?

In many cases, the grounds of complaint would be considered sufficient without the inclusion of such facts. The only difficulty with adopting that approach is that it might leave the applicant open to an application for further information from the respondent. In deciding how much to include, the applicant should consider which facts should be included to give the respondent a broad idea of the claim it has to meet.

The advantage of adopting the above approach is that it requires the factual basis of the claim to be marshalled around the legal issues, making the grounds of complaint instantly more comprehensible to the tribunal.

The consequences of incomplete/incorrect applications [7.6]

Particularly where the applicant has instructed a representative close to the deadline, there may be occasions when there is insufficient time to obtain details about the claim. The golden rule in these circumstances is to submit the original application in time in any event, even if it is only possible to give the barest details of the claim, and then make an application to amend at a later date. The reason for this is that making an application to amend the IT1 (provided it does not prejudice the other side) is usually far easier than making an application for an extension of time as the hands of the tribunal are tied by very strict criteria (see CHAPTER 6 – TIME LIMITS).

Under 'grounds of complaint' it is quite common to see the following: 'The applicant's claim is for unfair dismissal and sex discrimination arising from her employment with the respondent. Detailed grounds will be submitted to the tribunal within 14 days.'

Amending the originating application [7.7]

Any alteration or addition (such as submitting more detailed grounds of complaint) to the IT1 must be done through an application to amend. The majority of such applications are dealt with by a chairman alone reviewing the papers (see CHAPTER 10 (10.9)). The power to amend an originating application comes under the tribunal's general case management powers contained in *rule 4* of the *Employment Tribunals (Constitution and Rules of Procedure) Regulations 2001 (SI 2001/1171)*. The application to amend should include: (a) the amendment/addition; and (b) briefly, the reason why the information was not included in the original application.

Tribunals frequently allow amendments to originating applications and apply the overriding objective (see CHAPTER 9 – FAIRNESS: THE OVERRIDING OBJECTIVE) in deciding whether to do so. The main barrier to success is prejudice to the respondent. This means that the earlier the applicant makes the application the better, as the respondent will be less able to argue that they have been prejudiced in the preparation of their case.

When amending the grounds of complaint, it is common practice amongst professional representatives to make the amendments on the original grounds, which are then headed 'Amended Grounds of Complaint'. The practice is to underline additional words and strike through words that are being deleted so that they are still readable.

For example: The acts of discrimination took place on the 5, 7, 8, 9 and 10 of January 2002. The people responsible for discriminating against the applicant were Bill Jones, Laurie Smith, and Peter Parker.

The advantage of doing this is that the tribunal need only look at one document to get a complete view of the application, as opposed to looking at the initial grounds and then at the amended grounds, which can be confusing.

Do's and Don'ts

Do:

- Submit the IT1 in time, even if it is incomplete, and then amend later.

- Try and make applications for amendments in good time to avoid arguments of prejudice by the respondent.

Don't:

- Confuse the grounds of complaint with a detailed witness statement – give sufficient information for the respondent to know the case it has to meet.

- Forget that effective grounds of complaint can defeat an application for further information.

8.

The Employer's Response – the Notice of Appearance (IT3)

Introduction [8.1]

When a claim to a tribunal is made, the tribunal will send to the respondent a copy of the applicant's originating application and also a notice of appearance (known as form IT3) for the employer or its representative to complete. The IT3 is the first opportunity for the employer to tell both the tribunal and the applicant what its case is. An effectively drafted IT3, which shows an understanding of the legal principles upon which the tribunal will decide the case, is important for the following reasons:

- to win a case an employer often needs to show that, at the time of the relevant events, it acted with an awareness of essential employment law principles. If a poor understanding of such principles is exhibited in the IT3 the applicant will be given a head start;

- a carelessly completed IT3 may create the damaging impression that the employer has not taken the dispute seriously.

Tribunals tend to expect higher standards of drafting from employers than employees.

Time limits for submission of the notice of appearance [8.2]

A notice of appearance should be returned within 21 days of receipt of the originating application (*Employment Tribunals (Constitution and Rules of Procedure) Regulations 2001 (SI 2001/1171), rule 3(1)*). Sometimes this is impractical, in which case there are two options. First, to lodge a holding IT3 (incorporating such information as can be provided) with an indication that there will be application to serve an amended notice at a later date. Second, to apply for an extension of time for service. Both applications are made under *rule 4(1)*. In making the application, the employer should address the overriding objective (see **CHAPTER 9 –**

FAIRNESS: THE OVERRIDING OBJECTIVE). This means that such applications are frequently successful, provided they do not prejudice the other side.

If the 21-day limit has already expired, do not panic. Tribunals will apply the overriding objective in deciding whether to extend time for service of the notice of appearance (see CHAPTER 6 – TIME LIMITS). The reasons for the delay should be given in any application. It is also usually appropriate to assert that preventing the employer from appearing in the proceedings would be a disproportionately harsh penalty. The employer may, however, be vulnerable to an application for costs (see CHAPTER 24 – COSTS).

The consequences of non-submission of the notice of appearance   [8.3]

The basic rule is that a respondent who does not file a notice of appearance is not a party in the proceedings. The case will proceed to be heard and determined by the tribunal in the absence of the employer. Where it is demonstrated by the employer that it never received notice of proceedings, it can apply to have the decision reviewed under *rule 13(b)*.

Completing the notice of appearance   [8.4]

- *Box 1*: The respondent's address and title. This is self-explanatory, but ensure that the tribunal is informed where there is any change of address.

- *Box 2*: The respondent's representative. If this box is completed, all correspondence from the tribunal will be sent to the representative and not to the respondent itself.

- *Box 3*: State whether the application is resisted.

- *Box 4*: Is the dismissal admitted and, if so, what is the reason? Employers should be extremely careful when completing this box.

  'Is the dismissal admitted?': If the employment relationship has terminated, do not admit the dismissal if this was brought about by the resignation of the applicant. The reason for highlighting this is that, in a constructive dismissal claim, an admission that the applicant was dismissed is tantamount to an admission of defeat.

  'The reason for dismissal': If the fact of dismissal is admitted, as in the majority of unfair dismissal claims, then the employer needs

to give the reason for this. Again, complete this section with great care. If the dismissal is to be fair, the reason given must be one or more of the potentially lawful reasons set out in *section 98(1)* and *(2)* of the *Employment Rights Act 1996*, i e:

(a) capability or qualifications;

(b) conduct;

(c) redundancy;

(d) the employee could not continue to work in the position without contravention of a duty or restriction imposed by enactment; or

(e) some other substantial reason.

Ensure that the correct reason is selected as amending this section of the notice of appearance can be extremely problematic, unless it can be shown that the employer has, while relying upon the same set of factual circumstances, simply picked the wrong legal 'label'.

- *Box 5*: The applicant's dates of employment. The last date of employment is the date of expiry of the notice period. Where there was no notice period, or there has been pay in lieu or notice, the final date will be the actual date when employment ended. The dates of employment may be at issue, in which case particular care should be taken in completing this box. For example, in an unfair dismissal dispute, there may be doubts about whether the applicant has been employed for a period of a year. Alternatively, the date of dismissal/resignation could be a major issue.

- *Box 6*: The applicant's earnings. Any compensation the applicant eventually receives will be determined, at least in part, according to their earnings, which should therefore be accurately recorded, although amendments to this part of the IT3 are usually permitted. Note, the respondent can choose whether it wishes to give weekly, monthly or annual figures. The basic/wage salary is the pre-tax figure and the 'average take home' the net figure. Bonuses and benefits should include overtime and such matters as pension benefits. Where the wages of the applicant fluctuated, the respondent should provide the average of the previous twelve weeks' wages, and indicate this on the form.

- *Box 7*: The grounds of resistance. There are two documents which members of the tribunal will read with particularly close attention. The first is the grounds of complaint in the IT1 and the second is the grounds of resistance in the IT3.

A sample grounds of resistance can be found in **APPENDIX V – CASE STUDY**.

Drafting the grounds of resistance [8.5]

Remember to address the issues which the tribunal will have to decide, not to simply answer the specific allegations in the IT1, which may be minimal in nature. If, for example, the grounds of complaint simply state: 'I was unfairly dismissed because my manager continuously picked on me', the tribunal will ask:

- what was the reason for the dismissal?

- was it a potentially lawful reason?

- did the respondent act reasonably in all the circumstances in treating it as a reason to dismiss the applicant?

The grounds of resistance needs to address all of those issues. Drafting effective grounds involves, therefore, a two-step process.

Step one: Identify the basic legal issues that the tribunal will have to decide. Examples of typical issues in unfair dismissals can be found in the paragraph above. In a case of sex or race discrimination, the issues will often be:

(a) was the applicant subjected to less favourable treatment?

(b) if so, was this on account of their sex/race?

(c) if there was less favourable treatment on grounds of sex/race, did the respondent take all reasonable steps to prevent such treatment taking place?

Step two: Structure the facts which (if found to be proven by the tribunal) demonstrate the employer acted lawfully around those issues. For example, in relation to issue (a) above: The respondent denies that it subjected the applicant to less favourable treatment (=legal issue). The applicant was treated fairly by the respondent at all times. In May 2002, the applicant was disciplined for persistent late attendance at work in accordance with procedures which apply to all staff regardless of sex/race etc. (=facts in support of the case).

Preserving the employer's position [8.6]

Remember, where appropriate, to preserve the employer's position in respect of each of the issues in the case. This can be done through use of phrases such as 'if, which is denied', 'without prejudice to the contention that...', and even the slightly less legalistic 'in any event'.

Example

It is denied that the applicant was treated less favourably than her chosen comparator (include facts in support).If, which is denied, the applicant was treated less favourably, it is denied that this was on grounds of her sex (include facts in support). Without prejudice to this assertion, it is contended that the respondent took all reasonable steps to prevent its employees carrying out acts of discrimination (include facts in support).

It can be seen from the example that the employer is defending its position in respect of each of the hurdles which the applicant will have to cross with use of such phrases as 'if, which is denied' and 'without prejudice'.

How much should be admitted? [8.7]

Careful thought is required as to what, if anything, should be admitted by the employer in the grounds of resistance. Remember that issues can be conceded much closer to the hearing date. Equally, credit may be lost with the tribunal if the employer seeks to dispute an aspect of the case that ought to have been conceded from the outset. A general rule of thumb is this: ask whether, if the tribunal accepted the employer's position in relation to a particular issue, that would still result in a finding against it (on that issue). If the answer is yes, then it may be appropriate to concede on that issue, unless there is some hope of further evidence emerging.

Example

An employee claims that she has been victimised by a manager on grounds of her sex over a period of three months, including one instance of being sent home from work. An investigation has been carried out by the respondent under its grievance procedure, the outcome of which is a report by a senior manager that, whilst sex discrimination and victimisation did not take place, the employee was erroneously sent home on a particular occasion and told to return the next day. The senior manager has found, however, that the reason for that treatment was not the employee's sex, but rather the mistaken (yet honest) belief of the junior manager that she was due to work the night shift that day.

cont'd

How should the grounds of resistance be drafted? It should be admitted that the employee was mistakenly sent home. This should be conceded in a way which does minimum damage to the case, for example: 'The respondent denies that the applicant was victimised or treated less favourably on grounds of her sex over a period of three months' (then give facts in support, including investigation). 'The respondent accepts that on [...] the applicant was mistakenly sent home. The respondent's internal investigation found that the reason for this had no connection with the applicant's sex, but was due to the erroneous belief of the manager concerned that the applicant was due to work the night shift that day.'

How much detail should be provided in the grounds of complaint [8.8]

Just as the employer needs to know from the applicant what case it has to meet, likewise the applicant is entitled to have notice of the major facts and events upon which the employer will rely in support of its case. A failure to do so can have serious consequences at a later stage. It is necessary, therefore, to include, important events and facts in support of the employer's case, but it is often best to steer clear of detailed explanations as to precisely *how* the employer's case will be proved in relation to those events.

Example

The applicant maintains that he was dismissed after a single incident of gross misconduct on 6 January 2002. The employer, while stating that he was dismissed for gross misconduct, also relies upon several past incidents of misconduct. The applicant needs to be given notice of this in order to respond. Include: 'On 19 January the applicant informed the human resources manager that he was unhappy in his position and wanted a transfer'. There is no necessity to say: 'The respondent will produce minutes of the meeting and call evidence from the manager in support of the fact that such a request was made', although there may, in certain situations, be tactical advantages in doing so.

Do's and Don'ts in the drafting of grounds of resistance

Do:

- Include the essential facts which (if found to be proven by the tribunal) demonstrate that the respondent acted lawfully.

- Structure those facts around the legal test, which the tribunal will apply in deciding whether the respondent has acted lawfully.

- Remember that if you have not yet taken full instructions from your key players, consider submitting a holding IT3 and making a subsequent application to amend. Remember that applications to amend are easier to make the earlier they are submitted.

- Keep in mind the need to avoid a possible application for further information from the applicant when drafting the IT3.

Don't:

- Include detailed explanations as to how you will prove the above.

- Include detailed legal arguments.

- Be afraid to make an application to amend, giving your full reasons and having regard to the overriding objective.

9.

Fairness: the Overriding Objective

Introduction [9.1]

The tribunal, when it exercises its procedural powers (whether following an application by the parties or of its own volition), is required to give effect (so far as is practicable) to the *overriding objective*. This is a recent innovation in tribunal proceedings, brought in by the *Employment Tribunals (Constitution and Rules of Procedure) Regulations 2001 (SI 2001/1171)*.

The overriding objective, where there is a conflict, takes precedence over all previous case law relating to the exercise of procedural powers by the tribunal (see **9.7**). Its introduction has been widely welcomed, with a number of chairmen observing that it compels them to do what in practice they have been doing for years – namely exercise their powers in accordance with common sense principles of fairness between the parties.

The tribunal is required to give effect to the overriding objective when deciding (amongst other things) applications to amend, requests for further information, witness orders, applications for costs, applications to strike out, disclosure and issues of admissibility of evidence during the hearing. If making or defending any such applications, you will need to explain why your position is correct with reference to the criteria laid down in the overriding objective.

The tribunal must also give effect to the overriding objective when making case management decisions of its own volition, such as directing that there should be a preliminary hearing or pre-hearing review.

What is the overriding objective? [9.2]

Regulation 10(1) of the 2001 Regulations states that: 'The overriding objective of the rules is to enable tribunals to *deal with cases justly*.'

Regulation 10(2) provides the definition:

'Dealing with a case justly includes, so far as practicable –

(a) ensuring that the parties are on an equal footing;

(b) saving expense;

(c) dealing with cases in ways which are proportionate to the complexity of the issues; and

(d) ensuring that it is dealt with fairly and expeditiously.'

Ensuring the parties are on an equal footing: This is a broad concept which encompasses the following, ensuring that a party has:

- a sufficient understanding of the case it has to meet;

- sufficient time to meet it; and

- is not disadvantaged by the fact that it has less resources and legal expertise at its disposal than the other party.

In essence, it is about providing, so far as is practicable, a level playing field.

Saving expense: The expense referred is the expense of the parties as a consequence of a decision being taken (or not taken) under *regulation 10(1)*. Included in this might be administrative and legal costs.

Dealing with cases in a way which is proportionate to the complexity of the issues: A tribunal must have regard to the complexity of an issue in making a relevant decision under the *regulation 10(2)*. Burden/s should not be placed on either party which are greater than is necessary to fairly decide that issue.

Ensuring that it is dealt with fairly and expeditiously: Here there is recognition of the old adage that 'slow justice is no justice'. Tribunals should treat the need for swift determination of disputes as a relevant consideration.

The above are all matters which a tribunal will weigh in the balance in deciding how to 'deal with the case justly'. No single factor is conclusive in itself. The importance and influence of each will depend upon the facts of the individual case.

Applying the overriding objective in practice [9.3]

When making or defending applications to the tribunal, it is good practice to relate your arguments or submissions to the criteria contained in the overriding objective, since the tribunal is obliged to give effect to it in exercising its procedural powers.

Sometimes, applying the overriding objective will inevitably mean an application is granted.

Example 1

There is an application by the respondent to amend the notice of appearance seven days after submission of the original to include the fact that the applicant was dismissed as a consequence of stealing three brown envelopes full of cash, not one. Doing justice between the parties will invariably dictate that such an application is allowed. If not, the respondent could be prevented from relying on that information at full hearing, hampering the presentation of its case. By contrast, there is little or no unfairness to the applicant, who has been given ample time to prepare their response.

Sometimes, however, deciding what is in accordance with the overriding objective will involve the tribunal in a delicate balancing exercise, as in the following example.

Example 2

The applicant complains, in the IT1, of acts of discrimination by specific individuals.

In addition to the specific allegations, the applicant alleges that there is a 'widespread culture of discrimination' throughout the respondent organisation.

The respondent makes an application seeking further information of 'the facts upon which the allegation that there is a widespread culture of discrimination is based, including details of any acts of discrimination which have given rise to the alleged culture, the perpetrators of the acts, the dates upon which the acts took place and the places where the acts took place.'

cont'd

85

The applicant refuses a voluntary request from the respondent to provide the details. The matter proceeds to argument by the parties at a pre-hearing review, where the respondent seeks a formal direction from the tribunal.

The respondent's argument

The application is necessary to understand the case it has to meet and deal with the case justly. (*Regulation 10(2)* – the overriding objective of dealing with cases justly) – 'Culture of discrimination is a vague phrase which could mean anything'. It is not clear whether the applicant is going to rely upon additional acts of discrimination it has not raised in the IT1. The parties will not be on an equal footing if the case proceeds to full hearing and the applicant raises allegations at the last minute which the respondent has not had an opportunity to respond to (*10(2)(a)*). It will also be more expensive (*10(2)(b)*) and cause delay (*10(2)(d)*) if the application is not granted now but a postponement turns out to be necessary at full hearing.

The applicant's response

The respondent has ample information to understand the case it has to meet and the information requested is unnecessary to do justice between the parties. (*Regulation 10(2)* the overriding objective of dealing with cases justly) – Far from placing the parties on an equal footing (*10(2)(a)*, this request would place the applicant at a disadvantage, by compelling them to disclose at an early stage matters which are more appropriately included in witness statements. The applicant does not have the same resources as the respondent. Having made the allegation that there is a culture of discrimination, it is entitled to see what evidence the respondent produces in response, before giving further details. (*10(2)(a)*) – The phrase 'culture of discrimination' has a clear enough meaning, and to make an order would be out of proportion to the complexity of the issue (*10(2)(c)*).

How the tribunal decides: balancing unfairness [9.4]

It can be seen from the above example that both sides can formulate an arguable case applying the criteria laid down in the overriding objective. For the tribunal, which is deciding the matter, it is frequently a question of asking which side will suffer a greater degree of injustice (ie unfairness) if the order sought is/is not made. The decision that is made may vary according to the tribunal that hears it (see also **9.6**).

Balancing the unfairness [9.5]

Example 3

In an application by the applicant for disclosure of documents, the tribunal may ask:

(a) how important is the issue to which the application goes?

(b) what is the potential importance of the information in relation to that issue? and

(c) what are the administrative burdens and expenses that an order would impose on the respondent?

It will determine whether (c) is outweighed by the combined effect of (a) and (b). If the application is granted, it will be because it decides the potential importance of the information outweighs the costs that the respondent will incur as a consequence.

Example 4

A postponement becomes necessary in the middle of a hearing because the applicant, who is unrepresented, suddenly raises a new allegation to which the respondent has not had an opportunity to respond. The respondent seeks an order for its costs. The applicant says that they have no resources. They would have raised the allegation earlier, but did not know this was necessary. The tribunal will balance the respective unfairness, in making its decision. Relevant factors may include the following:

• Was there a pre-hearing review where the importance of raising all relevant issues was explained fully to the applicant?

• Could the respondent have pre-empted this situation by making a request for further information?

• What is the size and resources of the respondent?

• Might a costs award have the effect of making the applicant abandon the application?

Choosing a middle way [9.6]

Often, 'giving effect to the overriding objective' will mean that the tribunal does not do what either party wants, but instead adopts a middle way. So, in example 2, it *might* make an order simply that the applicant gives a general indication, no more than a paragraph long, of what it means by the phrase 'culture of discrimination.' In example 3, it could direct disclosure in much more limited terms than that which is sought by the applicant, for example that the respondent provides a written summary of the information which is sought, rather than all the original documentation. In example 4, a far smaller costs award than that which is asked for by the respondent may be awarded. If either party receives a strong indication from the tribunal that it is unwilling to make the order that is sought, it is often sensible to address the tribunal on a possible middle course.

The status of previous case law [9.7]

There is a large amount of case law predating the overriding objective which deals with procedural powers, such as the ordering of further particulars and disclosure, or discovery, as it was then known. The overriding objective takes precedence over this case law as it constitutes legislation.

It has not yet been decided the extent, if at all, to which a tribunal will continue to be entitled to have regard to previous case law. At the time of writing, the most likely course is that tribunals will have regard to it (where relevant) by way of guidance, but will not be obliged to follow it where it considers that it conflicts with the overriding objective.

Do's and Don'ts

Do:

- Treat the overriding objective as a tool when making and defending applications.

- Consider whether your concerns could be addressed by a costs order against the other side.

- Approach the issue by balancing the respective unfairness to the parties.

- If seeking to rely on case law predating the overriding objective, think about arguing that the overriding objective incorporates pre-existing principles of fairness which have long been adopted by tribunals.

Don't:

- Use case law predating the introduction of the overriding objective without considering the extent to which, if relevant, the principles in the case have been altered by the introduction of the objective.

- Forget that the overriding objective is intended to be flexible and is designed around the changing needs of individual cases.

10.

Communicating with the Tribunal

The tribunal's response [10.1]

Relatively quickly after the IT1 is sent to the tribunal, the applicant should receive an acknowledgement (on form IT5) giving the address for correspondence, the case number and notice of the fact that ACAS is available for the purposes of conciliation. The case number should be quoted in all future correspondence. It is normal for the applicant to wait until receipt of the respondent's notice of appearance (which will be sent to them by the tribunal) before contemplating further contact with the tribunal (see **10.5**).

Sending the IT3 to the respondent [10.2]

Upon receipt of the originating application, the tribunal will send a copy of it to the respondent, together with:

- a formal notice of originating application form (IT2, guidance notes on such matters as time limits); and

- a blank IT3 form for use as the notice of appearance.

The completed notice of appearance should be returned and entered within 21 days. The respondent might wish to give thought to making any appropriate applications at the same time as returning the notice of appearance (see **10.5**).

Action by the tribunal upon receipt of the notice of appearance

Entering details on the register [10.3]

A register, open to the public, is kept of all tribunal cases, giving the names of the parties and basic details about the claim. The outcome of the case is also recorded on the register. Upon receipt of the notice of appearance, basic details about the case will be entered by the Secretary of the tribunal.

In cases appearing to the Secretary which involve the allegation of a sexual offence, details of the names (or any other identifying factors) of the party or parties should be deleted from the register in order to preserve confidentiality (*Employment Tribunals (Constitution and Rules of Procedure) Regulations 2001 (SI 2001/1171), rules 2(5)* and *15(6)*). If a party wishes to benefit from such confidentiality, it would be sensible to alert the Secretary's attention to the fact upon submission of the originating application or notice of appearance. It should be noted, however, that this protection is only available in relation to allegations of a sexual offence.

Action by the chairman [10.4]

Upon receipt of the notice of appearance, both it and the originating application are usually placed before a chairman in order to review whether the case can proceed directly to full hearing, or whether there are preliminary matters which need to be addressed. Expect the chairman to have regard, in particular to the following:

- whether a directions hearing is necessary (see CHAPTER 13 – DIRECTIONS AND DIRECTIONS HEARINGS);

- whether there is an issue relating to jurisdiction (e g time limits) suitable for dealing with by way of a preliminary hearing (see CHAPTER 15 – PRELIMINARY HEARINGS);

- whether a pre-hearing review is warranted (see CHAPTER 14 – PRE-EMPTIVE STRIKES);

- whether further particulars are needed;

- whether there are any other steps which should be taken to ensure that the case can proceed to final hearing;

- the estimated length of hearing (see **10.7**).

In a growing number of cases, tribunals are listing cases for directions hearings of their own motion.

Early communication by the parties [10.5]

If a party seeks one of the above steps to be taken, it is sensible to make the appropriate application as early as possible. When the chairman comes to review the case upon return of the notice of appearance, he will have that application in front of him. So the respondent might, for example, want to accompany the notice of appearance with a relevant application or letter indicating dates to avoid, or with an application for further particulars.

Listing the case for full hearing [10.6]

A large number of tribunals, though not all, now use a pre-listing enquiry system. The parties are sent a form informing them of the month in which it is proposed the case will be heard and requiring them, within a short time-scale, to inform the tribunals of any dates upon which they (or their witnesses) are unable to attend. It is essential that this form is filled in accurately – failure to do so might well jeopardise an application for an adjournment due to non-availability at a later date. In cases where no pre-listing questionnaire is sent out, parties should inform the tribunal as early as possible of dates to avoid in the following six months. The majority of cases are now heard within a six-month time period, in accordance with the Employment Tribunal Service's (ETS) target.

Length of hearing [10.7]

The chairman, upon examination of the file, will usually form a view on the anticipated length according to the issues in the case. Often this will be difficult for him to do because, for example, there is no way of knowing the number of witnesses that will be called. It is sensible, if concerned that the hearing may be listed for less time than is necessary, to inform the tribunal of this as soon as possible. Where the chairman decides that the case should be listed for a directions hearing, it is here that a date will often be fixed for full hearing. Parties should therefore come to directions hearings with their dates to avoid an estimated length of hearing.

The notice of hearing [10.8]

In all cases, parties receive a notice of hearing giving the hearing date. As stated, steps should be taken, wherever possible, to ensure that the case is listed on a day that the parties can manage. Where, however, this is not so, and an application for a postponement is necessary, act promptly. The same applies if the case has been listed for insufficient time.

Making applications for orders [10.9]

There are various orders which can be made upon application by the parties, for example:

- for the provision of further particulars;
- for disclosure;
- for postponement;
- for the attendance of witnesses;

- for the case to be listed for a preliminary hearing or pre-hearing review; or

- an application that the other side show cause why their case should not be struck out.

Should the application be made orally or in writing? [10.10]

The vast majority of applications are made in writing in the first instance. Where the case has been listed for a directions hearing, it may be convenient to take advantage of this to make an oral application on the day itself. Further, something may happen on the day of a hearing that demands an oral application, for example an application for an adjournment to deal with an unexpected development. In most other circumstances, it is normal to make an application in writing first, unless circumstances dictate otherwise. In the case of urgent applications, it is often sensible to fax rather than post the application.

Unlike the County Court, there is no prescribed form that the parties should use to make an application. It is important, however, that both the *order which is sought* and the *grounds upon which it is sought* are clearly set out. Chairmen are inundated with letters from parties requesting various orders. If the order sought is attractively set out, with persuasive and clear reasons, the application is likely to stand out. This chapter provides a very brief guide to the making of an application to the tribunal. Each application should meet the following requirements:

- Identify the case name and number at the top of the page.

- Identify the order which is sought.

- Identify the grounds upon which the order is sought.

- Attach any relevant documents, such as the request for further particulars or schedule of documents of which disclosure is sought, relevant correspondence from the other side etc.

- The application should be accompanied by a covering letter addressed to the clerk to the tribunal asking that the application be brought to the attention of the chairman as soon as possible.

- A copy of the application should be sent to the other side and this should be confirmed in the application itself.

Example of structure of application

(An example of an application in a particular context, witness orders, can be found in APPENDIX V – CASE STUDY)

Re: Case No: 56940/2002 Jones v Smith and Co.

Order sought from the tribunal: The applicant/respondent seeks an order under [identify relevant tribunal rule] that the respondent/applicant [specify order sought]. For example, the applicant seeks an order, under *rule 4*, that the respondent provide the further particulars sought by the applicant and set out in the attached document dated [...] and headed 'Request for Further Particulars'.

Grounds for seeking the order: The grounds should be set out concisely, but persuasively. Any attempts that have been made to obtain voluntary consent by the other side to what is requested should also be set out, enclosing any relevant correspondence. The party making the application should have regard to the to the legal criteria which the chairman will apply in deciding whether to make the order (see relevant chapter relating to the power in question e g CHAPTER 12 – DISCLOSURE, CHAPTER 16 – WITNESS ORDERS AND ORDERS FOR THE PRODUCTION OF DOCUMENTS etc). The overriding objective is likely to be central in most cases.

The response from the tribunal [10.11]

When the chairman has considered the application, he will write to the parties with his decision, giving brief reasons.

Do's and Don'ts

Do:

- Address the legal criteria which the tribunal will apply in deciding whether to make a particular order.

- Address the overriding objective, including the prejudice to the respective sides if the order is/is not made.

- Present your applications clearly and attractively.

Don't:

- Phrase the application in a manner which assumes it will be granted.

The case management role of the tribunal [10.12]

'A tribunal may, at any time, on the application of a party or of its own motion, give such directions on any matter arising in connection with proceedings as appear to the tribunal to be appropriate'(*rule 4(1)*).

At the start of this chapter, attention was drawn to the fact that the chairman will normally review a file upon return of the notice of appearance. This is an example of the tribunal exercising its 'case management' role. With virtually every procedural power exercisable upon application of the parties, including orders for the provision of further particulars, disclosure and postponement, the rules provide that the same power may be exercised by the tribunal 'of its own motion'.

This reflects the modern role of the tribunal in actively managing cases. It is useful for the parties to be aware of this role for two reasons:

- One of the chief case management concerns of the tribunal in any case will be to avoid unnecessary delays, and to ensure that the full hearing is ready to proceed on the day upon which it is listed. Parties should manage their own cases, including the preparation of evidence and the making of any applications, with this concern in mind.

- The fact that the parties are in agreement over a particular course, such as an adjournment or the adducing of late evidence in breach of a direction, does not necessarily mean that the tribunal will agree (though it will always be a relevant factor). The independent case management role of the tribunal enables it to take decisions of its own as to the management of the case.

The tribunal, in managing the case, will seek to give effect to the overriding objective (see CHAPTER 9 – FAIRNESS: THE OVERRIDING OBJECTIVE). The case management role of the tribunal starts from the day upon which the application is received and continues until the conclusion of the case.

Case management during the course of a hearing [10.13]

The tribunal will continue to actively manage cases during the hearing itself. In many ways, this overlaps with its role in regulating its own procedure. So, if the chairman believes that a question is being asked of a witness which is unfair or which that witness is not in a position to answer, he may intervene regardless of whether the other party objects. Similarly, if one party seeks to adduce new evidence on the day of hearing which has not been disclosed, the tribunal may (depending upon the circumstances), refuse its admission of their own motion, particularly if it can only be accommodated by the granting of an adjournment.

The Employment Act 2002

New developments in the tribunal's case management role **[10.14]**

The new Act gives the President of the employment tribunals the power to make practice directions. Practice directions will constitute a further set of rules running alongside the existing procedural rules. The directions are likely to set out more precise criteria for how the tribunal will operate its powers under the rules and impose tighter procedural requirements on the parties. Areas where it is possible that practice directions will be made include the preparation of evidence by the parties (including such matters as the use/form of witness statements and the content of bundles and directions on the making of applications (including for postponements). It is not known, at the time of writing, when this provision will come in to effect, since the Act makes clear that an amendment to the procedural rules will have to occur first.

Communicating with the tribunal   [10.15]

Checklist

- Send important documents, such as the IT1 and IT3, by recorded delivery.

- Make a note of the case number and quote it on all correspondence.

- Think from the outset about the number of witnesses needed, dates to avoid and applications that need to be made.

- Make applications that clearly set out the order you seek and the grounds for seeking it.

- Keep in mind the administrative burden on tribunals and their desire to avoid unnecessary delays.

Contacting employment tribunals

Central website (includes guidance on making and resisting claims and has downloadable IT1s and IT3s): www.employmenttribunals.gov.uk.

England and Wales

- Ashford Employment Tribunal
  Tufton House
  Tufton Street
  Ashford
  TN23 1RJ
  Tel: 01233 621346
  Fax: 01233 624423

- Bedford Employment Tribunal
  8–10 Howard Street
  Bedford
  MK40 3HS
  Tel: 01234 351306
  Fax: 01234 352315

- Birmingham Employment Tribunal
  Phoenix House
  1–3 Newhall Street
  Birmingham
  B3 3NH
  Tel: 0121 236 6051
  Fax: 0121 236 6029

- Bristol Employment Tribunal
  Ground Floor
  The Crescent Centre
  Temple Back
  Bristol
  BS1 6EZ
  Tel: 0117 929 8261
  Fax: 0117 925 3452

- Bury St. Edmunds Employment Tribunal
  100 Southgate Street
  Bury St. Edmunds
  IP33 2AQ
  Tel: 01284 762171
  Fax: 01284 706064

- Cardiff Employment Tribunal
  Caradog House
  1–6 St Andrews Place
  Cardiff
  CF10 3BE
  Tel: 02920 678 100

- Exeter Employment Tribunal
  2nd Floor
  Keble House
  Southernhay Gardens
  Exeter
  EX1 1NT
  Tel: 01392 279665
  Fax: 01392 430063

- Leeds Employment Tribunal
  3rd Floor
  11 Albion Street
  Leeds
  LS1 5ES
  Tel: 0113 245 9741
  Fax: 0113 242 8843

- Leicester Employment Tribunal
  5a New Walk
  Leicester
  LE1 6TE
  Tel: 0116 255 0099
  Fax: 0116 255 6099

- Liverpool Employment Tribunal
  1st Floor
  Cunard Building
  Pier Head
  Liverpool
  L3 1TS
  Tel: 0151 236 9397
  Fax: 0151 231 1484

- London Central Employment Tribunal (see also Stratford
  Employment Tribunal for East London)
  Ground Floor
  19–29 Woburn Place
  London
  WC1H 0LU
  Tel: 020 7273 8603
  Fax: 020 7273 8686

- London South Employment Tribunal
  Montague Court
  101 London Road
  West Croydon
  CR0 2RF
  Tel: 020 8667 9131
  Fax: 020 8649 9470

- Manchester Employment Tribunal
  Alexandra House
  14–22 The Parsonage
  Manchester
  M3 2JA
  Tel: 0161 833 0581
  Fax: 0161 832 0249

- Newcastle Employment Tribunal
  Quayside House
  110 Quayside
  Newcastle Upon Tyne
  NE1 3DX
  Tel: 0191 260 6900
  Fax: 0191 222 1680

- Nottingham Employment Tribunal
  3rd Floor
  Byron House
  2a Maid Marian Way
  Nottingham
  NG1 6HS
  Tel: 0115 947 5701
  Fax: 0115 950 7612

- Reading Employment Tribunal
  5th Floor
  30–31 Friar Street
  Reading
  RG1 1DY
  Tel: 0118 959 4917
  Fax: 0118 956 8066

- Sheffield Employment Tribunal
  14 East Parade
  Sheffield
  S1 2ET
  Tel: 0114 276 0348
  Fax: 0114 276 2551

- Shrewsbury Employment Tribunal
  Prospect House
  Belle Vue Rd
  Shrewsbury
  SY3 7NR
  Tel: 01743 358341
  Fax: 01743 244186

- Southampton Employment Tribunal
  3rd Floor Duke's Keep
  Marsh Lane
  Southampton
  SO14 3EX
  Tel: 023 8071 6400
  Fax: 023 8063 5506

- Stratford Employment Tribunal
  44 The Broadway
  Stratford
  E15 1XH
  Tel: 020 8221 0921
  Fax: 020 8221 0398

- Watford Employment Tribunal
  3rd Floor
  Radius House
  51 Clarendon Road
  Watford
  Hertfordshire WD1 1HU
  Tel: 01923 281750
  Fax: 01923 281781

Scotland
Note: this book covers tribunal practice and procedure in England and Wales. Tribunals in Scotland operate under parallel, if slightly different, rules.

- Aberdeen Employment Tribunal
  Mezzanine Floor
  Atholl House
  84–88 Guild Street
  Aberdeen
  AB11 6LT
  Tel: 01224 593137
  Fax: 01224 593138

- Dundee Employment Tribunal
  13 Albert Square
  Dundee
  DD1 1DD
  Tel: 01382 221578
  Fax: 01382 227136

- Edinburgh Employment Tribunal
  54–56 Melville Street
  Edinburgh
  EH3 7HF
  Tel: 0131 226 5584
  Fax: 0131 220 6847

- Glasgow Employment Tribunal
  Eagle Building
  215 Bothwell Street
  Glasgow
  G2 7TS
  Tel: 0141 204 0730
  Fax: 0141 204 0732

11.

Post-claim Requests for Further Information

For pre-claim requests for further information, including the lodging of questionnaires in discrimination cases, see CHAPTER 5 – PRE-CLAIM REQUEST FOR INFORMATION.

The request for further particulars [11.1]

An order that one party provide further particulars of its case can be made upon application by either party or ordered by the tribunal of its own motion (the power to order further particulars arises under *Employment Tribunals (Constitution and Rules of Procedure) Regulations 2001 (SI 2001/1171), rule 4(1)* and *(3)*. The application may be made orally (for example at a directions hearing) or in writing (see CHAPTER 10 – COMMUNICATING WITH THE TRIBUNAL (10.9)). A request for particulars consists of a series of questions, usually relating to the grounds set out in the IT1 or IT3. The purpose is to provide the party making the application with information about the case it has to meet and/or the tribunal with information about the issues it has to decide. The possible advantage of such a request can be summarised as follows:

- It enables a party to properly prepare its case and not be 'ambushed' at full hearing.

- It may have the effect of exposing vulnerable areas in the other side's case which causes them to lose confidence at an early stage and settle or concede.

- Non-compliance with an order may enable an application to strike out under *rule 4(8)* to be made.

- A request and any reply received might serve as a useful forerunner to an application for a preliminary hearing (see CHAPTER 15 – PRELIMINARY HEARING) or for a deposit under *rule 7* (see CHAPTER 14 – PRE-EMPTIVE STRIKES).

As with all tactical decisions, the advantages have to be weighed against possible disadvantages. If there is an obvious weakness in an aspect of the other side's case, which it is for them to remedy, there may be advantages in not alerting them to it. Be careful, however, not to prejudice the preparation of your own case. Tribunals are required, under the overriding objective, to act in a way that places the parties on an equal footing. Where the other side is unrepresented, the tribunal may be unsympathetic to a party who claims to be taken by surprise at full hearing when the matter could have been clarified by an earlier request for further information. If, however, full particulars have been sought, the tribunal may refuse the other party permission to make the new allegation, or at the very least will be sympathetic to an application both for an adjournment to deal with the new issue and for the resulting costs (see CHAPTER 17 – POSTPONEMENTS AND ADJOURNMENTS and CHAPTER 24 – COSTS).

Making the application [11.2]

Factual examples of where a request for further particulars might be appropriate are given below. An example of how to lay out the request can be found in APPENDIX V – CASE STUDY, although there is no proscribed form for doing so.

When considering a written application, a tribunal will usually expect the party seeking the order to have first sought the particulars from the other side voluntarily. It may be possible to avoid this if making the request at a directions hearing, although the other party should generally not be taken by surprise at that hearing by a long and difficult request. An application for an order can be made either in writing or orally. If making the application in writing it is sensible to enclose the formal request for particulars with the application itself (the reasons in the application may be brief if the request speaks for itself) (see CHAPTER (10.9)).

If the application is made orally, a copy of the request for particulars requested is sufficient. Generally, such applications are more likely to succeed the earlier they are made, although in theory an application can be made at any time prior to the conclusion of proceedings. On occasions, the information in the IT1 will be so insufficient that the respondent will lodge a 'holding IT3', make a simultaneous application for further particulars and then amend once the particulars have been received (see CHAPTER 8 – THE EMPLOYER'S RESPONSE).

The criteria for making an order [11.3]

The tribunal will determine an application for further particulars in accordance with the principles set out in the overriding objective (see

CHAPTER 9 – FAIRNESS: THE OVERRIDING OBJECTIVE). It will balance the relevance of the request against such matters as prejudice to the other side by having to answer it. The case law in this area predates the overriding objective. The principles in the cases are likely, however, to remain relevant when considering the overriding objective. They include *White v University of Manchester [1976] ITR 143; International Company Ltd v Whiteley [1978] IRLR 318 EAT; Byrne v Financial Times Ltd [1991] IRLR 417*. In practice, a tribunal will usually make an order if it considers that it is necessary in order for one party to understand the case it has to meet at final hearing and prepare accordingly. If a request goes further than is necessary to achieve this objective, a tribunal will either not make the order or make it in modified form.

Traditionally, tribunals have not entertained requests that they consider are 'oppressive', a factor which, in practice, they will continue to have regard to when giving effect to the overriding objective. Oppressive requests usually ask not what the other side's case is but detailed questions about how they are going to prove it, for example which witnesses they intend to call and which documents they intend to adduce to prove an element of their case (see *P&O European Ferries Ltd v Byrne [1989] ICR 779; [1989] IRLR 254 CA)*. Remember that these matters, as crucial as they are, are best dealt with through processes such as disclosure and directions for exchange of witness statements.

In making and defending such applications, parties should make full reference to the overriding objective, including issues such as placing the parties on an equal footing, the expense of proceedings and doing justice to the complexity of the issues. These criteria can be used as tools both in making and defending applications. Tribunals will be particularly anxious to ensure that the issues are properly defined before the full hearing takes place in order to avoid delays and injustice at that stage.

Examples of requests

The applicant has alleged that managers within the respondent organisation 'continuously discriminated against her over a period of ten months, but has not gone into further details. The respondent might request all or some of the following information if it has not been provided in the grounds of complaint:

- who, in the respondent organisation, the applicant alleges discriminated against her;

cont'd

- the specific act/s of discrimination relied upon with dates; and

- the basis upon which the applicant asserts that she was subjected to less favourable treatment on grounds of sex/race, including details of any comparator upon whom the applicant wishes to rely.

It can be seen from this example, that each request relates to the issues which the tribunal will have to decide in the case.

In an unfair dismissal case, the respondent has relied upon capability as the reason for dismissal and alleged that the applicant's performance was inadequate over a period of six months, without giving further details. The applicant may wish to request: (a) details of the precise duties that the respondent alleges were carried out incompetently; and (b) details of dates. The tactical advantages of such a request are obvious, particularly if the applicant considers that the respondent will not be able to provide such information.

Allegations of inconsistency: where an applicant alleges that they were treated differently from other employees, and treats this as a ground for unfairness, the respondent will often be entitled to details of which employees the applicant alleges were treated more favourably.

Consequences of failing to comply with a request for further particulars [11.4]

Where a tribunal makes an order, it will give a deadline for the provision of further particulars. If that deadline is not complied with (or the particulars provided are inadequate), the party in whose favour the order was made can make an application under *rule 4(8)* that the other party show cause why the tribunal should not strike out the originating application or notice of appearance. In practice, a tribunal *may* be reluctant to impose such a draconian penalty applying, as it must, the overriding objective. It might make an award for costs, however, where one party has incurred additional legal costs arising from the enforcement. Alternatively, it could give rise to an application for a pre-hearing review and an order that a deposit be paid in respect of the aspect of the case which has not been particularised (see CHAPTER 14) or even, in certain circumstances, a preliminary hearing (see CHAPTER 15).

Where the case proceeds to full hearing, any default should be highlighted by the disadvantaged party, pointing out to the tribunal that the other side has been given every opportunity to particularise its case but has failed to do so. If particulars emerge at full hearing that should have been given in answer to an earlier request, the tribunal should be invited to attach no weight to those matters, or alternatively asked to grant an adjournment in order for the new matters to be met, with costs payable by the party in default.

The power to order written answers [11.5]

An alternative to the requesting of further particulars is a request for written answers (the power to order written answers is contained in *rule 4(1)* and *(3)*). In practice, there is considerable overlap between the two. There is no hard and fast rule as to when a request for written answers, as opposed to a request for further particulars, should be made. It is submitted that in the majority of cases there will be little practical difference between the two, and in those circumstances a request for further particulars is the most appropriate course. There is usually little that can be achieved through a request for written answers that cannot be equally well achieved by a well-drafted request for further particulars. One example of the use of written answers might be to obtain information in a discrimination case that has not been previously sought in a questionnaire, and where the time limit for filing a questionnaire has expired. Whether a tribunal accedes to such an application will, however, depend upon the circumstances. The tribunal may, of its own motion, decide to ask a party a series of questions about its case. Such questions will be for the purpose of clarifying the issues that the tribunal has to decide.

Do's and Don'ts in the drafting of particulars

Do:

- Decide what particulars to seek by reference to what is necessary to prepare the case.

- Make reference to the overriding objective in making the application.

- Make the request as early as possible.

- Ask for the particulars to be provided voluntarily first.

- Keep in mind the issues the tribunal will have to decide and phrase the requests with these in mind.

cont'd

Don't:

- Ask questions about what legal arguments the other side will adduce.

- Phrase the request officiously or aggressively.

Tactics

- An effective request for further particulars can expose weaknesses in the other side's case and encourage them to settle.

- Remember, it is one of a number of interlocutory tools at your disposal.

- If an order is made, include the request for particulars and any answers in the bundle at full hearing, and do not be afraid to refer the tribunal to it where appropriate. The wing members are unlikely to have copies of their own and the chairman may have lost sight of it amongst the mass of papers in the file.

12.

Disclosure

Introduction [12.1]

The process of disclosure enables each party to have sight of relevant documentation in the other's possession. Parties should give thought to disclosure as early as possible in proceedings. Very often, it is not until disclosure takes place that a party is able to properly prepare its case and gain a realistic view of its prospects. Parties should first agree matters of disclosure voluntarily and, if unable to come to agreement, seek an order from the tribunal. It will often be the employer who, for obvious reasons, has the majority of documentation in its possession. In such cases, it is essential to properly assemble and organise that documentation at an early stage.

Usually, disclosure relates to contemporaneous documents, such as notes of disciplinary hearings, memorandums between relevant managers and correspondence. Such documents often have greater evidential value than witness statements and oral evidence produced at the hearing. This is because they:

- are created nearer the time of the relevant events; and

- are not written directly for the purpose of a tribunal hearing.

Disclosure is traditionally thought of as a process that benefits the recipient of the information rather than the party disclosing it. The benefits can, however, run both ways. Disclosure of the documentation forces the parties at an early stage to assemble and organise the documents in their possession, an essential process in the preparation of the case. Although the respondent may hold most of the documents, it should never shrink from seeking disclosure of relevant papers in the applicant's possession.

The extent of the duty of disclosure [12.2]

There is no automatic duty of disclosure by the parties in tribunal proceedings. Disclosure takes place in the majority of cases, whether by voluntary agreement between the parties or as a consequence of an order or direction by the tribunal. Cases where there is no disclosure, whether formal or informal, are very few and far between. Disclosure usually takes one of three forms:

(a)   Disclosure by agreement between the parties.

(b)   Disclosure pursuant to an order from the tribunal.

(c)   Disclosure as a consequence of a direction to the parties to prepare an agreed bundle.

Even in (a), the parties often agree the extent of disclosure with reference to the powers of the tribunal (see **12.4**). Disclosure is one of the matters that the tribunal usually has regard to at the directions hearing (see CHAPTER 13 – DIRECTIONS AND DIRECTIONS HEARINGS), where a direction for disclosure is frequently included in a number of other directions intended to ensure that the case is ready for full hearing. A fair hearing usually cannot take place in circumstances where important and relevant documents are not before the tribunal. Tribunals strive to avoid the scenario where a full hearing begins but has to be postponed in order for disclosure to take place. If this does occur, and it is due to the fault of one of the parties, the tribunal may consider making a costs award against that party (see CHAPTER 24 – COSTS).

Which documents need to be disclosed   [12.3]

In a typical unfair dismissal or discrimination case, it is common to see disclosure (by one or of the means outlined above) of the following documents:

*   Letter of appointment.

*   Contract of employment, including any amendments.

*   Internal procedures and guides relevant to the dispute in question: e g disciplinary code, sickness absence procedure, redundancy procedure, redundancy (including selection criteria), equal opportunities policy.

*   Policy documents, such as company announcements, relevant to the dispute in question (most common in redundancy/business reorganisation cases).

*   Relevant correspondence, internal memorandums and emails between: (a) the respondent and the applicant; and (b) management within the respondent organisation.

*   Attendance notes of all relevant meetings concerning the applicant.

- Minutes of all relevant meetings, including disciplinary and appeal hearings.

This list is only intended to be indicative. Many such documents will probably be included in the bundle for full hearing. Parties should be proactive in identifying the documents they need in individual cases.

The power of the tribunal to order disclosure [12.4]

The *Employment Tribunals (Constitution and Rules of Procedure) Regulations 2001 (SI 2001/1171)* introduce an important change in the field of disclosure of documents. The tribunal's powers are stated in the new rules as being identical to the powers of the civil courts under the *Civil Procedure Rules 1998 (CPR), Part 31 (CPR 31) (SI 1998/3132)*.

CPR 31 states that there can be two types of disclosure: 'standard disclosure' and 'specific disclosure'.

Standard disclosure   [12.5]

Standard disclosure refers to general disclosure of relevant documentation. The tribunal may give a direction for standard disclosure (whether of its own motion or upon application from a party) at a directions hearing or otherwise. There may be a direction for 'standard disclosure by list' (see **12.15**). An application for standard disclosure, provided it is made in reasonable time, is likely to be successful since, applying the overriding objective, it entitles a party to documentation which, upon an application of the overriding objective, is necessary to do justice between the parties (see **12.8**).

The meaning of standard disclosure   [12.6]

The following documents must be disclosed in standard disclosure:

- the documents upon which a party relies;
- the documents which support their case;
- documents which support the other party's case.

Parties should not adopt a biased or partisan view in deciding whether a document supports the other side's case, but consider the issue from the perspective of an objective bystander. There is a duty to carry out a 'reasonable search' for documents in the last two categories, having regard to:

- the number of documents involved;

- the nature and complexity of the proceedings;

- the ease and expense of retrieval of a particular document; and

- the significance of any document which is likely to be located during the search (*CPR 31.7(2)*).

Non-disclosure (in a process of standard disclosure) of documents which assist the other side can have serious consequences, ranging from an order for costs against the offending party to more serious consequences if there is evidence of a deliberate attempt to conceal the documents in question. In practice, the documents 'upon which a party intends to rely' includes not simply documents that assist that party, but relevant background documents which are necessary in order to give the tribunal a complete factual picture of the case. It is best to avoid a situation where a case proceeds to final hearing and the tribunal requests to see a particular document as this causes delay and further expense.

Specific disclosure [12.7]

Specific disclosure, as the name suggests, relates to a particular document or category of document. Once again, such orders are usually made prior to full hearing (at a directions hearing or otherwise), but there is nothing to prevent a tribunal making them at a full hearing. Sometimes an application for specific disclosure follows a failure to disclose a document through standard disclosure. For the basis upon which a tribunal will make an order for specific disclosure, see **12.8**.

Disputes about disclosure [12.8]

Where the parties cannot agree, it is possible to make an application to the tribunal for an order for disclosure either of a specific document or a class of documents. A party can take advantage of a directions hearing (see **CHAPTER 13**) to make this application, or make it in writing to the tribunal (see **CHAPTER 10 – COMMUNICATING WITH THE TRIBUNAL** (**10.9**)).

The rules simply state that the tribunal's powers of disclosure are the same as those provided to the civil courts under *CPR 31*. It is necessary, therefore, to look at *CPR 31* to see what those rules are. *CPR 31* requires a court to exercise its powers in accordance with the overriding objective which applies to all of the civil procedure rules. This is worded in very familiar fashion to the overriding objective applicable to tribunals, with some notable differences. In the area of proportionality, a court, and hence a tribunal, must exercise its power in a manner which is not merely proportionate to the complexity of the issues (as under the tribunal rules), but also to the amount of money involved, the importance of the case and the financial position of the parties. Second, a court is required to ensure that a case is dealt with 'expeditiously and fairly'.

Applying the overriding objective in the CPR in deciding disputes over disclosure [12.9]

In deciding, in accordance with the overriding objective contained in the *CPR*, whether an order for disclosure is necessary in order to deal with the case justly, a tribunal is likely to ask all or some of the following questions.

- What degree of relevance (or potential relevance) and probative value do the documents sought have in relation to an issue in the case?

- Is the extent and volume of the disclosure sought out of proportion to its importance (or potential importance) to the issue/s in question?

- Is the extent and volume of the disclosure sought out of proportion to the importance of the case as a whole?

- Would making the order cause the proceedings to become longer and more protracted than justice demands?

- Is the application for disclosure premature?

A word of warning [12.10]

If a tribunal decides that the document in question falls in to one of the three categories covered by standard disclosure, then an application will be difficult to resist.

Case law predating the new tribunal rules [12.11]

The old test for disclosure (or discovery as it was then known) was whether it was necessary for disposing fairly of the proceedings. It remains to be seen the extent to which the tribunals will have regard to historic cases now that they are required to exercise their powers in accordance with the *CPR*. The likelihood is that tribunals will have regard to them, but that they will not constitute binding authority. For example, the old case law attached importance to whether a request for disclosure was oppressive, i e it placed too great a burden on the person required to disclose it compared to the potential importance and probative value of the documents in the case. This test is now likely to be subsumed within that of proportionality under the overriding objective, discussed above.

Examples of disputes about disclosure [12.12]

Many disputes concerning disclosure relate to allegations of unfair treatment in comparison to other employees. For example, there may be an allegation of disparate treatment in a dismissal case, giving rise to an application for disclosure of relevant papers in the cases where the applicant alleges there was more favourable treatment. In a discrimination and equal pay case, a comparison with other employees is commonly the means of proving discrimination. Because of its critical importance in these cases, tribunals are likely to be more sympathetic to such applications (for the special considerations which apply to discrimination cases see *Clwyd County Council v Leverton [1989] 2 WLR 47* and *[1989] AC 706;* and *West Midland Passenger Transport Services Ltd v Singh [1988] ICR 614*).

There is no hard and fast rule as to when tribunals will order disclosure. Individual tribunals will take different views as to the necessity of disclosure. The overriding objective contained in the *CPR* should be used as an instrument both in seeking and defending applications. A useful tip is to ask whether the application relates to a specific allegation that the applicant has already made, or whether it is simply what is known as a 'fishing expedition' – an attempt to trawl through the other side's documents in the hope of finding further material upon which to make new allegations.

Example

An employee in a company with 40 employees is dismissed for gross misconduct, namely hitting another employee.

Scenario (a): She seeks disclosure of documents relating to all gross misconduct dismissals in the past ten years. This is likely to be refused as dismissal of another person for a different reason in different circumstances is unlikely to be relevant to any issue the tribunal has to decide.

Scenario (b): She seeks disclosure of all documents relating to fights between employees. This, again, is likely to be refused, particularly if it does not relate to a specific allegation of disparate treatment.

cont'd

> *Scenario (c)*: She alleges in the IT1 that, six months before her dismissal, an employee, whose name she knows, was not dismissed following a more serious incident of violence. Disclosure of relevant documents in relation to the other incident is likely to be ordered because she has made a clear allegation of disparate treatment, and is probably entitled to sight of the documents relevant to this allegation.

Failure to comply with an order for disclosure [12.13]

The tribunal has the power to strike out the defaulting party from the proceedings if an order for disclosure is not complied with. The correct course in these circumstances, for the party in whose favour the order was made, is to make an application under *rule 4(8)* that the other party be invited to show cause why the originating application or notice of appearance should not be struck out. Representations as to why the party should be struck out should be made with that application. The tribunal will apply the overriding objective (see CHAPTER 9 – FAIRNESS: THE OVERRIDING OBJECTIVE) in deciding whether to strike out. An alternative course open to the tribunal is to draw an adverse inference from the non-disclosure of the document. Where there has been a failure to disclose, a party should draw it to the attention of the tribunal conducting the full hearing wherever appropriate.

Disclosure against third parties [12.14]

The power of the tribunal, under *rule 4(5)(b)*, to order the production of documents by a third party (and the attendance of that party), is dealt with in CHAPTER 16 – WITNESS ORDERS AND ORDERS FOR THE PRODUCTION OF DOCUMENTS.

Method of disclosure [12.15]

Disclosure can take place 'by list'. This means that a party is given a list of documents upon which the other intends to rely and it can then request copies of specific documents. Alternatively, all the documents can be physically supplied. The issue is one for the parties to agree or the tribunal to direct. Often, the applicant will not have seen much of the documentation and it is frequently in their interests to request copies of everything not in their possession. For an employer, its list for disclosure frequently takes similar form to the index for the bundle at full hearing, another reason why compiling an organised list at this stage can be both productive and time saving.

Privileged documents: documents protected from disclosure [12.16]

There are certain categories of document that the parties are not obliged to disclose and which they are entitled to keep confidential. Included in this are documents in the following categories.

Legal professional privilege [12.17]

The law recognises that, as a matter of public policy, parties should be free to seek legal advice without having that advice revealed to the other side. The protection extends to any communication made by or to a solicitor, barrister or legal executive in their professional capacity made for the purpose of giving or obtaining legal advice or assistance (see *O'Shea v Wood [1891] P.286 CA and Kennedy v Lyell [1883] 23 Ch .D. 387 at 404*). Note, however, that communications from unqualified lawyers are not privileged. Human resource managers should, therefore, be cautious when giving written advice on legal prospects of success to a manager within the same organisation as this document would not be covered by legal professional privilege, nor would written advice given by employment advisors who are not qualified lawyers (*New Victoria Hospital v Ryan [1993] I.C.R. 201, EAT*). By contrast, legal advice from a qualified in-house lawyer would be covered (*Alfred Crompton Amusement Machines Ltd v Commrs. Of Customers and Excise (No2) [1974] 2 All ER 1169 HL*). However, where proceedings are contemplated or pending, communications with unqualified advisors are likely to be privileged.

Communications (not limited to communications with lawyers) for the purpose of obtaining advice or evidence in contemplated or pending legal proceedings [12.18]

This must be the dominant purpose for which the document was created. Examples of where such privilege might apply are:

- the applicant writes to a former colleague in the respondent company asking them to be a witness in the case; and

- the respondent asks its own doctor to report on an assertion made by the applicant in the IT1 that they had a severe mental illness which rendered them disabled within the meaning of the *Disability Discrimination Act 1995*. Note, however, that if there was a report by the doctor on this issue before tribunal proceedings were contemplated, it would not be protected by privilege.

Medical reports and other confidential documents   [12.19]

The fact that a document is 'confidential' (whether medical or otherwise) is *not*, in itself, a bar to its disclosure in tribunal proceedings. There is no presumption against the disclosure of confidential documents. Where an objection is taken by a party to disclosure of a confidential document, the court will apply the overriding objective (*CPR* version) in deciding whether to order disclosure. For this reason, parties both making and defending applications for disclosure should have regard to whether such disclosure is necessary to do justice between parties in the case. The fact that the information is sensitive or embarrassing is unlikely, of itself, to prevent disclosure. Where sensitive material is involved, however, the tribunal ought to be concerned to ensure, before making any order, that:

• the information sought cannot be obtained elsewhere; and

• the disclosure only goes as far as is necessary; so, with an issue in relation to whether an applicant is disabled, a tribunal is unlikely to order disclosure of their entire medical records, merely records relevant to the issue of their disability. Similarly, the tribunal may order that the names of certain individuals be deleted to protect confidentiality. Parties should not forget that communications with experts, whether doctors or others, *will* be privileged if made for the purpose of obtaining advice or evidence in *contemplated or pending* legal proceedings.

ACAS officers   [12.20]

Communications with ACAS officers are privileged, unless expressly waived by the party involved (*Industrial Tribunals Act 1996, s 18(7)*).

Without prejudice communications   [12.21]

This is the phrase used to describe negotiations by the parties made with a view to settling or compromising a case. The courts have held that it is in the public interest that such communications, whether oral or written, are not disclosed save with the consent of both parties (*Independent Research Services Ltd v Catterall [1993] ICR 1 EAT, Cutts v Head [1984] 1 All ER. 597, CA*). The issue in respect of privilege is whether the communication contains genuine negotiations which constitute an attempt to settle the case. The fact that a document is, or is not, headed 'without prejudice' is not determinate of this issue – but rather the substance of the communication itself (*South Shropshire District Council v Amos [1986] 1 WLR. 1271 [1987] 1 All ER 340, CA*). That said, it is sensible for a party, when conducting such negotiations, to clearly mark any written document 'without prejudice'.

Public interest immunity (CPR 31.19)   [12.22]

This usually relates to documents in the possession of public bodies where disclosure may be withheld on the basis that it is harmful to the public interest. If satisfied that the document would, under ordinary principles be for disclosure, the tribunal is required to balance the public interest in concealment against the public interest which lies in the effective administration of justice. 'Public interest', in the former sense, includes the extent to which non-disclosure is necessary for the proper functioning of the public service in question (see *Evans v Chief Constable of Surrey [1989] 2 All E.R. 594*; *Barrett v Ministry of Defence, The Independent, January 23, 1989*; *R v Bromell, Re Coventry Evening Newspapers Ltd [1993] Q.B. 278*). Public interest, in the latter sense, includes issues such as the importance of the disclosure in the case and the extent to which it is necessary for the fair disposal of the case.

Immunity may be sought in respect of an entire class of document ('class claim') or merely in respect of the contents of a particular document ('contents claim'). With a class claim, it is irrelevant whether the contents of particular documents would be harmful to the public interest – 'the point being that it is the maintenance of the immunity of the class from disclosure in litigation that is important' (*Per Lord Wilberforce in Burmah Oil Co Ltd. v Governor and Company of the Bank of England [1980] A.C. 1090, 1111*). The fact that a class of documents is held to be for disclosure does not prevent a contents claim being made in respect of a particular document within it. In both class and contents claims, tribunals have been instructed by the Employment Appeal Tribunal to exercise extreme care in the making of any order (*Halford v Sharples (EAT) [1992] ICR 146*). In respect of the class claims, the power to order disclosure should not be exercised without the giving the party against whom it is made the opportunity to appeal (see *Halford* above).

National security   [12.23]

With a limited number of tribunal claims (*Employment Rights Act 1996, s 202(2)*), disclosure cannot take place if a minister of the Crown is of the opinion that it would be contrary to national security. The tribunal has no power, in those circumstances, to enquire further in to the reasons for the minister's opinion.

Even with claims which are not covered by this statutory prohibition, if a minister signs a certificate claiming immunity in respect of a document on grounds of national security, the tribunal should not exercise its right to inspect the document. The tribunal's duty is limited to assessing whether, with reference to the certificate, the immunity was being claimed in appropriate circumstances and with sufficient particularity to demonstrate that disclosure would constitute an actual or potential risk to national security (*Balfour v Foreign and Commonwealth Office [1994] I.C.R. 277*).

Waiver – disclosing privileged documents [12.24]

A party can waive the privilege attaching to a document and disclose it. Sometimes this will be the right course to adopt. For example, where a doctor has, in contemplation of tribunal proceedings, given clear and unequivocal advice that a person is or is not disabled, it might be best to disclose that advice if it is beneficial to the party involved. Once privilege on a document has been waived, it cannot be retracted. If a document is included in a list of disclosable documents by accident, immediate steps should be taken by the party involved to correct the error by informing the other side of the mistake. If a document is physically disclosed, any attempt to retract it will generally be unsuccessful, even if disclosed in error. Note, however, that without prejudice correspondence (see **12.21**) cannot be disclosed without the consent of both parties.

Disclosure: step by step [12.25]

- Remember, the earlier you address issues of disclosure the better. You should certainly address your mind to it after service of the IT1 or IT3, if not before.

- Make a list of all relevant documents in your possession – whilst not compulsory, it is probably best to apply the criteria for standard disclosure contained in the *CPR* since, if a dispute occurs, the tribunal will be bound by these rules in deciding whether to make an order.

- Decide which, if any, of those documents are privileged and do not need to be disclosed. Remove them from the list of disclosed documents.

- Structure the list as you would for a tribunal bundle – there is no need, unless so ordered by the tribunal, for parties to file a formal disclosure statement, as required under *CPR 31.10*.

- Make a list of all the documents you require from the other side.

- Write to the other side to agree when disclosure will take place and the method of disclosure – a normal agreement would be for standard disclosure (whether by list or supply of all documents) within, say, 14 days.

- Upon receiving disclosure, review whether you think it is complete. If it is missing documents (or if a review of the disclosed

118

documents reveals a need for further material), write to the other side requesting them.

* If the request is not complied with, consider applying for an order under *4(5)(b)*. Set out clearly which issue/s the documents are relevant to and the attempts which have been made to secure voluntary disclosure. This can be done in writing, or alternatively you can request an oral hearing.

Tactics

* Requesting disclosure from the other side can exert pressure on them and expose weaknesses in its case.

* If an application for disclosure is unsuccessful, make a full note of it, and bring it to the tribunal's attention at a later stage if relevant.

* If you accidentally fail to disclose a document, immediately bring it to the other side's attention, with an explanation.

* If you accidentally disclose a privileged document (whether by list or otherwise), immediately inform the other side that the disclosure was accidental and request its return.

13.

Directions and Directions Hearings

Introduction [13.1]

CHAPTER 10 – COMMUNICATING WITH THE TRIBUNAL described the wide case management powers of the tribunal. One of the central powers is that contained in *Employment Tribunals (Constitution and Rules of Procedure) Regulations 2001 (SI 2001/1171), rule 4(1)* which states that a tribunal:

> 'may at any time, on the application of a party or of its own motion, give such directions on any matter arising in connection with the proceedings as appear to the tribunal to be appropriate'.

Directions can be made by a tribunal orally or on the papers, either of its own volition or in response to an application from the parties. 'At any time' means just that, from the lodging of the application to the conclusion of proceedings.

What are directions? [13.2]

Directions are defined in the rules as:

> 'any requirement relating to evidence (including the provision and exchange of witness statements), the provision of further particulars, and the provision of written answers to questions put to a party by the tribunal'.

Directions hearings are interlocutory hearings, usually short hearings which take place at least a month prior to the full hearing (see **13.3**). Directions can, however, be made by the tribunal at any time, as described above (**13.1**)

The directions discussed in this chapter and throughout the book can, and frequently are, made upon written application by the parties, without the need for a hearing (see **CHAPTER 10 (10.9)**).

Directions hearings at the instigation of the chairman [13.3]

After submission of the IT1 and IT3, a chairman will invariably review the case.

In lengthy or potentially complex cases, he will usually decide that a directions hearing is necessary in order to ensure that the case is prepared for full hearing. The parties are informed of this by letter, often expressed in similar terms to the following:

'The chairman of the tribunals considers that a Hearing for Directions is desirable in this case. The hearing will take place at […] on […] before a chairman sitting alone to:

(a) clarify the issue in the case and give any necessary orders for further particulars (see **CHAPTER 11 – POST CLAIM REQUESTS FOR FURTHER INFORMATION**);

(b) consider what, if any, orders are required for disclosure of documents (see **CHAPTER 12 – DISCLOSURE**) and the attendance of witnesses (see **CHAPTER 16 – WITNESS ORDERS AND ORDERS FOR THE PRODUCTION OF DOCUMENTS**);

(c) arrange, if possible, for agreement as to documents;

(d) consider how long the case is likely to last and give directions as to the date and length of the hearing; and

(e) give any other directions which may be necessary for the fair and expeditious disposal of the case.'

The letter usually states that the parties should attend in person or through a representative and that, if there is no attendance, directions may be given in their absence.

In addition to the matters stated in the letter, parties should expect a chairman to give directions on the preparation of a joint bundle and possibly also a chronology (see **CHAPTER 19 – PREPARING FOR THE FULL HEARING**).

Directions hearings at the instigation of one or both of the parties [13.4]

There is nothing to prevent either party requesting a directions hearing themselves.

It is particularly sensible to do so where you consider that the other party is likely to present their case at full hearing in an unpredictable manner, raising new issues or calling unexpected evidence.

Generally, directions hearings listed at the request of the parties (or party) take place in three instances:

- Where an application has been made on paper by one or both of the parties which (in the view of the chairman) merits a hearing (note that such applications may merely be dealt with on the papers, see CHAPTER **10** (**10.9**)).

- Where one or both of the parties requests a directions hearing.

- Where a hearing is necessary for the purpose of enforcing earlier directions which have not been complied with (see **13.9**).

You should make use of a directions hearing to ensure that all outstanding pre-full hearing issues are dealt with, having regard to the checklist of issues described above.

Preparing for a directions hearing [13.5]

In preparing for a directions hearing each party should:

- define the issues in the case;

- decide what further information it needs from the other side (see CHAPTER **11**);

- consider what directions, if any, should be obtained in relation to disclosure (see CHAPTER **12**);

- consider if there are any other directions needed – for example consolidation with another claim/s which involve similar issues of fact or law, or issues relating to reporting restrictions etc;

- decide how many witnesses they will call;

- have in mind a time estimate for the hearing;

- make a note of dates to avoid for a full hearing (it is crucial to obtain accurate information prior to the hearing as to the dates upon which witnesses/representatives cannot attend. An application for a postponement at a later date may well be refused if the party was given a full opportunity to give dates to avoid).

A directions hearing need not necessarily be confrontational. Most chairmen will expect the parties to have had at least a brief discussion on what can be agreed. Such agreement may be:

- prior to the day of the hearing, by mail, fax, email or telephone; and/or

- immediately prior to the hearing, at the tribunal itself.

Where the dispute is complex, consider whether the tribunal would be assisted by the preparation of a chronology and/or short skeleton argument. These can assist in marshalling the arguments prior to the making of an application. Make sure that the skeleton argument is just that – i e skeletal (see **CHAPTER 19**). Ensure that both documents are provided to the opponent prior to the hearing – it may be that the chronology can be agreed.

Using the directions hearing to make applications [13.6]

One advantage of a directions hearing, particularly one instigated by the tribunal, is that it can (and should) be used by the parties to make applications for directions in areas where they cannot agree, without the necessity for giving advance written notice to the tribunal of the fact that an application will be made. An application can be made on the day (under *rule 4(1)*) for an order for:

- further information (see **CHAPTER 11**);

- disclosure (see **CHAPTER 12**);

- witness orders (see **CHAPTER 16**).

The structure of the hearing and the order [13.7]

Each chairman will conduct the hearing in his own way. It is common, however, for the chairman to start by asking upon which matters the parties are agreed. He will then form a view on whether the directions which have been agreed are appropriate from the tribunal's perspective, in accordance with the tribunal's responsibility for case management.

With areas of dispute, he will usually hear first from the party who is seeking a particular order or direction before hearing the response.

When seeking and defending such applications, parties will have to persuade the tribunal according to the criteria in CHAPTER 9 – FAIRNESS: THE OVERRIDING OBJECTIVE, and any relevant case law (see CHAPTER 10 (10.9)). Remember that the powers in question are intended to be operated flexibly by tribunals according to the specific factual circumstances before them.

The order [13.8]

The chairman will usually make his order orally on the day of the hearing, although there may be a short break after completion of the submissions before it is delivered. The order will also be written down and sent down to the parties. It is possible to appeal an interlocutory decision, although in practice this may be difficult (see CHAPTER 28 – STEPS AFTER THE DECISION II: APPEALS).

Setting aside directions

If a party is unhappy that a direction has been made they may apply to the tribunal to have it set it aside. The application should be in writing (see CHAPTER 10). Generally speaking, such applications will only be successful where the party has not had a full opportunity to present their case (for example because the directions was made following a written application) or if there has been a change of circumstances since the direction was made. It is possible to appeal to the Employment Appeal Ttribunal in respect of an order for directions, but this will only be successful if it can be demonstrated that the chairman acted irrationally (i e outside the ambit of his discretion), failed to take in to account a relevant factor or took in to account an irrelevant factor. In practice, this is difficult to show, since the reasons accompanying any order may be very brief.

Enforcing directions [13.9]

What happens if a party does not comply with directions or orders given by the tribunal? *Rule 4(8)* states that:

'If a requirement...is not complied with, the tribunal –

(a) may make an order in respect of the costs under *rule 14(1)(a)*; or

(b) before or at the hearing, may strike out the whole or part of the originating application, or, as the case may be, the notice of appearance, and, where appropriate, direct that a respondent be debarred from defending altogether.'

The rule then goes on to state that this power will not be exercised unless the party against whom the order is made has been given an opportunity either in writing or orally to make representations.

Where, as is relatively common, a party has failed to comply with a direction, the correct course is to write to the tribunal requesting that the other side show cause why the whole or the relevant part of the originating application or notice of appearance should not be struck out. The effect of either being struck out is that the application cannot be brought or defended. Sometimes the default will only relate to part of the claim, for example sex discrimination, in which case an application to strike out that part of the claim would be appropriate.

Whether to strike out the originating application or notice of appearance is a matter for the discretion of the Tribunal. It is a severe penalty and the tribunal will have regard to the overriding objective. Commonly, where an application under *rule 4(8)* is made, it has the effect of making the other party comply with the original order. In those circumstances, the tribunal may exercise its discretion not to strike out, in accordance with the overriding objective, on the basis that the other side has not suffered long-term unfairness as a consequence of the default. Sometimes, the tribunal will make an 'unless order', namely that a strike out will occur if the party in default does not comply within a further period of, say, 14 days.

Partial compliance [13.10]

There will be instances where a party has partially complied with an order. For example, the answer to a request for further information is incomplete, or disclosure is only partial. In those circumstances, it is still possible to take enforcement action under *rule 4(8)*. The tribunal will, generally, be less willing to strike out if there has been at least some compliance, depending on the degree of default.

In all cases where there has been non–compliance, it is sensible, at the very least, for the party who has obtained the direction to flag this up at the time, whether in correspondence or at a hearing. This can become extremely useful at a later stage.

Example

The respondent writes to the applicant requesting details of the additional employees within the organisation whom the applicant claims were discriminated against by a particular manager. She refuses. A directions hearing has already been listed at the instigation of the chairman in order to ensure the case is ready for full hearing. At that hearing, the respondent applies for a direction that further particulars of the individuals in question be provided, in order to understand the case it has to meet. The tribunal makes that direction, whilst stressing that the applicant has the alternative, if she chooses, of simply withdrawing the allegation. The particulars are not provided, and the respondent seeks to enforce the order through an application under *rule 4(8)* that the applicant show cause as to why the part of her originating application relating to discrimination against other individuals should not be struck out.

The chairman, exercising his discretion and applying the overriding objective, declines to make the order. He comments, however, that, if the applicant does not give such details, then less weight is likely to be attached to her evidence on that issue. The respondent expressly asks the tribunal to note that, if details are given on the day of the hearing, necessitating a postponement, it will make an application for costs. When the full hearing takes place, the allegation is repeated, but details are not provided. The respondent reminds the tribunal of the attempts which were made to seek particulars of the individuals concerned. It asks that, in the circumstances, the tribunal attach no weight to the applicant's evidence that others in the organisation were discriminated against by the manager in question. Note that chairmen have a wide discretion as to whether strike out. The approach to non-compliance will vary considerably according to the facts concerned and the individual chairman hearing the case.

Flagging up non-compliance [13.11]

Do's and Don'ts

Do:

- Remember that directions can be given orally or in writing by the tribunal.

- Make full use of a directions hearing to avoid the need for further interlocutory hearings.

cont'd

- Give consideration as to whether the time estimate for the directions hearing is sufficient.

- Make contact with the other party beforehand to establish areas of agreement.

- Request a directions hearing of your own volition where you consider it is useful and necessary, giving reasons why.

- Consider the issue of the directions you need immediately after submission of the notice of appearance.

- Prepare thoroughly for directions hearings.

- Give thought, before requesting a hearing, to whether you need an oral hearing or whether an application can be dealt with on the papers.

- Make a careful note of directions which are and are not made, and refer to them if they become relevant at final hearing, e g disclosure or further particulars.

Don't:

- Adopt a confrontational approach unless necessary.

- Forget the basic purpose of directions – namely to promote a fair hearing.

- Apply for orders or directions which are oppressive and go further than is necessary.

- Forget to ask, where appropriate, for costs arising from a party's failure to comply with directions.

14.

Pre-emptive Strikes: Pre-hearing Reviews and Strike Out Applications

Pre-hearing reviews [14.1]

Obtaining an order at a pre-hearing review (PHR) (the powers of the tribunal at a PHR are contained in *rule 7* of the *Employment Tribunals (Constitution and Rules of Procedure) Regulations 2001 (SI 2001/1171)*) is a useful method of deterring the progress, at an early stage, of exceptionally weak cases (or a particular aspect of a case) and paving the way for a successful costs application. A PHR can be sought (or ordered by the tribunal of its own volition) in relation to a contention contained in either the IT1 or the IT3, although, in practice, it is usually the former which is scrutinised in these circumstances. Parties should keep in mind the distinction between a PHR and a preliminary hearing (see **CHAPTER 15 – PRELIMINARY HEARINGS**). The latter is normally an appropriate option where there is an issue over whether the tribunal has the jurisdiction (i e power) to hear a claim. By contrast, a PHR is the right course if the tribunal is entitled to hear the matter, but there is an issue over whether it has reasonable prospects of success (see **14.5**).

The power of the tribunal at a PHR [14.2]

If the tribunal decides that a matter has no reasonable prospects of success, it may, under *rule 7(4)*, order a party to pay a deposit of up to £500 as a condition of continuing with the proceedings. Where it does so, the party in question will be warned by the tribunal that, if they pay the deposit and persist with the claim, they may both lose the deposit *and* have a costs order made against them at the conclusion of the full hearing (*rule 7(6)*). If the party in question succeeds at full hearing and/or avoids a costs award, the deposit will be refunded, as it will if the claim or contention in respect of which the order is made is withdrawn (*rule 7(8)*). The tribunal conducting the review must be different from the tribunal that conducts the full hearing (*rule 7(9)*).

PHR or strike out? [14.3]

The test for deciding whether to order payment of a deposit at a PHR, namely 'no reasonable prospects of success', is the same as that which the tribunal apply in deciding whether to strike out the claim (under *rule 15(2)(c)*) on the basis that it is 'misconceived' (see below). This may provoke the question 'what is the point in applying for a PHR, why not seek simply apply to strike the case out?' Each case will turn on its facts. In deciding whether to make either order, the tribunal must seek to give effect, so far as is practicable, to the overriding objective (see CHAPTER 9 – FAIRNESS: THE OVERRIDING OBJECTIVE). This usually makes it more likely that it will order payment of a deposit following a PHR rather than strike out. A strike out is, as the name suggests, a draconian measure that knocks out the other party's case permanently without giving them the opportunity of a full hearing. By contrast, an order for the payment of a deposit and a costs warning enables the party to proceed with the knowledge of the possible consequences. Much will depend, however, upon the facts of the case and the individual approach of tribunal members. Particularly where it considers that a claim is bound to fail, the tribunal might conclude that a strike out is the right course.

The material upon which the tribunal will base its decision [14.4]

The decision of the tribunal will be based exclusively upon an examination of the following (*rule 7(1)*):

- originating application or notice of appearance (in practice this will include any further particulars which have been provided); and/or
- any written representations from the parties; and/or
- any oral representations.

It is not possible to give evidence at a PHR, although extracts of written evidence (i e from documents or witness statements) may be quoted in any written representations which are submitted.

Meaning of 'no reasonable prospects of success' [14.5]

There is very little case law defining what 'no reasonable prospects of success' means. Broadly speaking, a claim or contention which has no reasonable prospects of success will fall into one or both of two categories.

(a) taken at its highest (i e even if accepted as true by the tribunal) the claim has no reasonable prospects of success; and

(b)   there are no reasonable prospects of the party in question proving their claim or contention. Note that in this context it is frequently sensible to precede the application for a PHR by seeking further particulars.

Example of (a): An employee resigns for the sole reason that his manager said to him 'sorry to see your team got hammered last night', relying upon this single incident as a repudiatory breach of contract entitling him to treat himself as constructively dismissed. A tribunal is likely to conclude at a PHR that, even if the employee's account is true, the incident in question is not serious enough to constitute a fundamental breach of the contract of employment and that the claim does not have reasonable prospects of success.

Example of (b): In a race discrimination case, the applicant claims that he was not selected for promotion because the manager was a member of the National Front. He has provided further particulars of this allegation, in which he simply states that he was told of it by 'reliable sources' whose names he is not prepared to disclose at any stage. The tribunal is likely to conclude, in these circumstances, that the applicant has no reasonable prospects of success in proving that the manager in question had National Front connections, and order the payment of a deposit in respect of that contention.

Cases that are not suitable for dealing with by way of a PHR   [14.6]

Where a case turns on an event or course of events in relation to which: (a) the parties are in dispute about what occurred; and (b) each party intends to call direct evidence, then a PHR is unlikely to be appropriate. Such issues can usually only be determined by hearing evidence.

Example

At a meeting with four senior managers, the applicant (in an unfair dismissal and sex discrimination case) claims that she was told: 'I am afraid the bottom line is we can't afford to employ pregnant women in your sort of job'. All four managers deny saying this.

It is unlikely, however, that a tribunal would order the applicant to pay a deposit because it is only in a position to determine whether the allegation is true by hearing the managers and the applicant give oral evidence about what occurred.

FACULTY SERVICES LIMITED

Advocates Library
Parliament House
Edinburgh EH1 1RF
Tel: 0131-226 2881
Fax: 0131-225 3642
Direct Line: 0131-260 5697
E.mail: iain.murray@advocates.org.uk
Website: www.murraystable.com

best regards,

Eng

11/4.

With the Compliments of
IAIN J. MURRAY, B. Com.
Advocates' Clerk

Applying for a PHR [14.7]

The first step is to make a written application to the tribunal that a PHR be held to determine whether a claim or contention has no reasonable prospects of success.

The application should:

- identify the contention in the other side's IT1 or IT3 in relation to which the review is sought – this might be the entire case or one particular aspect of it;

- explain why the contention has no reasonable prospect of success.

Upon receipt of the application, the chairman will, if he decides it appropriate, list the case for a PHR. If he decides that a PHR should not take place, he will write to the party seeking the review giving his reasons in summary form.

The hearing [14.8]

Parties (particularly the party seeking the review) are well advised to prepare a thorough skeleton argument for the purposes of a PHR setting out the basis upon which they bring their case. Where case law is to be relied upon, this should be set out in the skeleton and four copies of the relevant authority prepared for the tribunal and the other side (to whom the authority should be disclosed in advance). A skeleton argument is particularly effective because the tribunal will not hear live evidence at the hearing. It will assist the party seeking the review if the tribunal has had an opportunity to read the skeleton argument and posses a clear understanding of the basis upon which that party's case is brought. Such skeleton arguments should, if possible, be mutually exchanged between the hearing. If only one party is relying on a skeleton, then this should be disclosed before the hearing, giving the other party sufficient time to read it.

The case will usually be heard by a three-member tribunal. How the hearing is conducted will be a matter for the tribunal concerned, but will be founded upon the principle that each party has a fair opportunity to present its case. The party who have applied for the review should be prepared to address the tribunal first, although the chairman may start the hearing by asking the other party to address certain concerns which the tribunal has about their case.

Order for a deposit and costs warning [14.9]

If the tribunal decides that the contention of a party has no reasonable prospect of success, they may order that party to pay a deposit of up to £500, which must be paid within 21 days of the date upon which the order is sent to the party. In deciding upon the figure, the tribunal will take in to account the ability of the party to pay. Where an order for a deposit is made, the tribunal will record its reasons in summary form. This will be accompanied by a note explaining to the party concerned that if they choose to pay the deposit and persist with the contention in question they may have a costs award made against them at the full hearing, in addition to losing the deposit. In deciding whether to order payment of a deposit, the tribunal will also have regard to the overriding objective (see CHAPTER 9).

Failure to pay the deposit [14.10]

The party against whom the order is made must pay the deposit within 21 days of the date (recorded upon the order) when the order is sent to them. If they fail to do so, the claim or contention in respect of which the order was made will be struck out and the party in question prevented from pursuing it at full hearing. The tribunal has *no* discretion in this respect. The only circumstances where the 21-day limit might be extended is where the tribunal receive written representations from the party concerned within the 21-day period.

Costs if the matter proceeds to full hearing [14.11]

If the party pays the deposit and the case proceeds to full hearing, the deposit will be refunded unless the party both fails to succeed in respect of the contention or claim and has a costs order made against it under *rule 14*. The amount already paid as the deposit will, under *rule 14(8)*, be deducted from any costs award.

The basis upon which the tribunal decides whether to make a costs award at full hearing will differ from the usual criteria for deciding costs. First, the tribunal should consider whether such an order is merited according to the normal criteria contained in *rule 14(1)*. If it decides that no award is warranted under this paragraph, it will then proceed to consider making an award under *rule 14(7)*. This paragraph relates exclusively to parties against whom a deposit order has been made and which allows the tribunal to make a costs order if:

- the party acted unreasonably in pursuing the matter which was the subject of the deposit; and

- the reasons which led the tribunal to find against that party on the matter in question were substantially the same as the reasons given by the tribunal at the PHR. As already noted in **14.2,** no member of the tribunal who heard the PHR may sit at the full hearing.

Striking out [14.12]

The four different categories where the tribunal has the power to strike out the originating application or notice of appearance are as follows:

(a) the originating application or notice of appearance (or any part of it) is scandalous, misconceived or vexatious (*rule 15(2)(c)*);

(b) the manner in which a party has *conducted proceedings* is scandalous, *unreasonable* or vexatious (*rule 15(2)(d)*);

(c) there has been a want of prosecution on the part of the applicant (*rule 15(2)(e)*);

(d) there has been a failure to comply with a direction given by the tribunal (*rule 4(8)(b)*).

Note that a strike out, with the exception of (c) above, can apply to both the applicant and the respondent.

In respect of each of the four categories set out above, the tribunal will apply a two pronged test:

- have the criteria for striking out under that category been met (see below);

- is a strike out consistent with the overriding objective (see CHAPTER **9**).

Categories (a) and (b): 'scandalous, misconceived, vexatious and unreasonable'

Scandalous [14.13]

There is very little case law defining scandalous conduct, but it is likely to include the making of an irrelevant allegation, unsupported by evidence, with the intention of smearing the other side. In practice, there is considerable overlap between this and the 'vexatious' category.

Misconceived [14.14]

Misconceived includes claims (or part of them) which have no reasonable prospects of success. This means that the criteria for a strike out is the same as that applicable to an order for a deposit upon a pre-hearing review. Note, however, that, upon an application of the overriding objective, the tribunal may be more inclined to pursue the latter option. For a definition of 'no reasonable prospects of success' see **14.1**. It is submitted that a strike out is the more appropriate option where it can be demonstrated that a claim (or part of it) is bound to fail.

Vexatious [14.15]

In *Marler Ltd v Robertson [1974] ICR 72, NIRC* it was established that vexatious included situations where the parties were motivated by some improper motive. This might include situations where the party has no real expectation of success, but is simply bringing proceedings with the intention of harassing or embarrassing the other side.

The 'vexatious' category includes claims where an applicant attempts to re-litigate in the tribunal a matter which has already been finally determined in earlier proceedings. The strike out occurs on the basis that, applying the doctrine of estoppel (see below), the claim constitutes an 'abuse of process'.

Circumstances where estoppel arises: Estoppel can arise:

- Where the applicant brings the same factual complaint on a different legal basis (cause of action estoppel) (*Blaik v The Post Office [1994] IRLR 280, EAT*).

- Where

  'a particular issue forming a necessary ingredient in a cause of action has been litigated and decided and in subsequent proceedings between the same parties involving a different cause of action to which the same issue is relevant, one of the parties seeks to reopen that issue'.

  (*Arnold v National Westminster Bank plc [1991] 2 AC 93, HL*, see also *Munir and another v Jang Publications Ltd [1989] ICR1*). This is known as 'issue estoppel'.

- Where the applicant had the opportunity to bring the claim in earlier proceedings but failed to do so. This is known as 'the rule in Henderson v Henderson' (see *Divine-Bortey v Brent London Borough Council [1998] ICR 886*, also useful general case on estoppel).

An example of the latter might be a claim that a dismissal (which has already been the subject of a tribunal decision) was discriminatory. Note that estoppel operates as a defence in proceedings and should be taken as a point in the notice of appearance.

When alleging that a party is 'estopped' due to previous tribunal proceedings, it is necessary to show that there has been a relevant 'decision' in those proceedings. This is defined in *regulation 2* of the *Employment Tribunals (Constitution and Rules of Procedure) Regulations 2001* as:

> 'a declaration, an order, including an order striking out any originating application or notice of appearance made under rule 4(8)(b) or 15(2), a recommendation or an award of the tribunal, and a determination under rule 6 but does not include any other interlocutory order or any other decision on an interlocutory matter'.

Note that dismissal of an application upon withdrawal constitutes a decision, but the circumstances in which this will estop a future application vary (see *Barber v Staffordshire County Council [1996] IRLR 209 CA* (claim estopped), *Sajid v Sussex Muslim Society [2002] IRLR 113 CA* (claim not estopped) and *Ako v Rothschild Asset Management Ltd [2002] IRLR 348* (High Court claim not estopped after withdrawal of tribunal claim).

For cases on the exercise of discretion to strike out for abuse of process (including estoppel), see *Barber v Staffordshire Couny Council* (above), *Department of Education and Science v Taylor and Ors [1992] IRLR 308, Ashmore v British Coal Coporation [1990] ICR 485, QBD, Mulvaney v London Transport Executive [1981] ICR 351 EAT, Acrow (Engineers) Ltd v Hathaway [1981] ICR 510, Telephone Information Services Ltd v Wilkinson [1991] IRLR 148, EAT).*

Unreasonable [14.16]

The 'unreasonable' category only applies to the conduct of proceedings as opposed to the contents of the originating application and notice of appearance. It is difficult to see precisely what it adds to the 'scandalous and vexatious' categories for strike out.

Category (c): want of prosecution [14.17]

This category arises where an applicant has caused 'inordinate and inexcusable delay'. In the modern climate of pro-active case management of cases by the tribunal (including targets for bringing cases to full hearing), it is unlikely that a claim would be allowed to 'go to sleep' such as to engage a strike out under this rule. One example of where it was applied was where a postponement was granted upon the applicant's request in order to attempt settlement, but the applicant failed (despite frequent reminders) to keep the tribunal informed as to the current position (*O'Shea v Immediate Sound Services Ltd [1986] ICR 598, EAT*).

Category (d): striking out for failing to comply with orders [14.18]

Where the tribunal make an order, for example for the provision of further particulars or disclosure, and the party in question fails to comply, the other party may make an application to strike out either the originating application or notice of appearance. Parties should be aware that striking out tends to be regarded by the tribunal as a draconian penalty. A decision on whether to do so will involve consideration of the overriding objective, including such matters as the degree of fault and the prejudice caused to the respondent by the non-compliance. The tribunal may decline to strike out if they consider that this would be a disproportionately harsh sanction, but indicate to the party involved that their non-compliance may prejudice their case at full hearing. It may give further time for compliance of the order. Even in circumstances where a strike out application is unsuccessful, the party making it should consider asking for its costs arising from the non-compliance.

Regardless of whether a strike out application is made or is successful, the party in whose favour the original order was made should not hesitate to flag up non-compliance at a later stage should it be relevant to do so. For example, if a party seeks to adduce during the course of a full hearing matters which should have been disclosed through the provision of particulars or disclosure, an objection should be taken by the other party.

Making an application to strike out [14.19]

The correct formulation is not to make an application to strike out, but rather an application that 'the applicant/respondent show cause why the originating application/notice of appearance should not be struck out' (*rule 15(3)*). The application can be made orally or in writing. In the former instance, it is sensible to put the other party on notice that it is to be made. The order in which the party is in breach of should be clearly set out (and if possible attached in its original form) as should the basis upon which the breach is alleged (e g failure to provide the particulars sought) (see **CHAPTER 10 – COMMUNICATING WITH THE TRIBUNAL**). The other party must be given the opportunity, either in writing or orally, to show cause why the claim should not be struck out.

Do's and Don'ts

Do:

- Remember that an order at a PHR can be limited to a particular contention of a party and need not extend to the whole claim.

- Remember that evidence cannot be called at a PHR and you are limited to consideration of the IT1, IT3, written representations, oral representations and probably also further particulars.

- Make any application in writing setting out why the matter in respect of which the PHR is sought has no reasonable prospects of success.

- Prepare a skeleton argument/written submissions for use at a PHR, quoting written evidence within it where appropriate.

- Remember that if the deposit is not paid within 21 days (and no extension of time sought within that period), the matter will be struck out.

- Address the tribunal at the conclusion of a future full hearing on what occurred at the PHR, with a view, if successful at that hearing, to obtaining a costs order under *rule 14(7)*.

- When applying to strike out for non-compliance with an order, set out the full history of default, including any letters of reminder sent.

- Consider whether it would be most appropriate to strike out or apply for a pre-hearing review.

- Address the overriding objective – minor default is unlikely to lead to a strike out.

- Consider making a simultaneous application for costs arising from the other side's non-compliance.

- Remember that, with claims which have no reasonable prospects of success, but are not completely hopeless, the tribunal may be more willing (applying the overriding objective) to order payment of a deposit at a PHR.

Don't:

- Attempt to call evidence at a PHR.

cont'd

- Make an application unless it has some prospect of success – this may be counterproductive.

- Be casual when faced with a strike out application but demonstrate to the tribunal that you have take it seriously.

- Seek to deny mistakes or administrative errors when they occur.

15.

Preliminary hearings

Introduction

[15.1]

Rule 6(1) of the *Employment Tribunals (Constitution and Rules of Procedure) Regulations 2001 (SI 2001/1171)* enables the tribunal to hold a preliminary hearing for the purpose of determining a party's entitlement to bring or contest proceedings. In essence, such hearings are appropriate where there is a self-contained legal issue which is capable of deciding the entire case or, as the Employment Appeal Tribunal (EAT) has put it, 'a knockout point which is capable of being decided after only a relatively short hearing' (*CJ O'Shea Construction Ltd v Bassi [1998] ICR 1130, EAT* and *Wellcome Foundation v Darby [1996] IRLR 538, EAT*).

The tribunal will give effect to the overriding objective in deciding whether there should be a preliminary hearing (see CHAPTER 9 – FAIRNESS: THE OVERRIDING OBJECTIVE). Preliminary hearings are intended to be a *time saving process*, relinquishing the need for the tribunal and the parties to deal with a range of issues when there is one, self contained issue which can be fairly determined and, if decided in favour of a particular party, will (or is likely to be) determinative of the entire case. They are not appropriate where the preliminary point cannot be separated from other issues in the case or can only be fairly determined by hearing all of the evidence.

Examples of issues suitable for determination at a preliminary hearing are:

* Whether the claim has been made within the time limit (see CHAPTER 6 – TIME LIMITS).

* Whether the applicant is employed or self-employed.

* Whether the applicant has the necessary qualifying period of continuous employment for an unfair dismissal claim.

* Whether the applicant was dismissed or resigned.

* Whether an essential statutory element for bringing the claim has been fulfilled.

- Whether the claim is of a type the tribunal has jurisdiction to hear.

Parties should note that, sometimes, there will be an issue which falls into one of the above categories, but which is not suitable for determination at a preliminary hearing because it cannot be properly separated from other issues in the case.

Issues suited for a preliminary hearing

Time limits [15.2]

The issue of whether a claim has been brought out of time is usually suitable for determination at a preliminary hearing. This is particularly so in cases, whether unfair dismissal or discrimination, where there is no dispute that the claim has been brought outside the three-month time limit. Also, that the only issue is whether it is just and equitable (in a discrimination case) to extend the time limit, or whether it was reasonably practicable (in an unfair dismissal case) to present the claim in time. In discrimination cases, the position may be more complex, for example where it is alleged there has been a continuous course of discriminatory conduct such that events which took place more than three months before the claim are not out of time. In this instance (particularly where it is alleged that the respondent carried out a discriminatory policy), it is submitted that the tribunal may wish to hear all the facts before forming a view, and therefore decline to proceed with a preliminary hearing (see CHAPTER 6 and APPENDIX I – CLAIMS A TRIBUNAL CAN HEAR).

Employed or self employed [15.3]

In this instance, the preliminary issue, if decided against the applicant, will be determinative of the case.

Qualifying period of employment [15.4]

The tribunal will make a finding at the preliminary hearing in relation to issues such as when the effective date of termination was and whether the employment was continuous (see CHAPTER 6 and APPENDIX I).

Dismissal or resignation [15.5]

In principle, this is an issue suitable for a preliminary hearing provided it is determinative of the case. Caution should be exercised, however, to ensure that it can be separated from other issues in the case. Parties should note that the issue of whether a person was constructively dismissed is *not* suitable for dealing with at a preliminary hearing.

Essential statutory element not fulfilled [15.6]

Examples of where a statutory element has not been fulfilled include where the applicant is not an employee or, in an unfair dismissal case, does not have the necessary qualifying period of employment. Another example is whether the named respondent is the relevant employer for the purposes of proceedings. The parties should look at the particular provision of substantive law under which the claim is brought and decide whether there is an isolated issue, capable of being determinative of the claim, which is suitable for dealing with by way of a preliminary hearing.

The type of claim is one which the tribunal has no jurisdiction to hear. Occasionally, the claim is of a type which the tribunal simply has no power to hear (see APPENDIX I). An example is where an applicant brings a claim for personal injury, or fails to define in the IT1, a claim which the tribunal is entitled to hear. In these circumstances, a preliminary hearing is appropriate and may well be directed to take place by the tribunal of its own motion.

Applying for a preliminary hearing [15.7]

It is sensible, if possible, to first agree with the other side as to the necessity for a preliminary hearing before making the application. The application should be made in writing specifying:

• the issue which the party seeks to have determined by way of a preliminary hearing;

• why this relates to the entitlement of a party to bring or contest proceedings.

It is also usually appropriate to address the criteria in the overriding objective, which the tribunal is obliged to give effect to in deciding whether such a hearing should take place, in particular, *regulation 2(b)*, *(c)* and *(d)* of the *Employment Tribunals (Constitution and Rules of Procedure) Regulations 2001* (see CHAPTER 9).

The hearing [15.8]

The hearing may be conducted either by a chairman alone or by a three-person tribunal. Unlike pre-hearing reviews, the tribunal may hear evidence and will frequently need to do so in order to decide the case. It is advisable in cases involving a number of factual issues to prepare witness statements and a bundle of relevant evidence. Similarly, if the case involves complex issues of law, it is useful to prepare a skeleton argument which cites the relevant authorities, all of which should be disclosed to the other side in advance, with copies prepared for the tribunal. How the hearing is conducted will be a matter for the tribunal, although each party should be given a fair opportunity to present their case. In time limit cases, the tribunal will usually hear from the applicant first.

Do's and Don'ts

Do:

- Consider whether there is a self-contained point suitable for dealing with by way of a preliminary hearing.

- Apply your mind to the overriding objective.

- Make the application as early as possible.

- Prepare for a hearing properly, if necessary using witness statements, a bundle of relevant evidence and a skeleton argument.

Don't:

- Request a preliminary hearing if the point in question cannot be separated from the other issues in the case.

16.

Witness Orders and Orders for the Production of Documents

Introduction

[16.1]

Rule 4(5) of the *Employment Tribunals (Constitution and Rules of Procedure) Regulations 2001 (SI 2001/1171)* states that a:

> 'A tribunal may, on the application of a party or of its own motion, – (a) require the attendance of any person in Great Britain, including a party, either to give evidence or to produce documents or both and may appoint the time and place at which the person is to attend and, if so required, to produce any document; or (b) require one party to grant to another such disclosure or inspection (including the taking of copies) of documents as might be granted by a court under *rule 31* of the *Civil Procedure Rules 1998.*'

Parties should note that the two powers are not mutually exclusive – it is possible to obtain an order for the attendance of the witness and/or the production of documents.

It is a criminal offence for the person named in an order not to comply with it.

Witness orders   [16.2]

There are three requirements which need to be fulfilled before a tribunal will exercise its discretion to make a witness order (*Dada v Metal Box Co Ltd [1974] ICR 559; IRLR 251*):

- An order is necessary because the witness will not, or may not, attend voluntarily.

- The witness is able to give relevant evidence.

- There is a specific date for the tribunal hearing which can be inserted into the order.

An order is necessary: A witness should, at first instance, be invited to attend voluntarily. If they decline, equivocate, fail to respond or state that it would be easier for them to attend if there was a formal order, then a party will be in a position to argue to the tribunal that an order is necessary.

The witness is able to give relevant evidence: The party seeking the order will need to demonstrate that the witness is in a position to give relevant evidence in relation to an issue which the tribunal will have to decide in the case.

Specific date: The tribunal will not make an order unless there is a specific date for the hearing the witness is required to attend. Parties should note that if the hearing date changes following a postponement, an application will need to be made for a revised order with the new date added.

Example of application to the tribunal

The order sought [16.3]

The applicant seeks an order, under *rule 4(5)*, that Bill Smith attend the tribunal on 9 January 2003 to give evidence.

Example: the grounds for making the application

The order is necessary because the applicant wrote to Bill Smith on […] asking him to confirm, as a matter of urgency, that he was willing to give evidence on the applicant's behalf (copy of letter attached), and there has been no response. The applicant believes that an order is necessary to secure his attendance.

Bill Smith (a colleague of the applicant at the relevant time) is able to give relevant evidence in relation to the issue of whether the applicant was fairly dismissed for theft. The applicant's case is that the respondent was told by Bill Smith, whilst carrying out the investigation, that the applicant was present with him outside the premises at the time when the theft was committed. The applicant alleges that the respondent failed to take this in to consideration in reaching its decision.

The hazard of hostile evidence: The power of the tribunal to compel the attendance of witnesses provides an important tool to the parties, but one

144

which should be exercised after a careful analysis of whether, if that witness is compelled to attend, they will give helpful evidence. Take the above example, but with the difference being that Bill Smith is *still* an employee of the company. He has not answered the applicant's letters. The applicant believes there is a danger that, if he attends, he will not give helpful evidence.

Whether to seek an order presents a tactical dilemma in which the potential value of the evidence to the applicant needs to be balanced against the risk that different evidence will be given to the tribunal. Such a judgement can only be made on the facts of each individual case. Parties should note that a witness who attends pursuant to an order they have secured is still 'their witness', and their evidence forms part of their case. Only in very limited circumstances will a tribunal give a party permission to treat a witness of their own as 'hostile' and cross-examine them as if they were giving evidence for the other side. Parties should note that, if the tribunal perceives that the order seeks to compel the attendance of a hostile witness, it may exercise its discretion and refuse to make the order (*Pasha v DHSS EAT 556/80*).

Orders for the production of documents [16.4]

Such an order can be made either against a party to the proceedings or a third party. Again, two conditions need to be complied with:

- the witness has not provided the documents voluntarily;

- the documents are relevant to an issue the tribunal have to decide.

Example

The applicant has resigned and claimed constructive dismissal. The respondent believes that the applicant, prior to the resignation, had already applied for a post in another company which he now occupies.

The order sought: The respondent seeks an order that Anne Jones, personnel director of Jones and Co, provide within 14 days all documents in the possession of Jones and Co (or any associated or subsidiary company) relating to the application of Peter Murray for a position within Jones and Co (or any subsidiary or associated company), including (but not limited to):

(a) the application form submitted and/or letter of application;

(b) the CV and covering letter;

cont'd

(c)   any letters sent by Jones and Co pursuant to the application, including letter of appointment; and

(d)   the contract of employment and/or statement of particulars of employment.

The grounds for seeking the order. A formal order is sought because Ms Jones has failed to respond to a letter (attached) requesting the above information.

The documents sought are relevant to the following issues:

(a)   whether Mr Murray (the applicant) left the respondent organisation in consequence of the alleged breach of contract or due to the fact he secured a position elsewhere;

(b)   the extent of the applicant's loss.

The respondent has reason to believe that the applicant was intending to leave the respondent's organisation in any event and that he did not act on the alleged breach of contract. Ms Jones is the personnel director of Jones and Co and has access to all of the documents requested.

Notifying the other side of the application and resisting orders: There is no obligation to serve a copy of the application on the other side. If the tribunal make the order sought, the other side will be served with it. If they have not had an opportunity to make representations prior to the order being made, it is open to them to make an application for the order to be set aside but they will need to show reasons why, on the merits of the application, the order should not have been made. It is normally sensible to serve the other side with a copy of the application, unless there is a reason for not doing so, for example that relevant documentation may be destroyed before an order is made. Where the other side have been notified, this should be referred to in the body of the application.

Do's and Don'ts

Do:

- Name an individual in the application: organisation names alone are not sufficient.

- Be precise in the wording of the proposed order. The witness is only obliged to comply with the strict wording of the order, so make sure it is tightly worded and covers, where appropriate, such matters as subsidiary or associated companies.

- Obtain a revised witness attendance order where the case is postponed.

- Consider whether it is necessary to obtain both a witness attendance order and an order for the production of documents.

Don't:

- Forget to include in the application:

  (a) attempts which have been made to obtain what is sought voluntarily;

  (b) the relevance of what is sought to the issue/s the tribunal has to decide;

  (c) the name of the individual against whom the order is made;

  (d) (in the case of a witness attendance order) the date of the tribunal hearing they are required to attend; and

  (e) (in the case of production of documents) the time span in which you want the documents provided (e g 14/21 days).

17.

Postponements and Adjournments

The criteria for granting postponements or adjournments [17.1]

There will be occasions when one party cannot or does not wish to proceed with a hearing, whether interlocutory or full, on the date upon which the hearing has been listed.

Rule 15(7) of the *Employment Tribunals (Constitution and Rules of Procedure) Regulations 2001 (SI 2001/1171)* states that:

> 'A chairman may postpone the day or time fixed for, or adjourn, any hearing (particularly where an enactment provides for conciliation in relation to the case, for the purpose of giving an opportunity for the case to be settled by way of conciliation and withdrawn) and vary any such postponement or adjournment.'

The difference between postponements and adjournments [17.2]

In tribunal proceedings, a postponement is a decision to move to a different date a hearing which has not yet begun. An adjournment applies to a partially completed hearing which the tribunal decides should be completed on another day, for whatever reason.

The criteria for deciding whether to grant an application [17.3]

The tribunal will apply the overriding objective in deciding whether to grant a postponement or adjournment (see **CHAPTER 9 – FAIRNESS THE OVERRIDING OBJECTIVE**), including the requirement to deal with cases expeditiously. Parties seeking adjournments should do so aware of the tribunal's reluctance to delay proceedings. They should also have regard to the guidance in the notice of hearing which states that, other than in exceptional circumstances, an application for an adjournment made less than 14 days before the hearing will not be successful. In deciding whether, under the overriding objective, a postponement is necessary to deal with the case justly, chairmen can be expected to ask some or all of the following the questions:

- Is the reason sufficiently important to affect the chances of a fair hearing?

- Has the party acted promptly in seeking the postponement after the reason became known to them?

- Is the application being made close to the hearing date?

- Are the parties in agreement that there should be a postponement?

- Might the other side be adversely affected if the application is granted?

- Could the application have been avoided if the party seeking it had acted diligently at an earlier stage?

- Is this the first application for an adjournment in the case?

None of the above matters are conclusive, but will be balanced by the chairman in making the decision. Where a postponement is in the interests of justice, but there has been default on the part of one of the parties, the chairman can make an order that the party in question pay any costs incurred by the other side which arise as a consequence of the postponement, under *rule 14(4)* (see CHAPTER 24 – COSTS).

There are a number of different reasons why a tribunal might grant a postponement. This chapter looks at some of the most common.

Non-availability of witnesses [17.4]

It is important for parties to avoid applications for this purpose by:

- accurately completing listing questionnaires sent out by the tribunal;

- if no listing questionnaire is sent, informing the tribunal prior to listing of periods of non-availability; and

- if the case is to be set down for full hearing at a directions hearing, come to that hearing with a list of dates to avoid.

Where a witness cannot attend at a hearing that has already been fixed, the party seeking the postponement should address in its application for a postponement the general criteria set out above to see if it applies in their case. There are a number of possible reasons for non-availability:

- Ill health, a doctor's certificate should be provided when making the application.

- Holiday absence – speed in making the application, and the date when the holiday was arranged (i e before or after the listing of the hearing), are likely to be important factors.

- Economic/organisational reasons – a postponement for these circumstances is likely to prove more difficult. Tribunal proceedings are inconvenient and costly for the majority of employers. In practice, a tribunal will need to be persuaded that there are compelling economic or organisational reasons why the witness cannot attend on that day. Promptness in making the application upon receiving notification of listing and the closeness of the hearing are likely to be relevant factors in any decision.

Alternatives where a postponement is refused [17.5]

- Make use of documentary evidence as a substitute. For example:

   (a) prepare a witness statement and ask the tribunal at the outset of the hearing for permission to adduce this as evidence (see CHAPTER 19 – PREPARING FOR THE FULL HEARING) – note the tribunal may attach less weight to the statement due to the fact that the witness cannot be cross-examined;

   (b) make full use of contemporaneous notes and records, such as notes of disciplinary appeals hearing, which you have included in the bundle (see CHAPTER 19).

- Consider renewing your application during the hearing if it becomes obvious that a fair hearing cannot be achieved in the absence of that witness. Be prepared for a possible argument on costs in these circumstances (see CHAPTER 24 – COSTS).

There is a pending appeal to the EAT [17.6]

On occasions, there is an appeal against a ruling by the tribunal on a preliminary or interlocutory matter, or an appeal against the tribunal's finding on liability in circumstances where the remedies hearing has yet to take place. There is no automatic right to a postponement in such circumstances. Whether one is granted will be a matter for the discretion of the chairman, in relation to which the Employment Appeal Tribunal (EAT) will be reluctant to interfere. The tribunal should be addressed on the overriding objective when making and defending such applications (see CHAPTER 9). Two examples of where the EAT has refused to interfere with the exercise of the chairman's discretion are:

- where an adjournment of the full hearing was refused in circumstances where there was a pending appeal against the tribunal's preliminary ruling as to the identity of the employer (see *Sperty Corporation (incorporated in USA) v Morris EAT 528/80*); and

- where the chairman refused to postpone a remedies hearing in order to await the outcome of the appeal on liability (see *Nevin Lonsdale Ltd v Saunders EAT 388/79*).

The parties are engaged in related proceedings in the High Court or County Court [17.7]

Such situations are now less common as tribunals have jurisdiction to hear claims for wrongful dismissal and contractual disputes (arising from the termination of employment) which used to be heard in the civil courts. They are more likely to occur in cases where the amount claimed is in excess of the total amount the tribunal is allowed to award for unfair or wrongful dismissal. So, in a case concerning a company director who is paid £150,000 a year and is entitled to one year's notice of termination, it may make sense for tribunal proceedings for unfair dismissal to be stayed pending determination of a High Court claim for wrongful dismissal. If that claim is successful, it is likely that the claim for unfair dismissal will be discontinued. There will be other instances where the two proceedings 'overlap' in the issues they have to decide. Where identical issue/s are concerned, the Court or tribunal hearing the case second is likely to be bound by the findings of the first (see *Divine-Bortey v Brent London Borough Council 1998 ICR 886*).

The case concerns a point of law that is awaiting resolution elsewhere [17.8]

Whether the tribunal postpones for this reason will be a matter for its discretion, which will be exercised in accordance with the overriding objective. Whether the case turns wholly on the point of law in question (*Pearson v British Airports Authority EAT 324/82*) and the closeness of 'decision day' on the other case are both likely to be important factors. Parties should note that a tribunal may be reluctant, except in the most compelling circumstances, to grant postponement for this reason, partly because it is not able to control what goes on in other proceedings, which may be settled or withdrawn. The tribunal will not grant a postponement in order to await the coming in to force of new legislation (*Willow Wren Canal Carrying Co Ltd v British Transport Commission 1956 1 All ER 567*).

Examples

Example one: A company receives a notice of hearing. The hearing has been listed in the middle of the holiday of the manager who made the decision to dismiss and is its leading witness. The day after receiving notification of the hearing, the respondent makes an application to the tribunal for a postponement, listing any further dates on which its witnesses cannot attend. A postponement will probably be granted. Applying the overriding objective, the case cannot be dealt with justly without the presence of the manager in question. The application has been made promptly, and will not cause more than minimal unfairness to the other side.

Example two: As above, except that the holiday in question is booked two weeks after the company receives notification of the hearing date and the company delays three weeks after receiving such notification in making the application to postpone. The application *may* be refused, on the basis that the company had the opportunity to avoid the postponement and has delayed too long in making the application.

Example three: A case is listed for a three-day hearing, starting on a Monday morning. On the Friday, one of the applicant's most important witnesses contracts a severe bout of flu. The applicant does not send in a medical certificate but applies for a postponement to which the respondent objects. The tribunal may refuse the application, but indicate that the individual's evidence can, if necessary, be taken 'out of turn' at the end of the hearing, or an adjournment can be ordered at a later stage if it becomes clear that the individual cannot attend and their evidence is material. Note: even if these indications are not made, a party should consider making such applications themselves once the full hearing has started.

Procedure for applying for a postponement prior to the hearing [17.9]

It is sensible to send a copy of your application for an adjournment to the other side and indicate this fact to the chairman. The tribunal will invariably do so in any event, but this can cause considerable delay.

It is normal for such applications to be made in writing. The application should set out in full the grounds for the postponement (see **CHAPTER**

10 – COMMUNICATING WITH THE TRIBUNAL (**10.9**)). It is sensible to fax the application. In moments of total desperation, the tribunal can be telephoned, the clerk will record in writing the reasons for the application and place them before the tribunal. For obvious reasons, this is a measure of last resort.

Upon receiving the application, the tribunal will invariably seek the response of the other side (if these have not already been received). The application will be placed before a chairman, who will then make a decision accompanied by brief reasons.

Adjournments during a hearing [17.10]

Sometimes it becomes necessary, during the course of a hearing, to request that the case be adjourned to another day. Commonly, this is in order to deal with an aspect of the case which has arisen unexpectedly and one party needs time to obtain evidence to respond to. It may be, for example, that a witness makes a new allegation in giving oral evidence. Alternatively, the other side may suddenly produce a document which has not been disclosed before and which requires the gathering of evidence in response. Again, the tribunal will apply the overriding objective (see **CHAPTER 9**) in deciding whether to grant the adjournment. If it concludes that a fair hearing demands the granting of an adjournment, it is likely to make that order. Expect the tribunal, however, to make a costs order if the adjournment is due to the default of one of the parties, such as failure to prepare their case properly at the outset, give details of their case to the other side, or make proper disclosure of relevant documents.

Alternatives to adjournments during a hearing [17.11]

Tribunals are resistant towards adjourning cases part heard. Quite apart from the additional delay and the unsatisfactory effect of the hearing being broken up, it causes severe administrative problems for the tribunal since it requires finding a new date when all those involved – the chairman, lay members and the parties – can attend. For that reason, the tribunal will expect parties to strive to find an alternative, including the following:

- If you need to obtain additional documentary evidence, see if there is any viable way of obtaining that document during the remaining course of the hearing.

- Where it is necessary to call an additional witness, explore whether there is scope for that witness appearing at any time in the course of the hearing, even if the evidence is taken out of turn.

153

- Do not be afraid of saying to the tribunal that a new matter has arisen which requires a short adjournment of say, 30 minutes, for you to consider with your colleagues/client.

Do's and Don'ts

Do:

- Try and avoid the need for postponements by giving the tribunal dates to avoid prior to a case being listed and notifying your witnesses promptly as to when they need to attend.

- Make applications for postponements promptly.

- If time is short, fax the application to the tribunal.

- Concentrate on why not granting the postponement would adversely affect the fairness of the proceedings.

- Ensure you give complete information, including the reasons why the application could not have been avoided.

- If the application is one the other side are likely to consent to, obtain their agreement before making the application, enclosing copies to the tribunal of relevant correspondence.

- Consider renewing your application during the full hearing if it becomes clear that fairness cannot be achieved unless an adjournment is granted.

- If refusal is maintained, make a clear note of the reasons why. Politely draw the tribunal's attention to refusal to grant an adjournment/postponement in final submissions if appropriate, for example stating that you would have wanted the opportunity to adduce evidence in response to a particular issue.

- Consider the alternatives where a postponement is refused, such as relying on documentary evidence and witness statements.

Don't:

- Assume that a postponement will be granted – this is always at the discretion of the tribunal.

- Attempt to gloss over lack of diligence or errors on your part

cont'd

---

that will be obvious to the chairman – admit them frankly and then move on to saying why a postponement is necessary in order to deal with the case justly.

- Forget to apply the overriding objective – including balancing the respective unfairness to the parties if the postponement is/is not made.

18.

Settlement of Claims

Advantages of settlement prior to hearing   [18.1]

A large number of cases settle prior to full hearing. Settling a case has the advantage of:

- dispensing with the risk, cost, disruption and anxiety of proceeding to determination by the tribunal;

- enabling the applicant to avoid having state benefits deducted from a tribunal award, a factor which can also serve to reduce a payment by an employer (see **18.11**);

- enabling the parties to agree matters which the tribunal has no jurisdiction to order, such as a reference and/or confidentiality clause.

Settlement is an option which should be explored in every case, a fact reflected by the automatic involvement of ACAS in virtually every tribunal dispute (see **18.10**). It can take place at any stage, from before an application is made to the conclusion of a remedies hearing. Further, tribunals usually decide the issue of remedy after reaching a decision on the substantive dispute. In these circumstances, they often give the parties an opportunity to reach a settlement in order to avoid a remedies hearing.

Parties should be aware that negotiations aimed at settlement are privileged and not for disclosure to the tribunal. If one party does disclose the content of negotiations to the tribunal hearing the case, it is open to the other party to apply for the case to be listed in front of a new tribunal on the basis that their case has been prejudiced, with all of the attendant costs implications.

A decision on whether to settle usually involves *assessing the risks of proceeding to full hearing* and deciding upon a figure for settlement which reflects those risks. In addition, it may involve a consideration of one or more of the following factors:

- *The cost of proceeding to full hearing.* This includes the impact, for both the employer and the employee, of attending the hearing and being taken away from normal duties. It also includes legal costs, time spent in preparation, and the anxiety and disruption of proceeding to full hearing, which should not be underestimated.

- *Issues of principle*. Occasionally, an employer believes a case is so unmeritorious that little or no money should be spent on settlement, or an applicant is determined to obtain a positive finding from a tribunal in their favour, regardless of an offer in settlement from the other side. Whilst legitimate, such stances should be adopted with caution and any decision taken rationally as opposed to emotionally.

- *The possibility of negative publicity*. A very small minority of cases attract publicity. The press do have access to the tribunals and are on the look out for cases which will be of interest to their readers. The possibility of publicity is a factor which can affect settlement.

A settlement usually includes one or more of the following features:

- a sum of money (common in most cases);

- an offer to reinstate (more unusual);

- a further benefit, such as an agreed reference, which can be important for applicants yet to find new employment (see **18.4**);

- a confidentiality clause, in cases where the employer and/or employee are concerned to keep the settlement and/or dispute confidential (see **18.5**).

Features of a settlement 1: sum of money   [18.2]

Deciding upon the right sum for settlement usually involves a two-stage process for both parties:

(i)   assessing what compensation the applicant would receive if successful, including any reductions for contributory fault/Polkey. It may be sensible to draw up a provisional schedule of loss (see **CHAPTER 26 − REMEDIES: CALCULATING LIKELY AWARDS**); and

(ii) assessing what percentage chance the applicant has of being successful.

The settlement figure usually constitutes (ii) as a percentage of (i). The party should then consider, with reference to the factors outlined above, whether there are any additional reasons why the figure should be reduced or enhanced.

Example

The applicant brings a claim for unfair dismissal. The respondent considers that, due to a procedural defect, there is a 40% chance that the dismissal will be considered unfair. The respondent calculates the award which the applicant is likely to receive, if successful, as £5,000 (see **CHAPTER 26**). It concludes that a reasonable settlement would be 40% of this figure, namely £2,000. The respondent is concerned about the disruption to its operations of two senior managers having to attend the tribunal at a busy time in their year. It decides, however, that the dismissal was meritorious, and it will not increase its 'bottom line' figure of £2,000 (a decision which will vary according to the circumstances). In reaching this view, it is also concerned not to give the impression to other employees that the organisation is an 'easy touch'.

Note, however, that although this represents a logical approach to negotiating, the process is not mechanistic and many subjective (and emotional) factors will come into any 'horse-trading' (see also **18.6**).

Features of a settlement 2: reinstatement [18.3]

Agreements to reinstate or re-engage are relatively rare since a decision by a party to terminate the employment relationship is usually one they are not willing to retract. A tribunal is limited to ordering either reinstatement in the original position (with continuity of employment preserved) or re-engagement (a more flexible option). The parties, through a settlement, are not so bound. It is, however, essential (for the sake of avoiding future disputes) to spell out in the terms of any agreement:

- the nature of the employment;

- the remuneration;

- whether continuity of employment is preserved;

- the effect of the settlement on previous rights and privileges accrued by the employee (including pension and seniority rights); and

- any payment which is to be made to compensate the employee in respect of the period when they were out of work.

Features of a settlement 3: reference [18.4]

Where the employee has not obtained new employment, an agreed reference can be extremely important. It can also be a useful bargaining tool for the employer.

The usual practice is for the parties to agree upon the terms of a written reference through a process of negotiation. It is increasingly common for references to be taken up on the telephone and applicants should attempt to protect themselves in this respect. Parties might consider using the following wording in an agreement:

> 'X shall, upon request from any prospective employer of Y for a written reference, provide a reference in identical terms to that contained in schedule (1) to this agreement and in no other terms. The employer shall respond to all oral (whether by telephone or otherwise) and email enquiries from prospective employers concerning the applicant's aptitude, performance and reasons for leaving the employment of x in accordance with the terms and spirit of the reference in schedule (1).'

From the applicant's perspective, the agreed reference should refer to as many of the following as possible:

- duration of employment;
- description of job and duties carried out;
- quality of performance in job;
- character and personality, particularly honesty;
- reasons for leaving.

The extent to which it is possible for an agreed reference to incorporate the above features will, of course, depend upon the circumstances of each case. Tribunals have no powers in regard to references and will not normally wish to see them.

Features of a settlement 4: confidentiality clause [18.5]

It is frequently the employer who wishes to keep the terms of a settlement confidential. This is not always so, however, for example if the employee does not wish the settlement to be revealed to prospective employers. One difficulty with a confidentiality clause is identifying the consequence of the breach. If no consequence is specified, then the party in breach will be liable for any economic loss flowing from the breach of confidence, along normal contractual principals. Such loss may be difficult to prove. An alternative option, often attractive to the employer, is to require repayment of the sum paid in settlement if the confidentiality clause is broken. Such a clause requires careful drafting. Parties may wish to consider adapting the following:

> 'The employee will not disclose, whether directly or indirectly, to any third party other than a professional advisor the terms of this settlement. The employee acknowledges that the payment of [include settlement figure] by the employer is conditional upon the employee's compliance with this clause, and that, in the event of a breach of the said clause, the said sum will become repayable to the employer.'

Negotiating a settlement [18.6]

The parties and/or their advisors can negotiate directly amongst themselves, or utilise the services of ACAS to act as conciliator (see **18.10**). As a basis for negotiations, it is often sensible for the applicant to set out their loss in a schedule, which is sent to the respondent. The respondent can then accept or challenge aspects of that schedule. This may also have the advantage of enabling the parties to prepare for a future remedies hearing. How to conduct negotiations is, of course, a question of tactics which will vary according the circumstances of each case. Commonly, each party will decide upon a 'bottom line', beneath which it will not go.

The form of the settlement [18.7]

The right to take a claim to a tribunal is a statutory right, which can only be contracted out of if strict criteria are met. This means that a settlement which purports to prevent an employee from making or pursuing a claim will only have that effect if it is incorporated into:

(a)   a valid compromise agreement to that effect; or

(b)   an order or decision of the tribunal with the consent of the parties;

(c)   an agreement made through ACAS (see **18.10**).

An agreement which purports to prevent an employee from making or pursuing a claim, but which does not fall in to any of these categories, will not achieve this purpose. It may, however, lead the tribunal to conclude, at a remedies hearing, that it would not be just and equitable to make any award for compensation, or to make a lesser award than it otherwise might make. In addition, the employer will almost certainly be given credit for any sums (other than those contractually due) which have been paid. An important factor in deciding whether to make no award for compensation where a previous settlement has not been validly concluded is likely to be whether any undue influence has been exerted on the employee to settle. It is submitted that a further factor would be if the tribunal accepted an employee's evidence that, had they received legal advice, they would not have agreed to the original settlement, since the purpose of the legislation is to enable employees to benefit from such advice.

(a) A compromise agreement [18.8]

(An example of a compromise agreement can be found in APPENDIX VI – SAMPLE COMPROMISE AGREEMENT, but should not be used without reading the guidance below.)

A compromise agreement can be entered in to before or after an application to a tribunal is made. The requirements of a valid compromise agreement are as follows:

(a) it must be in writing;

(b) it must relate to particular proceedings;

(c) the employee must have received advice from a relevant independent advisor as to the terms of the proposed agreement and, in particular, its effect on their ability to pursue their rights before an employment tribunal;

(d) there must be in force, when the advisor gives the advice, a contract of insurance or an indemnity provided for members of a profession or professional body covering the risk of a claim by the employee or worker in respect of loss arising in consequence of the advice;

(e) the agreement must identify the advisor; and

(f) the agreement must state that the conditions regulating compromise agreements under the relevant Act are satisfied.

In relation to (b), above, a compromise agreement can relate to more than one possible complaint (e g unfair dismissal and sex discrimination) to a tribunal, but these should be specified. It is not sufficient to state that the employee is prevented from taking 'any claim before a tribunal'. The agreement should specify the particular claim/s with reference to the

section of the statute under which that claim can be made (see
APPENDIX I – CLAIMS A TRIBUNAL CAN HEAR).

In relation to (c), a 'relevant independent advisor' includes:

- a solicitor with a practising certificate or a barrister (who is either in independent practice or employed to give legal advice);

- a worker at an advice centre who has been certified in writing by the centre as competent to give advice and is authorised to do so on behalf of the centre;

- an officer, official, employee or member of an independent trade union who has been certified in writing by the trade union as competent to give advice and is authorised to do so on behalf of the trade union; and

- a person specified in an order made by the Secretary of State.

(b) Orders or decisions of the tribunal made by consent [18.9]

This form of settlement is popular when a case settles on the day of a hearing, which is relatively common, but can be utilised at any stage after an application has been made. Usually, the most effective type of decision is a 'Tomlin order', named after the judge who invented this form of order. This is a decision by the tribunal to stay proceedings upon the terms set out in a schedule attached to the order. A Tomlin order has three principal advantages:

- it enables the applicant to avoid the recoupment provisions (see **18.11**);

- it enables the parties to include in the schedule matters, such as an agreed reference or a confidentiality clause, which the tribunal has no jurisdiction to order;

- if the employer does not comply with a Tomlin order, the case can be reinstated before the tribunal, provided the decision provides for there to be liberty to apply.

The alternative is for the settlement to be incorporated in to the main body of a tribunal order. In these circumstances, the tribunal is limited to ordering remedies that are within its jursidiction, and the recoupment provisions (see **18.11** below) will bite on any sum which the tribunal orders to be paid.

(c) ACAS [18.10]

Details of the vast majority of employment tribunal claims are automatically passed to ACAS in order to facilitate a settlement. In most cases, the ACAS officer assigned to the case will contact the parties. Where this does not happen, the parties can find out who has been assigned to their case from the relevant ACAS office (see CHAPTER 3 – GETTING ADVICE).

Where the parties have initially declined the assistance of ACAS, there is nothing to prevent them making use of it at a later stage.

ACAS can be an attractive option both in terms of conducting the negotiations and drawing up a binding agreement. The ACAS officer will not only act as a conciliator, but also draw up a formal agreement for the parties to sign (called a COT3) which complies with statutory requirements. The officer will further contact the tribunal to inform them that the case has settled. ACAS can be asked to become involved even at a late stage in negotiation when the parties have substantially agreed upon the terms of a settlement, but require the assistance of an ACAS officer to finalise the details and incorporate them in a binding agreement. Parties should be aware, however, that ACAS may not allow itself to be used simply as a 'rubber stamp'. It will usually require there to be some areas which still require negotiation, even if these relate to the details of the settlement or agreement.

Parties using ACAS should be aware of the following:

- it is independent;

- it will not advise either party on the merits of their case or advise them that a particular offer should be rejected or accepted;

- communications made to it by either party will be communicated to the other party in an attempt to facilitate settlement;

- communications with ACAS are normally privileged and not for disclosure to the tribunal;

- once an agreement has been made through ACAS, it will be extremely difficult to set it aside, unless it can be shown that the ACAS officer acted in bad faith or adopted unfair methods;

- ACAS may suggest standard wordings for such matters as provision of agreed references and confidentiality clauses, but these can be adapted by agreement;

- an agreement concluded through ACAS can operate to bar more than one claim or prospective claim but, as with compromise agreements, all such claims should be precisely specified.

The recoupment provisions [18.11]

Where the employee has received either job-seekers allowance or income support in the period between termination of employment and the date of the remedies hearing, such amounts are liable to be deducted by the benefits agency from any award which the tribunal makes. No other social security benefits which are received will be deducted. If there is a voluntary settlement between the parties, no deduction will be made.

Recoupment is a factor which both applicants and respondents should bear in mind when negotiating a settlement. It is in the applicant's interests to avoid recoupment. The respondent may legitimately, however, seek to use this fact to reduce a payment made in settlement. So, if the parties estimate that £2,000 will be deducted from the award, they might agree to 'split the difference' and reduce the amount of the settlement payment by £1,000. The parties should note that, to avoid the recoupment provisions, they must either conclude a compromise agreement, a settlement through ACAS, or agree to a Tomlin order (see **18.9**) being made by the tribunal. If the amount of the settlement is incorporated in to the main body of a tribunal consent order, the recoupment provisions will bite on any sum which is awarded.

Enforcement of the settlement [18.12]

A compromise agreement or an agreement concluded through ACAS is a binding agreement enforceable in the County Court. Similarly, breach of an agreement scheduled to a Tomlin order is directly enforceable in the County Court, as is any order for payment of a sum made by the tribunal. The tribunal does not itself deal with enforcement. Where, however, the employer has failed to comply with the terms attached to a Tomlin order, the applicant is fully at liberty to apply to the tribunal for the stay on proceedings to be lifted, and the claim be reinstated. To enable this to happen, the applicant should ensure that there is a clause stating that the parties have liberty to apply in the event of non-compliance with the terms of the agreement scheduled to the order.

Do's and Don'ts

Do:

- Ensure that any settlement is incorporated in to a valid agreement or order.
- Bear in mind the recoupment provisions when deciding whether to settle.

cont'd

- Calculate as precisely as possible what the applicant is likely to receive if successful at tribunal, and then decide what percentage of that figure to settle for based upon the prospects of success.

- Give thought to an agreed reference and confidentiality clause.

- Consider using ACAS to conciliate and draw up the final agreement.

- Remember that negotiations aimed at settlement are privileged and cannot be revealed to the tribunal.

Don't:

- Interpret a desire to settle as a sign of weakness.

- Conclude a settlement without incorporating it in to a valid form.

- Open negotiations with your 'bottom line' figure (unless the circumstances demand otherwise).

- Tell the other side that something is your final offer unless that is genuinely the case – this will weaken your credibility.

19.

Preparing for the Full Hearing

Introduction [19.1]

Preparation is the key to the effective presentation of your case in a tribunal. Preparation involves:

- knowing the facts of the case and the issues;

- ensuring that your case is ready to proceed to full hearing;

- presenting your case in a well-prepared and professional manner with an organised bundle and, where appropriate, a chronology and skeleton argument.

This chapter looks at some of the key steps in preparing the case for tribunal namely:

- ensuring you have complied with directions;

- preparing an effective bundle;

- drafting a chronology;

- drafting witness statements.

In addition, matters such as the drawing up of a *dramatis personae* and a skeleton argument are examined.

Some or all of the matters mentioned in this chapter might, in addition to constituting good practice, be the subject of a formal direction by the tribunal. It goes without saying that all directions should be complied with. Where the direction involves a measure of cooperation between the parties, ensure that you have done what is required and you will be able to demonstrate (i e through correspondence) objectively that any failure to comply is due to default on the part of the other side.

The bundle

What is the bundle? [19.2]

The bundle comprises the documentary evidence (except witness statements) upon which you rely in the case. There is frequently a direction that the parties compile an agreed bundle of evidence so that the tribunal does not have to refer to two different ones. Even where there is no such direction, it is sensible for the parties to attempts to agree a bundle. If this proves impossible, each party should prepare their own. Either way, six bundles are required – three for the tribunal, one each for the parties and one for the witness table.

The contents of the bundle [19.3]

A bundle should be:

- indexed (in the form of a contents page at the start of the bundle);
- paginated, with every page numbered, as opposed to every document;
- typically it should contain:

  (a) the IT1 and IT3;

  (b) the contract of employment;

  (c) relevant company procedures (such as disciplinary procedures and equal opportunities policies);

  (d) correspondence – i e letters, emails, memos, file notes;

  (e) minutes of meetings;

  (f) pay slips and relevant proof of earnings;

  (g) any relevant company announcements, for example a house notice announcing a redundancy situation, transfer of ownership, change of location etc.

An example of a contents page can be found in APPENDIX V – CASE STUDY. You will see that it divides the above into different sections (which may be conveniently separated by colour dividers), with the exception of correspondence and minutes of meetings, which are combined into one section. Note that it is usual to place the documents in each section in *chronological order*, particularly the correspondence section – tribunals find it irritating and confusing if letters, memos and minutes are not presented in a logical order.

Note: the above constitutes broad guidance only. Each bundle will vary. In discrimination cases, for example, there may be the need to add to the first section of the bundle the questionnaires. In all cases whether there have been requests for further particulars, these (together with any answers) should be added in to the first section. Further, it may be, in a discrimination case, that an analysis has been undertaken of the ethnic group or sex of certain section/s of staff – where these are included is a matter for the compilers of the bundle, but an obvious place would be in either the first or second sections.

Preparing an agreed bundle [19.4]

Parties should communicate as early as possible in order to:

- decide (if there has been no direction to that effect) upon whether there should be an agreed bundle;

- who will prepare it; and

- the procedure for agreeing the bundle.

Example

Since, in practice, the relevant documentation in a case tends to be predominately in the hands of the employer, a common route is for the employer to compile a provisional bundle and send to the applicant the contents page, listing all the documents which it has included. The applicant should then reply stating which additional documents (both in its possession and that of the respondent) it wishes to see included and where in the bundle they should be placed. Provided there is no objection from the respondent, those documents are then incorporated, either in a separate section in the bundle, or within the body of the existing bundle.

Note to both parties: by agreeing to the inclusion of the other side's documents in an agreed bundle does not mean that the document becomes part of 'your' evidence, or that you will be taken by the tribunal to be relying upon it. A bundle is simply a collection of the relevant evidence for the tribunal to consider. Objections to inclusion should only be based on irrelevance or evidential unfairness.

The consequences of coming to a tribunal without a bundle [19.5]

Where it is not possible, or there is insufficient time, to agree your bundle, you should still prepare one for use at the tribunal. This should include all relevant documentation, both helpful and unhelpful, to the case whilst excluding privileged documentation (see CHAPTER 12 – DISCLOSURE). Tribunals increasingly assume that a proper bundle will be prepared. A party, particularly a respondent, who has not prepared one may create an impression of disorganisation, sloppiness or inexperience. Compilation of the bundle also helps you in the process of effectively marshalling the facts of the case and identifying the relevant documentation.

The chronology [19.6]

A chronology lists all relevant events in a case in chronological order, with the date on the left and the event in question on the right. An example of a chronology can be found on in APPENDIX V. Sometimes, there will be a direction from the tribunal that the parties agree a chronology in a particular case. Even where there is not such a direction, it is useful to prepare a chronology (preferably an agreed one).

The purpose of a chronology [19.7]

A chronology not only assists the tribunal in gaining an understanding of the sequence of events in a case, but is also an essential tool in the personal preparation of a case – whilst time consuming and frequently laborious, it enables the advocate to organise the facts in their head and, in the process, identify key weaknesses and inconsistencies in the other side's case.

Precisely how you draft the chronology is a matter for individual style, but bear in mind the following:

- it should include all relevant events, not just events helpful to your case; and

- it should not be phrased in a biased or self-serving way.

Dealing with disputed events [19.8]

Frequently, each side will have different versions of what occurred on the same date. How this is dealt with is a matter of style.

Example

18.5.02: Meeting at office between Mr Harris and the applicant. The parties are in dispute as to what occurred on this date. The applicant claims he was told to resign. This is denied by the respondent.

Alternatively, if you consider this is going to make the chronology too difficult, long and cumbersome, simply describe the event itself.

18.5.02: Meeting at office between applicant and the respondent. [You might consider adding]: The contents of this meeting are heavily in dispute between the parties.

Clearly the first style has the advantage of offering the tribunal more information, but may prove impractical on occasions. Whatever style you adopt, try to draft the chronology in a consistent manner.

Chronologies as a tool in personal preparation   **[19.9]**

You are likely to find, as you prepare a chronology, that good ideas for cross-examination and final submissions spring to mind. Some barristers even go so far as to say that compiling an effective chronology constitutes 50% of their preparation.

Think about, for your own purposes only, putting an additional third column on the page, so that, as you draft the chronology, you can write down ideas that come to mind.

Example

2.4.02: Meeting between applicant and Joe Bloggs. Note: claims in her statement to have had no meetings with management after 1 April.

A 'who's who' in the case   **[19.10]**

It is extremely useful if a 'cast' list is compiled for the tribunal detailing the names and positions of all relevant people (on both sides) in the case. Again, this is not a purely altruistic gesture. It will assist in the organisation and preparation of your own case and create an impression of competence to the tribunal.

Witness statements

What are witness statements? [19.11]

The evidence of the witness is contained in written form, which is then usually read out to the tribunal. The major advantage of their use is that the statement can be written and planned in advance, ensuring that the evidence which the witness gives is both complete and presented in as attractive a manner as possible. Unless the other side are prepared to agree to mutual exchange, you should think carefully about disclosing a witness statement to them in advance as to do so gives them the advantage of knowing what you are going to say without you having the same benefit in relation to their case. Sometimes the tribunal will give a direction for advanced mutual exchange.

Advantages of a witness statement:

- it is written in advance and can be carefully planned;
- it can be phrased in a persuasive and structured manner;
- it reduces the level of uncertainty in relation to your own evidence;
- it acts as a prop for the witness concerned;
- it may reduce the nerves of that witness;
- it can be drafted by representatives or advisors (but see warning below).

Drafting witness statements [19.12]

An example of a witness statement in an unfair dismissal case can be found in APPENDIX V.

An effective witness statement usually bears the following characteristics:

- It includes *all* of the relevant events on which that witness is able to give evidence.
- It does not stray into giving evidence about events and incidents which are outside the direct knowledge of that witness, for example events which the person did not witness.
- It is structured around the issues the tribunal has to decide.
- It reads persuasively.
- It is written in numbered paragraphs.

Achieving the above involves a three-stage process on the part of the representative:

- define the issues in the case;

- take instructions from the witness in relation to those issues; and

- attractively setting out those instructions in a well structured and persuasive statement.

Structuring the witness statement [19.13]

Example

In a sex discrimination case, the manager is accused of denying the applicant promotion due to her sex. The manager's case is that the reasons for non-promotion bore no relation to the applicant's sex, but that she was less able in her job. The statement could be structured in the following way:

- First section – sets out the position and duties of the manager (including the number of employees he has charge of), how long he has held that post, any relevant prior experience, and any training in equal opportunities.

- Second section – sets out when the manager first met the applicant, how long they have worked together, the frequency and nature of the contact, with the aim of demonstrating that the manager had ample opportunity to gauge the applicant's performance.

- Third section – brief description of the applicant's performance in the job.

- Fourth section – description of the higher post, i e how the vacancy arose, the duties of the job.

- Fifth section – description of the criteria he adopted for deciding who would occupy the position.

- Sixth section – description of the extent to which the applicant met that criteria and the extent to which she did not.

- Seventh section – description of the other candidates, including how many applied and who was interviewed.

- Eighth section – description of the qualities of the candidate who was chosen.

cont'd

- Ninth section – comparison between the selected candidate and the applicant, explaining why there were reasons unrelated to the applicant's sex for the decision that was made.

- Tenth section – final paragraph detailing witness' personal reaction to being accused of sex discrimination.

The above statement is structured around the legal issue in the case, namely whether there has been less favourable treatment on grounds of sex.

The role of the representative in the drafting of a statement [19.14]

It is common in cases where a party is represented for the representative to draft the statement after taking instructions from the witness concerned. Note, however, that the evidence in the statement is that of the maker alone. If the witness is 'fed' a version of events by the representative, this is likely to come across in the tribunal, with potentially devastating consequences for the credibility of the witness and the integrity of the representative. At the more extreme end of the scale, inviting a witness to fabricate evidence constitutes attempting to pervert the course of justice, a criminal offence.

The role of the representative should be limited to matters of style and structure, that is to say relating the witness' version of events to the legal and factual issues which the tribunal has to decide and phrasing it in as strong and persuasive a manner as possible. A prerequisite for this is the taking of effective instructions from the client, namely asking the client what took place in relation to all the relevant issues in respect of which that client can give evidence.

Does a witness statement dispense with the need for the witness to attend? [19.15]

Witness statements do not dispense with the need for the witness to attend at the hearing to be questioned both by the tribunal and the other side. There is, however, nothing to prevent you making an application for the statement to be adduced as evidence in the absence of the witness concerned, explaining why the witness cannot attend. Unless you are sure that the contents of the statement are not going to be contentious, failing to call the maker of the statement to give oral evidence is not a wise course, unless completely unavoidable. The tribunal will be bound to consider any unfairness to the other side as a result of not being able to question the witness. If the statement is allowed in, the tribunal may well attach less weight to it due to the fact that the witness cannot be questioned. Be particularly careful when the contents of the witness statement conflict with the evidence of a witness who is able to give oral evidence – the tribunal will usually be inclined to prefer that evidence.

Skeleton arguments [19.16]

Skeleton arguments, something used for some time by barristers and solicitor advocates, are becoming more common in tribunal proceedings. A skeleton argument sets out your case in relation to some or all of the issues in outline form.

It enables the tribunal, prior to hearing from you, to gain an understanding of your argument.

Advantages of a skeleton argument:

- It forces you to carefully plan and structure your submissions.

- It is a good opportunity to influence the tribunal from the outset.

- It provides the tribunal with a readily accessible account of your case.

- It can be used as a prop when making submissions.

Warning: ensure that the skeleton argument does not become a hostage to fortune by tying you to a position or argument which by the end of the hearing you no longer wish to rely upon. For this reason, skeleton arguments are more safely deployed either when the evidence has been heard (i e for final submissions), or in a hearing which involves submissions rather than evidence (for example a legal dispute about whether the tribunal has jurisdiction to the hear the evidence in question.

An example of a skeleton argument can be found in APPENDIX V.

List of issues [19.17]

At the start of the full hearing (or before), it is extremely useful if you can agree a list of issues with the other side and place it before the tribunal. Many chairmen do this of their own motion and will be grateful if this is done in advance.

Do's and Don'ts

Do:

- Prepare and seek to agree the bundle as early as possible.

- Ensure that you have complied with directions.

- Prepare a chronology and a cast list (see **APPENDIX V**) – invaluable tools in personal preparation.

- Consider using, where appropriate, a skeleton argument, *dramatis personae* and list of issues.

- Ensure that a witness is completely happy with the contents of their statement before signing it.

- Always ensure that a bundle is to be prepared either by yourself or (in the case of a joint bundle) by the other side.

- Ensure your witnesses have copies of their witness statements well in advance of the hearing.

- If possible, where referring to a document in a witness statement, include the page number in the bundle where it can be found.

- Generally, do not agree to advance disclosure of witness statements unless there is mutual disclosure.

- Consider if there is any default on the part of the other side that has prevented you preparing properly for the hearing, and if necessary refer the tribunal to it, with evidence.

Don't:

- Panic if you come to the tribunal without a witness statement (unless there is a direction to this effect) – witness statements are important but not mandatory.

- Feel obliged to volunteer a skeleton argument unless confident about doing so.

- Forget that thorough preparation is the key to knowing and understanding both your case and that of your opponent.

- Assume that because a matter is not the subject of a formal direction, it is unnecessary.

20.

The Hearing I: the Order of Proceedings

Introduction [20.1]

This chapter looks at the order in which proceedings are conducted and also encompasses the steps parties should take upon arrival at the tribunal. It should be read in conjunction with the next two chapters, which address the manner in which tribunals approach issues of procedure and evidence, and describe some of the essential qualities of tribunal advocacy from the opening through to final submissions.

Arrival at the tribunal [20.2]

- Upon arrival at the tribunal you should check in at reception, indicating which party you appear for. You will then be directed to either the respondent's or the applicant's waiting room. Some tribunals have private conference facilities, of which you may wish to take advantage. Tribunals strive to cater for those with disabilities, including hearing difficulties. It is sensible to contact the tribunal well in advance of the hearing to confirm what arrangements are in place.

- Make contact with the clerk, who will usually introduce themselves to you in the waiting room, giving them copies of all documentation that you wish to place before the tribunal. Commonly, this will be the bundle (whether agreed or otherwise) and any skeleton arguments, skeleton arguments, legal authorities, statements of issues or chronologies (see CHAPTER 19 – PREPARING FOR THE FULL HEARING). The last two should, if possible, be agreed with the opponent.

- Where appropriate, make contact with your opponent, both as a courtesy and with the aim of giving the tribunal a clear idea of the areas of agreement and disagreement between the parties. When speaking to you opponent, bear in mind the following:

  (a) Avoid heated arguments, do not re-run the dispute, do not allow yourself to be pressurised, and never inform the tribunal

176

that the parties are in agreement over a matter unless you are sure that this is the case.

(b) Disclose statements of issues, chronologies and skeleton arguments (see **CHAPTER 19**) to the opponent, agreeing the first two where appropriate.

(c) Ensure that each side is in possession of the relevant evidence.

(d) Ascertain whether the other side has an objection to a particular course which you are proposing, such as calling a witness out of turn, or a proposal not to call a witness but to rely on written evidence.

(e) Disclose any legal authorities upon which you wish to rely so they have had a full opportunity to read them prior to the occasion when you refer the tribunal to them (sometimes this necessitates disclosure of such authorities prior to the day of the hearing).

Note that if you do not wish to have any direct contact with the other side, you can ask the clerk to pass documentation to them.

• Speak to your witnesses before the start of the hearing to describe the order of proceedings and practical matters such as the Oath, where to sit and who's on the tribunal. You should also clarify aspects of the case which you do not understand or upon which, if acting as a representative, you need further instructions.

Order and structure of proceedings [20.3]

Formalities: The chairman is addressed as sir or madam. The parties will be directed where to sit as they enter the room, but it is usual for the respondent to sit on the left (as you face the tribunal) and the applicant on the right. Witnesses occupy the table in between the parties (or, in some tribunal rooms, to one side). Proceedings are conducted, in their entirety, sitting down (apart from witnesses being required to stand when taking the oath/affirming).

Who presents their evidence first? [20.4]

It is usual for the party upon whom the burden of proof lies to call their evidence first. Below is an account of who usually goes first in different disputes, such as unfair dismissal and discrimination. Sometimes, for example in a claim for unfair dismissal, the burden of proof shifts according to the issue that the tribunal has to decide. In these circumstances, it is usually the party upon whom the initial burden lies who will go first.

Unfair dismissal: Provided the parties agree that there was a dismissal the respondent will normally present their evidence first, since the burden is on them to prove what the reason for dismissal is. In many cases, the reason for dismissal, e g misconduct, will not be in dispute, and the only issue will be whether the respondent acted reasonably in dismissing for that reason (in relation to which the burden of proof is neutral). Even in these circumstances, it is usual for the respondent to present their evidence first.

Where the fact of dismissal is in dispute: The employee presents their evidence first. Included in this category are claims for constructive dismissal, where, in all cases, it is for the applicant (in order to demonstrate that a constructive dismissal took place) to prove that they acted reasonably promptly upon a repudiatary breach of contract by the respondent.

Discrimination: The applicant will go first (since the burden lies on them to prove discrimination) unless, for example, the respondent concedes that there has been indirect discrimination, but wishes to assert a defence of objective justification, whereupon the respondent may give its evidence first.

Mixed unfair dismissal and discrimination claims: Who goes first in these circumstances will be for the tribunal to decide. It will listen, however, to the views of the parties. The applicant may be better placed, particularly in claims of direct discrimination, to argue that they should go first, since the burden of proving discrimination falls solely on them, in contrast to unfair dismissal, where the burden of proof in deciding reasonableness is neutral.

Equal pay cases: The applicant will usually present their evidence first, since the burden is on them to prove the principal components of their claim (shifting to the employer, where applicable, to prove a material factor defence).

Going first: advantage or disadvantage? [20.5]

On balance, going first is preferable, but the issue is by no means clear cut and often the reverse can be true. It is important, whether you are going first or second, to maximise the advantages available to you, which are different in kind.

Advantages of going first:

- You have the first and (usually) the last word. The party who goes first will deliver their final submissions last. It may be, however, that the other party will ask for a right to reply in relation to matters raised in those submissions, which they have not had an opportunity to make submissions.

- You can create a positive first impression of your case in the minds of the tribunal.

Advantages of going second:

- Your witnesses can respond directly to matters raised in evidence by the other side before they are raised in cross-examination.

- You know the case you have to meet and can, if necessary (and provided there is a natural pause in proceedings), review your original plan of attack, although the scope for doing so may be restricted by your existing witness statements.

The order of proceedings: step by step

Step one: introduction by the chairman   [20.6]

Brief introduction by the chairman to deal with such matters as establishing whether there is agreement over the effective date of termination, clarifying the issues, establishing the batting order, organising the documentation (e g bundles etc) and confirming whether the parties are ready to proceed or if there are preliminary issues which need to be resolved. If the applicant is unrepresented, the chairman will normally explain the legal basis upon which the tribunal will decide the case.

Step two: (optional) opening speech from the party who is calling their evidence first (party A)   [20.7]

The desirability of making an opening speech is discussed in CHAPTER 22 – THE HEARING III: THE ESSENTIALS OF EFFECTIVE TRIBUNAL ADVOCACY.

Step three: party A calls its evidence   [20.8]

Witnesses should be called, if possible, in a logical order. The witness is first asked questions in chief by their own side and is then cross-examined by the other side. For guidance of examination in chief (including the use of witness statements) and cross-examination, see CHAPTER 22.

179

Step four: party B calls its evidence [20.9]

Exactly the same process as is described above in relation to party A is then carried out by party B.

Step five: closing submissions [20.10]

Each party, or their representative, addresses the tribunal, at the conclusion of the evidence, as to why the tribunal should find in their favour. The party who has adduced their evidence last (i e party B) speaks first. Guidance on making final submissions is contained in CHAPTER 22.

Step six: the decision [20.11]

The tribunal will ask the parties to return to their waiting room whilst they make their decision. Upon being asked to return, the parties will usually be informed that the decision they are about to hear is an oral decision, but that they will be sent a written decision in due course (see CHAPTER 28 – STEPS AFTER THE DECISION II: APPEAL). Parties should not confuse the written summary of reasons with the extended written reasons, which should be obtained within 21 days of receipt of the summary of reasons to allow for a possible appeal.

Step seven: remedies hearing/costs [20.12]

If the applicant is successful in relation to all or part of their claim it is currently the practice of the tribunals, provided there is time, to proceed straight into a remedies hearing (see CHAPTER 26 – REMEDIES: CALCULATING LIKELY AWARDS), and cases are usually listed with this in mind. Therefore, always come prepared and ready to prove and argue the case on remedies

21.

The Hearing II: the Conduct of Proceedings by the Tribunal

Introduction [21.1]

Tribunals have the power to regulate their own procedure (*Employment Tribunals (Constitution and Rules of Procedure) Regulations 2001 (SI 2001/1171), rule 11(1)*). This means that they have a discretion to conduct proceedings in the manner in which they see fit, including deciding what evidence they hear, the order in which it is heard and the manner in which it is adduced. There are, however, two important limitations upon this discretion. First, tribunals must conduct proceedings in accordance with the rules of natural justice, in relation to which the Employment Appeal Tribunal (EAT) and higher courts have, over the years, laid down guidelines. Second, they must do so in accordance with their own procedural rules. A feature of the 2001 Regulations is the duty to give effect to the overriding objective (see CHAPTER 9 – FAIRNESS: THE OVERRIDING OBJECTIVE) when conducting the hearing, a matter the parties should address wherever appropriate.

Failure to be aware of some of the key features of a fair procedure could lead to a party being seriously disadvantaged in the presentation of its case. In particular, parties should bear in mind the following:

- Parties have the right to give evidence, call witnesses, question witnesses and address the tribunal (*rule 11(1)*).

- It is for the parties, not the tribunal, to ensure that all relevant evidence is placed before the tribunal (see *Craig v British Railways (Scottish Region) [1973] ITR 636* and *Derby City Council v Marshall [1979] IRLR 261; [1979] ICR 731, EAT*). Even if a matter is raised in the IT1 or IT3, it is incumbent upon the party concerned to adduce evidence in relation to it, although the tribunals may assist parties by reminding them (particularly those who are unrepresented) of this. If no evidence is adduced, the tribunal will have no factual material upon it in which it can make a finding for, or against, a particular party.

- The party who calls their evidence first should call *all* of their evidence and not, subsequently, put in cross-examination to the other side's witnesses matters which have not been first adduced in chief from their own (see CHAPTER 22 – THE HEARING III: THE ESSENTIALS OF EFFECTIVE TRIBUNAL ADVOCACY – *Aberdeen Steak Houses v Ibrahim [1988] IRLR 420; [1988] ICR 550, EAT*).

Example: The applicant has given evidence about a meeting that took place between her and the manager in the respondent organisation. She alleges that the manager told her she would shortly be made redundant. When the manager gives evidence, the applicant's representative suggests to him that, in addition to saying this, he also told the applicant that she was hopeless at her job. This had never been said by the applicant in evidence and the representative is therefore putting in cross-examination something which has not formed part of her case in chief.

- The party who calls their evidence second must, in cross-examination of the first party's witnesses, put to them all factual matters which are in dispute in relation to which it proposes to call evidence of its own (see *Aberdeen Steak Houses* above). The reason for this is the principle that each party must be given a fair opportunity to deal with the other's case (see CHAPTER 22).

Example: The applicant gives evidence saying that he was unfairly dismissed for an allegation of fighting. It is the respondent's case that this was the second incident of fighting which the applicant had been involved in, a matter which is in dispute. The respondent, in cross-examination, does not ask the applicant about the prior incident. When the respondent's manager gives evidence, he mentions it as a factor he took into account in reaching his decision. The allegation in relation to the prior incident of fighting ought to have been put to the applicant in cross-examination to give him an opportunity to deal with it.

- Parties must not be taken by surprise by serious allegations which are made at the last minute and which they have not had time to prepare for (*Hotson v Wisbech Conservative Club [1984] IRLR 422; [1984] ICR 859, EAT*). Where this occurs, the party against whom the allegation is made is entitled, if necessary, to seek an adjournment. Again, this is based upon the principle that each party should be given a fair opportunity to deal with the other's case.

- It is for the tribunal to decide who presents their case first and second, but within the confines of fairly strict guidelines laid down by the EAT (*Gill v Harold Andrews (Sheepbridge) Ltd [1974] IRLR 109; [1974] ICR 294* and *Oxford v Department of Health and Social Security [1977] IRLR 22; [1977] ICR 884*). (see CHAPTER 20 –

- It is generally for the parties to decide the order in which they call their own witnesses (*Barnes v BPC (Business Forms) Ltd [1975] IRLR 313; [1975] ICR 390*).

- Where evidence is relevant to the issue/s the tribunal has to decide, then it is obliged to hear it, even if it is in hearsay form (*Rosedale Mouldings Ltd v Sibley [1980] IRLR 387, [1980] ICR 816*). The form in which the evidence is presented is relevant only to the weight, or importance, which the tribunal attach to it (see **21.2–21.4**).

- The chairman is under a duty to take a note of the evidence in the case, which may be ordered to be produced on appeal by the EAT (see CHAPTER **28** – STEPS AFTER THE DECISION II: APPEAL) (*Houston v Lightwater Farm Ltd [1990] IRLR 469 [1990] ICR 502*).

Calling evidence [21.2]

Evidence is the factual material upon which the tribunal reaches its decision. The rules of fairness dictate that there are limitations upon the types of evidence that can be adduced in tribunal proceedings. It is within the tribunal's discretion not to allow a party to adduce certain evidence or, if has already been adduced, to exclude it altogether from their minds in coming to a decision. Such evidence is described as 'inadmissible'. By contrast, evidence which can be legitimately placed before the tribunal is described as 'admissible'. 'Admissible' merely means that the tribunal is entitled to consider the evidence and take it into account in reaching its decision. It may ultimately decide to accept, reject, or attach no weight (i e importance) to it.

Admissible and inadmissible evidence

Irrelevant evidence [21.3]

For evidence to be admissible, it must be relevant to one or more of the issues which the tribunal has to decide. The reliability or accuracy of a piece of evidence is *not* a factor in assessing its relevance. Nor does a party need to show that it is important evidence. All such considerations go to weight.

In assessing relevance, parties should ask whether it is 'probative' of one of the issues that the tribunal has to decide – that is to say capable, in any respect, of assisting the tribunal in deciding that issue. If it is so capable, even in a very limited way, it will normally be admissible. If the relevance is limited, this is a factor which goes to weight, but not admissibility.

It is important for parties to bear in mind the distinction between relevance and weight. On many occasions, evidence will be of dubious, or very limited relevance. In these circumstances, it will usually be admissible. The opposing party will, however, be well placed to argue that, given its marginal relevance, the tribunal should attach little or no weight to it.

Examples: relevance and weight compared   **[21.4]**

Example one: An employee is dismissed for theft from his employer which he denies. The respondent discovers, after the hearing, that he has a criminal conviction for theft ten years ago and seeks to adduce this in evidence. The applicant attempts to get the evidence of theft excluded on the basis that it is irrelevant. It is likely that the applicant will succeed in getting the evidence excluded on grounds of irrelevance. In the circumstances of this case, the past conviction is not relevant to the issue which the tribunal has to decide, which is the information that was before the employer at the time and upon which the employer based its decision.

Example two: As above, except that the theft was a factor which the employer took into account in reaching its decision to dismiss. The evidence is, in these circumstances, clearly admissible, as the tribunal is assessing the reasonableness of the employer's decision at the time, and the theft is one of the factors which the employer took into account. The applicant is likely to want the evidence admitted in any event, in order to argue that it was unreasonable for the employer to take into account such an (arguably) irrelevant factor.

Example three: In a discrimination case, the applicant argues that they were denied promotion on account of race and that a less well qualified person accepted the job. The applicant seeks to adduce evidence that, at a Christmas party, which took place after the selection process, the manager responsible was heard making a racist joke.

The evidence of the joke is likely to be admitted because it is relevant to the issue of whether there was a racial motive for the non-selection. This does not prevent the respondent arguing, in final submissions, that the tribunal should attach no weight to the evidence, for example on the basis:

cont'd

- that the evidence is untrue (if applicable); and/or

- that, in any event, no tribunal could safely infer from the making of such a joke that the manager would adopt a racist selection procedure.

Without prejudice communications [21.5]

Offers and negotiations relating to the settling of proceedings are not admissible evidence in tribunal proceedings. For this reason, it is important that documents relating to such negotiations or offers are not included in the evidence presented to the tribunal and that no reference is made to them during the course of proceedings. On occasions, an applicant who is not represented will be unaware of this rule, and will draw the tribunal's attention to an offer which has been made. The chairman will, in these circumstances, indicate to both parties that such evidence is not admissible and will direct the lay members to exclude such evidence from their minds in reaching any decision. The respondent may still consider, however, that the tribunal has been prejudiced by the disclosure of the information in question. It is open to the respondent to make an application to the tribunal that the hearing be abandoned and the case listed in front of a newly constituted tribunal. Whether this course is adopted will depend upon a number of factors, including the size of any offer that has been made.

Tribunals are aware that parties do attempt to settle cases and that fact, in itself, is unlikely to prejudice them. Where, however, the offer is sufficiently large to suggest that the respondent recognises there are serious weaknesses in their case, then serious thought should be given to making such an application, which should be made as soon as possible (and preferably immediately) after the wrongful disclosure has taken place. If successful, the respondent should consider making an application for costs arising from the postponement.

Challenging inadmissible evidence [21.6]

In the criminal jurisdiction, a challenge to the admissibility of the evidence is made in the absence of the jury. This prevents the unsatisfactory course of asking the jury to exclude from their minds evidence which they have already heard.

This option is not available in civil or tribunal proceedings. The fact remains, however, that the best course is to prevent inadmissible

185

evidence from coming to the attention of the tribunal which makes the decision.

The advisable course is to:

- Agree with the other side in advance of the hearing the evidence which the tribunal will hear. In the majority of cases this will be possible.

- If possible, resolve any disputes about the relevance of evidence at a directions hearing, obtaining a ruling from the chairman as to what evidence can be adduced at full hearing. Such disputes are likely to be particularly prevalent in discrimination and equal pay cases.

During the hearing:

- Sometimes the other side's representative will ask a question of a witness which will put you on notice that inadmissible evidence is about to be adduced. The best course is to object to the question there and then, before the answer is given. State that a question is being asked about an irrelevant matter and explain why. The chairman will then give a ruling on whether the question is permissible. Sometimes, it is best to let such questions 'go by' if they are innocuous in nature and you are confident that the answer will not harm your case.

- If inadmissible evidence is adduced, you have a choice whether to refer to it there and then, or to wait until your final submissions. If you believe that an answer has been given which will lead to the adducing of further inadmissible evidence, it is best to object immediately in order to prevent this occurring.

- When addressing the tribunal during final submissions, draw its attention to any evidence which, in your submission, it should exclude from its mind as being irrelevant or incapable of assisting in deciding the case.

Do's and Don'ts

Do:

- Remember the fundamental principle in tribunal proceedings that each party should have a fair opportunity to present their own case and respond to that of the other side.

- Apply for an adjournment (with costs where appropriate) if a new matter is raised by the other side which you have not had an opportunity to respond to and in relation to which you need time to prepare evidence in response. Alternatively, if appropriate, ask for a short break to take instructions.

- If you are going first, ask for a witness to be recalled if the other side give evidence about a matter which ought to have been put to them first in cross-examination.

- Attempt to resolve issues of inadmissible evidence prior to the hearing.

- Use the overriding objective as a tool when challenging the fairness of proceedings.

Don't:

- Forget that it is the duty of the parties to place all relevant evidence before the tribunal.

- Be afraid to ask for a witness to be recalled if you have failed to put a matter to them – although the tribunal have a discretion to refuse.

22.

The Hearing III: the Essentials of Effective Tribunal Advocacy

Introduction [22.1]

Advocacy is, in essence, the art of persuasion. Whilst experience is an invaluable asset for any advocate, there are certain key features of good advocacy which this chapter seeks to address.

Pre-hearing preparation [22.2]

The importance of thorough preparation cannot be overestimated. Many are impressed by the ability of good advocates to 'think on their feet'. The capacity to respond to a witness effectively in cross-examination, answer questions from the tribunal and deal with unexpected developments comes, at least in part, from a having a thorough knowledge of the facts of the case and a clear idea of the chronology in which relevant events occurred. It also comes from having given careful thought in advance to how the case should be presented. The following are some of the key features of effective preparation.

Prepare a chronology [22.3]

It is a myth that preparing an effective chronology lengthens your preparation time,– usually the reverse is true. In most circumstances, you will do this anyway for the tribunal, so there will be no duplication of effort. A chronology is an invaluable way of ensuring that you have a thorough knowledge of the documentation in the case. It will enable you to organise and marshal the evidence in your own mind. The chronology should contain all relevant events in the sequence they occurred. Where the event is recorded in a document, e g notes of a disciplinary hearing, the document should be referred to in the chronology.

Chronologies are usually drawn up using the following:

- the bundle of documentary evidence (such as letters, disciplinary notes etc);

- witness statements;

- any additional instructions you may have.

Many advocates prepare chronologies in draft form as they are reading the documents. As you prepare the chronology and marshal the facts, useful thoughts on the presentation of your case will frequently come to mind. For example, you might notice an inconsistency or weakness in the other side's case which provides a useful avenue for cross-examination, or a point may occur to you which could be used in final submissions. Note these down as they occur. How this is done is a matter of choice. You might, for example, wish to have separate sheets of paper headed 'points for cross-examination', 'points for final submissions' and 'matters to be asked of own witnesses'.

After completing your chronology you should be able to turn to any document in the case and be satisfied that, if it is relevant, the event to which it refers is recorded in the chronology.

Identify the issues in the case   **[22.4]**

It is essential to identify the issues which the tribunal will have to decide. Only then can you plan how to persuade the tribunal how to find in your favour in relation to those issues. In order to identify the issues, you will need to have a knowledge of the relevant area of law. So, in an unfair dismissal case, you will need to be aware that the tribunal must decide:

(a)   what the reason was for the dismissal;

(b)   whether this was a potentially lawful reason; and

(c)   whether the employer acted reasonably in dismissing for that reason.

In many such cases, (a) and (b) are not in dispute and the only live issue is (c).

Plan your objectives   **[22.5]**

Once you have identified the legal issues, plan your objectives in relation to those issues based on your factual knowledge of the case. An applicant in an unfair dismissal case might, therefore, wish to demonstrate that the employer failed to adopt a fair procedure by:

- not interviewing relevant witnesses;

- not giving the applicant a proper opportunity to respond to the allegations;

- failing to take in to account relevant considerations, for example the applicant's good record up to that point.

Or, in a case of alleged discrimination by non-promotion, the objective of the respondent might be to demonstrate that they carried out a fair selection procedure through open advertisement and interview, and that the non-selection of the applicant was due to their qualifications and experience. Under each area you might want to make notes of the areas of evidence which are likely to support each proposition, highlighting matters to put in cross-examination and which need to be adduced from your own witnesses in support of your case.

Plan your examinations in chief and cross-examinations and, using your objectives, have a broad framework in mind as to what your final submissions will be.

Advocacy at the hearing [22.6]

The importance of note taking: It is essential to take a thorough note of the evidence as it is heard. Proceedings are not tape recorded and your note will (unless you ask the chairman to recite his) be the only record you have of what has taken place. It is surprising how mundane evidence can become relevant at a later stage, for example if a witness contradicts themselves when giving evidence. It is also important, when making final submissions, to be able to accurately recite to the tribunal important pieces of evidence upon which you rely.

Unqualified people, representing themselves or their companies, are well advised to bring a friend or colleague to help take notes – it is sometimes hard to write, listen and think at the same time.

The opening speech [22.7]

There is no obligation upon a party to make an opening statement and this is frequently unnecessary in straightforward cases where the issues are adequately defined at the outset. The objective of your opening speech should be limited to:

- defining the issues in the case; and

- giving the tribunal a very broad outline of your case in relation to those issues.

The latter can be useful, particularly in complex cases, if you wish the tribunal to approach the evidence with a clear idea of what your case is. It is crucial, however, that you do not stray into giving evidence in your opening or make submissions about the strength of the evidence.

Do's and Don'ts

Do:

- Keep your opening concise.

- Make an opening statement only if you feel that it is necessary to clarify the issues from the outset.

- Confine your remarks to giving a broad view of what your case is in relation to the issues, or the 'theme' of your case.

Don't:

- Describe in detail the evidence which the tribunal is going to hear.

- Make submissions about the strength of your case and the weakness of the other side's – save this for final submissions.

- Allow your opening to become a hostage to fortune by making predictions about the evidence – cases are inherently unpredictable.

Examination in chief [22.8]

Examination in chief is when you ask your own witness to give their version of events to the tribunal. As an advocate, your task is to ensure that the evidence they give is:

- complete in relation to all issues in relation to which they are able to give evidence is complete;

- presented in as persuasive a manner as possible.

It can be a considerable advantage if a witness statement is prepared. This can then be read out by the witness, accompanied by supplementary questions (if necessary) to clarify or expand upon the matters in the statement. Where a statement is not prepared, you will have to elicit the necessary evidence from the witness through a series of questions. Where questions are asked of a witness in chief (whether supplementary to a witness statement or otherwise) these questions should be 'non-leading' – the answer must not be suggested in the question (see **22.13**).

Preparing an examination in chief [22.9]

Before your witness gives evidence, you should be clear about all of the matters which you require that witness to cover. This involves you identifying which of the issues in the case the witness is able to give direct evidence about.

Typically, evidence in chief (whether through a witness statement or otherwise) should cover:

- all relevant events and conversations which that person witnessed;

- the basis upon which that person reached any relevant decision, including the matters they took in to account (note, in an unfair dismissal case, it is common for these to be recorded by the manager in a contemporaneous memo. Where the memo is complete, the witness statement need simply refer to that document as being an accurate reflection of the basis for the decision);

- any other matters upon which that witness is able to give relevant evidence.

Examination in chief: step by step [22.10]

- Inform the tribunal who you are calling.

- The witness, while standing by the witness table, will be asked to take the oath or to affirm, as administered by either the chairman, one of the lay members or the clerk, at the chairman's discretion. The witness then sits for the rest of the proceedings.

- The witness will then usually be asked to confirm their name and address by the chairman. If he does not ask, make this your first question.

- If the witness has a statement, ask that witness to confirm:

  (a) that they have made a statement in the case;

  (b) that they have a copy of that statement in front of them;

  (c) that the signature at the bottom of the statement is theirs;

  and

  (d) that (subject to any corrections made today) the contents are true.

- Where there are parts of the statement which are incorrect – for example a date is wrong – take the witness to that part immediately, ask them to correct it, and ask the tribunal to make a note of the correction.

- Then indicate to the tribunal that the witness will read out the statement. (It should be noted, however, that some chairmen prefer witness statements to be taken as read by the tribunal, especially when the time-management of a case is presenting difficulties.)

- As the witness reads out the statement, stop them at any point where an additional question or point of clarification is warranted, or alternatively wait until they have read the statement and ask additional questions at that point, referring them back, where necessary, to the relevant numbered paragraph.

The purpose of supplementary questions where a witness statement is used [22.11]

The purpose of supplementary questions is to:

- correct anything which is inaccurate;

- update the statement in relation to recent events;

- add to or clarify particular parts of the statement;

- respond to new points given in evidence by other witnesses;

- refer the tribunal to a document in the bundle which is mentioned in the statement.

The questions can be asked either after the statement is read out or as it is being read out, with the witness being stopped at the relevant stage. The latter is usually the best course when you are stopping to refer the tribunal to a particular document in the bundle mentioned in the statement. In these circumstances, you should ask the witness to refer to the page in the bundle and confirm that the document is the one he is referring to in the statement. With important documents, give the tribunal an opportunity to read it there and then, before asking the witness to continue.

- Where there is no witness statement, elicit the relevant evidence from your witness through a series of questions, which in contentious matters (i e matters in dispute) should be non-leading.

- The best means of preparing the questions is to write down all the matters upon which you need that witness to give evidence, and then formulate the questions.

Leading questions [22.12]

Any question asked of your own witness, including (where there is a witness statement) supplementary questions, should not be leading in respect of any contentious matter. A leading question is one where the answer is suggested in the question. As a good rule of thumb, a question which can be answered with a simple 'yes' or 'no' may indicate that a leading question has been asked. Similarly, questions starting with 'is it right to say...' or 'would you agree...' are strongly indicative of a leading question. By contrast, questions starting with the words 'why' or 'to what extent...' are unlikely to be leading. Leading questions can do a disservice to your own witness. A tribunal is likely to attach less weight to an answer which is given to a leading question.

Example

You are acting for the respondent. You want to bring out in evidence both that the seriousness of the misconduct and that the applicant's previous formal warning for misconduct were important factors in the decision to dismiss.

Example of a leading question: Is it right to say that the most important factors in coming to the decision to dismiss was both the seriousness of the misconduct and the fact that the applicant received a formal warning three months previously? Answer: Yes.

Example of a non-leading question: What were the principal factors in deciding that dismissal was warranted? Answer: The seriousness of the misconduct and the fact that he had been warned three months earlier.

Effectively directing your witness [22.13]

Adducing the evidence you want from a witness without asking leading questions can be extremely difficult. The following should prove useful:

- Use your materials – often you can direct the witness to the area you want by referring them to a particular document. This can act as a signpost. You can ask, for example, what their reaction is to a particular document, whether it is accurate or inaccurate, whether they wish to add something etc.

- Direct your witness to a particular aspect of the other side's case which you want them to deal with. For example, 'what is your reaction to the assertion by x that you lost your temper at the meeting on the 12?'.

- Plan your questions in advance: this is important, but remember that evidence frequently does not go according to plan so you need to retain an element of flexibility.

Challenging leading questions asked by your opponent: Do not be afraid to object to a leading question (preferably before the answer is given) if one is asked by your opponent of their own witness. Sometimes, you can nip the question in the bud, for example if you hear the words 'is it true to say that the main reason...'. Interrupt and politely point out to the tribunal that the question is being phrased in a leading manner. Tribunals differ in their approach to the asking of leading questions. They will, rightly, be much more lenient to an applicant who is representing themselves and is unfamiliar with proceedings, than a legally qualified representative. A tribunal will also be keen to prevent proceedings becoming oppressive and will therefore usually only restrict leading questions in relation to matters that go to the heart of the dispute between the parties.

Cross-examination and putting your case   [22.14]

The aim of cross-examination is:

- to elicit the evidence helpful to your case from the other side's witness, usually (in contrast to examination in chief) through a series of leading questions;

- to give that witness an opportunity to deal with your case where it is inconsistent with or at odds with their own. This is an aspect of procedural fairness – namely giving both sides the opportunity to comment on the other side's evidence. This is particularly important with allegations of dishonesty (note, if your side is going first, your own witness should already have given the inconsistent version when giving evidence in chief – it is usually not permissible, in these circumstances, for the allegation to be put for the first time in cross-examination).

A successful cross-examination involves the examiner eliciting the answers they want from the witness through very precise questioning. This involves:

- careful planning;

- an appreciation of the issues in relation to which that witness evidence is relevant;

- the identification of weaknesses in that evidence which you can bring out;

- the setting of realistic objectives for your cross-examination;

- the formulation of precise questions – usually leading in nature.

In contrast to examination in chief, leading questions are not only permitted, but are generally preferable. They allow you to control the witness and elicit the answers you want from them.

Example

You appear for the applicant in an unfair dismissal case where an employee of eight years standing was dismissed for being three hours late for an important meeting. Whilst preparing the case, you have noticed that the contemporaneous memorandum recording the reasons for dismissal makes no mention of the employee's previous good attendance record. One of your objectives is to demonstrate that this was an important factor which the manager failed to take into account in reaching his decision.

Q: Do you agree that the applicant's previous good record was a relevant factor for you to consider when taking the decision to dismiss?

A: Yes.

Q: Please turn to page 40 in the bundle. This is a contemporaneous memorandum which you prepared recording the factors you took into consideration in deciding to dismiss the applicant?

A: Yes.

Q: Did you take care in writing that memorandum?

A: Yes.

Q: Yet you make no mention of that previous good record?

A: No.

Q: suggest the reason is that you didn't consider it?

A: ....

Explanation of example   [22.15]

There is an old saying: 'never ask a question in cross-examination unless you know the answer'. This would probably be better phrased as 'never ask a question in cross-examination unless you are fully prepared for any possible answer'. Using the above example, some of the questions do admit of more than one answer, but the planning of your questions should ensure that, where possible, the witness is 'cornered' into giving evidence that assists you. If, for example, the witness answers that the previous good record is not a relevant factor, this does not matter. You have still obtained a potentially damaging admission from the manager that he failed to take in to account a relevant consideration. You can simply note this down for final submissions and proceed to the next theme in your cross-examination.

Putting your case [22.16]

The obligation to put your case to a witness is an important one. It stems from the principle that each party should have the opportunity to respond to the other side's evidence. This is particularly so when you are first to cross-examine and your own side's evidence is being called second. If you have failed to put an aspect of your case in cross-examination, the tribunal may refuse to admit evidence from your own side in relation to that matter. Alternatively, the other side's witness may have to be recalled in order to give them the opportunity to deal with it. The obligation to put your case extends especially to circumstances where:

- you are alleging that the witness said or did something which has not been mentioned in their evidence in chief; or

- has failed to give a truthful account of an event.

Parties, especially those who may be appearing before a tribunal for the first time, should not, however, be too daunted by the obligation to put their case – important though it is. No one can predict with certainty the course which evidence may take, and even the most conscientious and experienced advocate cannot count on being able to eliminate the risk of surprise altogether. Provided that you do your best to avoid any possibility of unfair surprise to your opponent in the way your evidence is presented, you need not expect the tribunal to be too harsh and censorious if, for any reason, your case has not been fully put. Given a spirit of goodwill all round, consequent risks of injustice can normally be removed through the tribunal authorising the recall of a witness or some other direction, though it is under no obligation to do so.

Example

You represent the respondent in an unfair dismissal case where the respondent maintains that the applicant was not dismissed but resigned. One of the crucial events is a meeting on the final day of the applicant's employment. The applicant gives evidence that, at this meeting, he

cont'd

---

was told to pack his bags and leave. Your case is that this was never said and further that the applicant said: 'I have had enough of this place, I'm leaving – send me my P45'. You must give the applicant the opportunity to deal with this allegation and you should further challenge his evidence that he was told to pack his bags and leave. Try and do this, however, in a way that is advantageous to your case.

Q: You were told that the purpose of the meeting was to find a way of resolving your problems at the company (refer to document in bundle)?

A: Yes.

Q: At the meeting, you were present, together with two members of management?

A: Yes, John Jones and Bill Smith.

Q: During the meeting, Bill Smith offered you a number of practical solutions for working out your problems at work?

A: No.

Q: You were angry and upset during the meeting?

A: Yes, because of the way they had been treating me.

Q: Both managers remained calm throughout the meeting?

A: I suppose so.

Q: You had been in the room for 30 minutes before you left?

A: Yes.

Q: When you left you were angry and upset?

A: Yes I was.

Q: You were so angry and upset that you told them you were leaving and they should send you your P45?

A: I never said that.

Q: You've since come to regret saying that and you've invented the story that they told you to pack your bags and leave?

A: No, I'm telling the truth.

Note that, with this example, you have built up to the moment of asking the relevant questions by establishing two facts favourable to your version. First, that the applicant was angry and upset and therefore liable to say something in the heat of the moment. Second, that he had been in the room for 30 minutes, something arguably inconsistent with a dismissal. Both these points can be noted down for final submissions.

Finally, it is important to be realistic when planning your cross-examination of a witness. There will be occasions when cross-examination is unnecessary altogether, for example because the witness' evidence is uncontentious. If you consider that asking questions will not assist your case, do not ask them, unless you have to in order to give the witness an opportunity to deal with your case.

Do's and Don'ts

Do:

- Plan a clear set of objectives for your cross-examination.
- Ensure that your objectives are realistic.
- Ask precise (preferably leading) questions.
- Plan for every conceivable answer.
- Be purposeful in your style of questioning.

Don't:

- Be aggressive.
- Engage in an argument with the witness – move on when the time is right.
- Assume that a cross-examination *has* to be hostile in tone: if you can get the witness to freely agree with you, this is often an advantage.
- Make comments on the witness' evidence there and then note these down and save them for final submissions.

Re-examination [22.17]

Every party calling a witness has the right to re-examine the witness after cross-examination from the other side. Re-examination must be limited, however, to matters which have been raised in cross-examination. It cannot, without the permission of the tribunal, be used to introduce evidence which should have been given in chief and which does not arise from the cross-examination. Re-examination is a right to be exercises sparingly and should *not* be used to persuade the witness to repeat, or to change, evidence they have already given. It is frequently unnecessary, and often inadvisable, to re-examine a witness at all.

Examples of where re-examination might be useful include the following:

- To give an opportunity to the witness to say something which you know forms part of their evidence but which they either inadvertently failed to mention in cross-examination or were not given an opportunity to do so.

  Example: You act for the applicant in an unfair dismissal case. In cross-examination, the applicant admits that she was warned for misconduct in 1996. Your instructions are that she was told by a senior manager prior to the dismissal hearing that the warning would not count against her. To remind her of this, you might ask: 'Did a manager discuss with you the 1996 warning prior to your disciplinary hearing?'

- To correct an straightforward factual error which the applicant has made in cross-examination.

  Example: You stated that you wrote to the applicant at the beginning of March complaining of her attendance. Could you turn to page 41 in the bundle. Is that the letter you were speaking of? The letter is dated 1 May – could you confirm to the tribunal what the correct date was.

Closing submissions [22.18]

Closing submissions take place after the evidence has been heard. Their purpose is to persuade the tribunal to find in your favour. The party who adduced their evidence second speaks first, with the other party responding. The tribunal has a discretion whether to allow a further response from the first party.

Effective submissions should contain a clear and obvious structure. It is usual to structure your submissions around the issues the tribunal has to decide, explaining why, in relation to each one, the tribunal should find in your favour. This involves referring to the evidence which has been heard and:

- drawing the tribunal's attention to evidence which supports your case;

- where there is a conflict on the evidence, suggesting why the tribunal should accept your side's version of what took place.

Do not forget the value of referring the tribunal to undisputed evidence which supports your case. This will not simply be evidence from your own witnesses which has not been challenged, but also advantageous answers which you have been able to obtain from the other side's witnesses in cross-examination.

Where there is a dispute about the evidence, reference to the undisputed facts can again be useful. So, to adopt the example used in cross-examination, in asking the tribunal to find that the applicant was not sacked but stormed out of the room and resigned, you can refer them to the undisputed evidence that he was angry at the time of the meeting, that he had been present in the meeting for 30 minutes before he left (a fact which, depending on the circumstances, could be inconsistent with dismissal). You will, in addition to that undisputed evidence, refer them to the account of what took place by both of your managers.

Provided that submissions are structured, relevant and persuasive, it is a matter of personal choice as to how they are presented to the tribunal. The following is a short illustration of how you might set about approaching such submissions in a particular case. In practice, your submissions are likely to be longer and to refer to considerably more evidence. Copies of any legal authorities (leading cases etc) on which you intend to relay should be provided to the tribunal and the other party (that is, four copies) no later than the beginning of your submissions.

Example

You act for the applicant in an unfair dismissal case. Your client has been dismissed for misconduct after an incident in which he was caught fighting at work. You concede, on behalf of the applicant, that the reason for dismissal was misconduct, and that this is one of the potentially lawful reasons under the *Employment Rights Act 1996*. You remind the tribunal that the only live issue before them is whether the respondent acted reasonably, in all the circumstances, in dismissing for that reason.

You state, for the following reasons, that it was not.

First, the dismissal was procedurally unfair because the respondent did not carry out a fair investigation.

cont'd

- There is undisputed evidence that the respondent made no effort to interview bystanders of the fight whom the applicant had told them would support his version that he had been severely provoked. Without doing so, the respondent could not have gained a proper understanding of a relevant factor, namely the degree of provocation which the applicant faced.

- The respondent failed to take in to account a relevant consideration in reaching its decision – namely that the applicant had an immaculate record until this incident. Whilst the respondent maintained in evidence that this was taken in to account, the weight of the evidence before the tribunal suggests otherwise – there is no mention of it in the memo recording the factors taken in to consideration in making the decision to dismiss and it was not until he was referred to it in cross-examination that the dismissing manager mentioned it.

Second, without prejudice to the contention that the dismissal was procedurally unfair, the decision to dismiss was outside the range of reasonable responses open to the employer.

- The applicant had an immaculate record.

- On the applicant's evidence, he faced severe provocation, an assertion which is likely to be correct given his previous good record.

- The undisputed evidence is that he immediately acknowledged that his actions, in fighting, were wrong and showed remorse for them.

- Two months prior to the applicant's dismissal, three employees were giving written warnings for being involved in fighting, but were not dismissed. No reasonable employer would have been so inconsistent as to give those employees a mere warning and subject the applicant to the extreme penalty of dismissal.

This example, in skeleton form, is intended to illustrate how you might set about dealing with the two main issues for the tribunal to decide, namely whether the employer carried out a fair investigation and whether dismissal was within the range of reasonable responses open to the employer.

Do's and Don'ts

Do:

- Make notes of points for final submissions as the case proceeds on separate piece of paper.

- Structure your submissions logically around the issues the tribunal has to decide.

- Use a skeleton argument in complex cases if you have time to prepare one.

- Plan your submissions carefully – with the aim of persuading the tribunal to find in your favour.

Don't:

- Repeat your best points *ad nauseam* – this will undermine their effectiveness.

23.

Private Hearings and Restricted Reporting Orders

Introduction [23.1]

The general rule is that tribunal proceedings are heard in public (*Employment Tribunals (Constitution and Rules of Procedure) Regulations 2001 (SI 2001/1171), rule 10(2)*). It is thought to be in the public interest that hearings be open to public scrutiny rather than take place behind closed doors.

There are two means of restricting publicity in tribunal proceedings. First, the tribunal has the discretion, in very limited circumstances, to order that a hearing (or part of a hearing) be heard in private. Second, there is provision, in cases concerning allegations of sexual misconduct (and cases concerning evidence of a personal nature in disability discrimination cases) for the tribunal to make a restricted reporting order. This, as the name suggests, does not prevent access to the tribunal by the public and media, but prevents the publication, until promulgation of the decision, of identifying details of individuals.

Hearings/evidence in private [23.2]

A tribunal may sit in private (*rule 10(3)*) for the purpose of hearing evidence which, in the opinion of the tribunal, is likely to consist of:

(a) information which cannot be disclosed without constituting a breach of a specific statutory prohibition;

(b) information which has been communicated to a witness in confidence or which has otherwise been obtained in consequence of the confidence reposed in them by another person; or

(c) information the disclosure of which would cause substantial injury to any undertaking of the witness or any undertaking in which they work.

In addition, a tribunal must sit in private where directed to by the Secretary of State in the interests of national security (*rule 8(1)*).

In relation to (b), this not only potentially includes medical practitioners or solicitors operating under a professional duty of confidentiality, but may also include those in business and other organisations who, when they receive the information, are under a duty to keep it confidential. An example of the latter might be where the witness is obliged to disclose details of confidential business transactions or trade secrets which they have received subject to a duty of confidentiality. The wording of the rules further suggests that the relevant moment in time for ascertaining whether a duty of confidentiality exists is the moment when the witness received the information. The disclosure of business transactions, trade secrets and confidential negotiations might also engage (c) – namely causing substantial injury to the undertaking.

Sensitive or embarrassing allegations [23.3]

The rules deliberately refer not to the making of allegations but to the disclosure of information by a witness. The mere fact that a damaging allegation is made will not, of itself, enable the hearing to take place in private. Serious allegations are frequently made in tribunals, sometimes without proper evidence, which are embarrassing and/or damaging for those involved. That is unless, in defending that application, the respondent is obliged to disclose information which is likely to cause substantial damage to the undertaking or involve the disclosure of confidential information. The situation could conceivably be different, however, in a (non dismissal) case where the applicant is still employed by the undertaking and wishes to give reveal evidence which could be damaging (this is because the protection extends to any undertaking of the witness or one in which they work).

Making applications for a case to be heard in private [23.4]

The application should be made immediately before the commencement of the full hearing. It has been held that it is not appropriate for the application to be decided by the chairman alone, but by the full tribunal (*Milne and Lyall v Waldren [1980] ICR 138, EAT*). It is sensible to highlight both to the tribunal and the other side, in advance of the day of the hearing, that the application will be made unless it is thought that this will 'put ideas into their head' about generating publicity. If the parties are in agreement that the hearing be in private, this will not necessarily be conclusive. Restricting the right of the public to observe proceedings is considered to be a serious matter and the tribunal will not make such an order unless satisfied that the criteria in *rule 10(3)* are met. Further, the tribunal has a discretion, even if the criteria in *rule 10(3)* are met, to decline to sit in public. In deciding how to exercise this discretion, it will take into account the overriding objective (see CHAPTER 9 – FAIRNESS: THE OVERRIDING OBJECTIVE) and will balance the need for privacy against the public interest which lies in proceedings being open.

Restricted reporting orders [23.5]

Restricted reporting orders have the effect of preventing publication of any information which might lead to members of the public identifying a particular person or people in a case. (The jurisdiction of the tribunal to make such orders arises both under *rule 16* and the *Employment Tribunals Act 1996, s 11*). Such orders can be made only in cases involving:

- allegations of sexual misconduct; or

- evidence that is likely to be of a personal nature in disability discrimination cases.

'Personal nature' means 'evidence of a medical or other intimate, nature which might reasonably be assumed to be likely to cause significant embarrassment to the complainant if reported'. In either case, the order from the tribunal will specify the persons who must not be identified, and a notice to that effect will be displayed on the tribunal door and the notice board displaying the list of proceedings.

The order can be made either of the tribunal's own motion or upon the application of the parties. The tribunal has a discretion whether to make the order and must consider whether it is in the public interest that the press be able to communicate the information to the public. There has been considerable debate about whether a restricted reporting order can be made in respect of a corporate body as well as an individual. Whilst there is some conflict in the case law on this point, on balance it is unlikely that corporate bodies can so benefit (see *Leicester University v A [1999] IRLR 352, [1999] ICR 701, EAT* (no protection for corporate bodies) and *M v Vincent [1998] ICR 73, EAT* (order protecting corporate body permissible)). Such bodies should be aware, however, that if publication of their name is likely to lead to a particular individual being identified, then this would constitute a breach of any order in respect of that person – something which offers them some protection.

In contrast to an application for a private hearing, which should be made immediately prior to the commencement of that hearing, an application for a restricted reporting order can be made at a much earlier, interlocutory stage in proceedings, and can be determined by the chairman alone exercising his powers under *rule 15(8)*.

Do's and Don'ts

Do:

- Consider at an early stage whether an order under *rule 10* is required or a restricted reporting order.

- Consider making contact with the other side to see if they would agree to an order.

- Make an application for a restricted reporting order as early as possible in proceedings.

- Make an application for a private hearing on the day of the full hearing, but, if at all possible, give the tribunal and the parties notice of the fact that the application will be made.

- In difficult or complex cases, consider seeking specialised legal advice on whether evidence (documentary or otherwise) is likely to be considered confidential.

Don't:

- Assume that because the criteria in *rule 10* or *rule 16* are met the tribunal will make the order.

- Forget that the general principle is that proceedings should be held in public.

24.

Costs

Introduction [24.1]

Unlike civil courts proceedings, there is no general rule in employment proceedings that the successful party has the right to recover their legal costs. Tribunals, in fact, have no inherent power to award costs and may only consider making an award in the restricted circumstances set out in the procedural rules (*Employment Tribunals (Constitution and Rules of Procedure) Regulations 2001 (SI 2001/1170)*).

The historic reason for not awarding costs was to ensure that tribunals were accessible to all parties, in an area of dispute where there is often a huge imbalance between the financial means of employees and employers. In practice, however, those employees who incurred no professional legal charges, effectively found themselves in a 'no lose' situation whereby if they succeeded with their claim, they received an award, whilst if they lost, it cost them nothing financially.

As public awareness of employment rights and employment proceedings grew, tribunals found themselves increasingly swamped with unmeritorious cases, whilst lacking the tools to discourage such applications. In an effort to redress the balance, the Government recently amended the regulations, granting tribunals wider powers to award costs. The 2001 Regulations have significantly increased the maximum level of costs that a tribunal can award and have widened the criteria applicable to assessing whether an award should be made.

Although the regulations have now made it mandatory for tribunals, in certain circumstances, to consider awarding costs, the tribunals' discretion as to whether to make an award remains largely unfettered (they require tribunals to consider the overriding objective when making any decision – see **CHAPTER 9 – FAIRNESS: THE OVERRIDING OBEJECTIVE**). The question that arises, therefore, is now that the tribunals have been given these additional powers, to what extent will they use them?

One thing that is clear, however, is that the 2001 Regulations have maintained the general presumption that costs are not recoverable. Unless there is a significant change in attitude, tribunals are likely to continue to be reluctant to award costs against unrepresented employees with genuine grievances, but whose claims are inadvertently misguided.

It remains vital to consider costs from the outset of a dispute and to bear in mind that, in most circumstances, you are unlikely to recover expenses arising from employment proceedings.

General grounds for awarding costs [24.2]

Parties need to be aware of the important distinction between costs occasioned by a *postponement or adjournment*, which are generally much easier to recover, and costs arising from the *bringing or conducting of proceedings*. It should be noted that the latter category, whilst generally more difficult to obtain a costs order under, also includes costs arising from *applications to strike out and other costs arising from non-compliance with tribunal orders*. Where there has been such non-compliance, a tribunal may well be more willing to find that there has been unreasonable conduct. Postponements and adjournments are considered in detail below.

Costs relating to the bringing or conducting of proceedings [24.3]

Costs under this head will involve the tribunal in a two-stage process. It will first ask whether a costs order should be made.

The new provisions relating to costs are found in *Schedule 1, rule 14* of the 2001 Regulations which provides that a tribunal may award costs where, in its view:

- a party, has in bringing the proceedings, or a party or a party's representative has, in conducting the proceedings, acted vexatiously, abusively, disruptively or otherwise unreasonably; or

- the bringing or conducting of proceedings by a party has been misconceived.

The second limb in *rule 14* effectively replaces the old criterion of 'frivolous' with the wider, more neutral test of 'misconceived'.

What is meant by 'vexatiously, abusively, disruptively or otherwise unreasonably' [24.4]

Under the first limb of *rule 14*, tribunals are allowed to award costs against parties who knowingly or recklessly bring a claim that amounts to an abuse of process. Practical examples include circumstances where a person brings a claim that they know/or is obviously without merit, or where a claim is brought out of spite or for some other improper motive (see *Beynon & ors v Scadden & ors [1999] IRLR 700 EAT* where the Employment Appeal Tribunal (EAT) held that the union was improperly using the proceedings to bring pressure on the employers to agree to union recognition).

In order to succeed in an application for costs under this limb a party will have to establish a degree of fault on the part of their opponent. In most cases, this will require some evidence as to:

- the other party's actual knowledge of the weaknesses of their case; and

- their subsequent conduct in the light of that knowledge.

In general, a tribunal will only make an award on the basis that a claim is 'vexatious' or 'abusive' where it is satisfied that there was some improper motive underlying the bringing or subsequent conduct of the claim. This is a stringent test and awards for costs under these headings are uncommon.

Bringing or conducting a claim 'unreasonably' is a slightly wider test that covers situations where, taking into account a party's knowledge, their subsequent decision to proceed with a claim is objectively difficult to justify. So, for example, costs were awarded against an employee who persisted with a claim for unfair dismissal after having been told that a fellow employee, who had been dismissed on the same day for the same offence, had had their claim dismissed and costs awarded against them.

What is meant by 'misconceived' [24.5]

The second limb undoubtedly provides a far wider basis for awarding costs. Just how much wider will depend on how the tribunals chose to exercise their discretion.

The term 'misconceived' is defined as including 'having no reasonable prospect of success' (*Regulation 2(2)* of the *Employment Tribunals (Constitution and Rules of Procedure) Regulations 2001)*. Under this test tribunals are allowed to award costs where there is no suggestion of fault or unreasonableness. Whether a claim is misconceived is an objective test based on an assessment of legal/factual criteria. It requires no evidence as to a party's conduct, knowledge and/or motives. Put simply, where a tribunal is satisfied that, despite a party's genuinely held belief as to the validity of their claim/defence, the application never had any realistic prospects of success, it *must* then consider whether to award costs.

It is clear that it will be easier to establish that a claim was misconceived as opposed to 'unreasonable' or 'vexatious'. In fact, it is difficult to imagine circumstances where an application could succeed under the first limb and not the second. It is likely, therefore, that most awards for costs will be made on the basis that a claim was misconceived, and certainly any application for costs should include a reference to this criterion.

Costs arising from non-compliance with interlocutory orders [24.6]

Suppose there has been a failure by a party to comply with a direction for the provision of particulars, disclosure or any other direction made by the tribunal. This necessitates the other party taking action to enforce the direction. Such action might include making an application to the tribunal that the other party show cause why their case should not be struck out under rule *15(2)(d)*, or the other strike out provisions. Alternatively, it might include a less drastic course, such as writing to the other party to remind them of their default.

Costs can be claimed in these circumstances against the other party on the basis of the unreasonable conduct principles set out above. Note, however, that the tribunal has a discretion whether to award costs in these circumstances, which will be exercised in accordance with the overriding objective. Tribunals differ in the approach which they take to such applications.

Example

The respondent, who is legally represented, secures a direction that the applicant provide further particulars of the grounds of complaint within 21 days. The applicant fails to comply. The respondent makes an application to the tribunal that the applicant be asked to show cause why the originating application should not be struck out under *rule 15(2)(d)* for unreasonable conduct. The chairman lists the case for hearing of that matter. Two days prior to the hearing, the applicant provides the further particulars. The respondent chooses to proceed with the strike out application. At the hearing, the chairman decides that, in view of the fact that the particulars have now been provided, on an application of the overriding objective the originating application should not be struck out. The respondent makes an application for their costs arising from the enforcement action. The chairman decides that he will not award the respondent their costs of the strike out hearing, since it ought to have known that, once the particulars were provided, the application was unlikely to succeed. He does award, however, costs of £50 in respect of making the application that the applicant show cause.

Specific situation where costs are recoverable

Rule 14(4), (5) – postponements or adjournments [24.7]

Where an application to adjourn a hearing is granted, tribunals may award either party the *extra* costs incurred *as a result* of the adjournment. Which party, if any, will be awarded costs will depend on the tribunal's view as to whose conduct gave rise to the need to adjourn.

It is to be noted that under *rule 14(4)* a tribunal does not need to be satisfied that the party who is requesting the adjournment has acted unreasonably or vexatiously before making an order for costs (a tribunal's discretion under *rule 14(4)* is separate and distinct from its discretion under rule *14(1)*). This is because the power to award costs under *rule 14(4)* is intended to be compensatory and not punitive. A tribunal can therefore make an award under this rule whenever it is satisfied that the adjournment will actually lead to extra costs being incurred.

Under rule *14(5)*, in an unfair dismissal case, a tribunal *must* make an order for costs against an employer, where:

- an employee has notified the employer at least seven days before a hearing that they wish to be reinstated or re-engaged; and

- the employer, without a special reason, at a subsequent hearing is unable to adduce reasonable evidence as to availability of the employee's old job or of alternative suitable employment.

The net effect of this rule is that, unless an employer can establish 'a special reason', it will be liable for the costs that the employee incurs as a result of any adjournment needed to allow the necessary evidence to be obtained.

Where a party has been required to pay a deposit [24.8]

If a party thinks that some or all of the arguments put forward by the other side have no reasonable prospects of success, it can make an application at a pre-hearing review for the tribunal to order that party to pay a deposit (see **CHAPTER 14 – PRE-EMPTIVE STRIKES** for a more detailed analysis of when it is appropriate to make an application for a deposit). Under *rule 7(4)* the maximum deposit that a tribunal can order was increased from £150 to £500.

A tribunal is required to record the reasons why it has ordered a party to pay a deposit and in reaching its decision a tribunal must also have regard to the means of the party who will have to pay the deposit.

If the party who has been required to pay the deposit subsequently loses the substantive application for the same or similar reasons as were given when ordering the payment of the deposit, a tribunal will usually award costs against that party on the grounds that it has acted 'unreasonably in persisting with having the matter determined by a tribunal '(*rule 14(7)*). Whether the costs awarded exceed the deposit will be a matter for the tribunal's discretion.

Extension of time for entering a notice of appearance [24.9]

Where a respondent either:

• fails to present their notice of appearance within the relevant time limit; or

• obtains an extension of time for presenting their notice of appearance;

a tribunal may, if satisfied that it was reasonably practicable for it to have been presented in time, make an order for costs against the respondent (pursuant to *14(2)*) where a tribunal is satisfied that it would have been reasonably practicable for the notice of appearance to have been presented in time, a respondent's failure to comply with the time limits amounts to unreasonable conduct contrary to *rule 14(1)*). Rather curiously, there is no specific requirement that the tribunal be satisfied that the delay has caused the employee actual loss or prejudice. Theoretically, therefore, once it is established that a respondent has delayed unreasonably, a tribunal retains a purely punitive power to award costs.

Equal pay claims [24.10]

Under *Schedule 3, regulation 5* of the *Employment Tribunals (Constitution and Rules of Procedure) Regulations 2001*, in an equal pay claim, a party can be compensated for the cost of instructing an expert to investigate and prepare a report explaining any alleged discrepancies in pay.

Considerations relevant to awards of costs

The overriding objective [24.11]

Whilst *rule 14* makes it mandatory for a tribunal to consider making a costs order against a party where it is satisfied that one of the criteria in that rule is met, whether it does so and the amount of costs that are awarded will depend upon a number of factors, including consideration of the overriding objective (see CHAPTER 9). It can be seen from the chapter on the overriding objective that the definition of 'dealing with the case justly' includes 'placing the parties, so far as possible, on an equal footing.' In practice, the tribunal may have regard to a number of issues when applying the overriding objective, including:

- whether the costs award might have a prohibitive effect on that party continuing with proceedings;

- the extent of the default or culpability of that party, having regard to whether they are legally represented and whether they warned about the possible consequences of their actions; and

- the size and resources of the parties. Parties would be wise to use the overriding objective as a tool both in making and defending costs applications.

Historically, due to the criteria applicable under the old rules, tribunals attached great weight to the 'reasonableness' of a party's action and or failure to act when determining whether to award costs. Tribunals were also extremely reluctant to 'penalise' applicants who, not being represented, had unintentionally issued or continued with proceedings that were unlikely to succeed. These concerns are still likely to be relevant in applying the overriding objective.

Tactics

Tribunals, applying the overriding objective of dealing with cases justly, are still likely to require some evidence of unreasonable behaviour before awarding costs against an unrepresented party. In this context, the steps taken to notify and to explain to the other party the reasons why their application is 'misconceived' will be particularly relevant. It is important, therefore, to give the other party reasonable notice, preferably in writing, of:

- the fact that you intend to apply for costs; and

- the reasons why you are making the application.

An added advantage in writing down the grounds upon which costs will be sought is that the letter can be used as a form of 'skeleton argument' in any subsequent application to the tribunal. Clearly, it will sometimes be impossible to put the other party on notice of a costs application, for example where their actions necessitate an application for an adjournment during the course of a hearing.

A presumption in favour of awarding some costs [24.12]

Rule 14 makes it *mandatory* for tribunals to consider awarding costs where they are satisfied that one or more of the criteria in *rule 14* are met. This duty would appear to arise irrespective of whether an application for costs has been made. In practice, where a tribunal is satisfied that an application was both misconceived and resulted in additional costs being incurred, it must then consider:

- whether to award costs, offering both sides the opportunity to make representations; and

- give reasons as to its decision to make/not make an award of costs.

This effectively creates a presumption (especially where both parties are legally represented) in favour of awarding costs, since a tribunal will be forced to justify its decision not to compensate a party for losses incurred by reason of mistakes made by the other side (see above – likely reluctance of tribunals to award costs against unrepresented 'genuine' applicant). A decision either way is likely to be made with reference to the overriding objective. Clearly, where the unsuccessful party has been given prior written notice setting out similar reasons to those that subsequently form the basis for the dismissal of their application, a tribunal will find it difficult to justify not making some award.

Compensation n [24.13]

It is important to b(compensate the party the party ordered t make an award wh to be incurred. The itself, justify an award of costs. ι award of costs is to le, and not to *punish* t tribunals can only cause *additional costs* :d badly will not, of

Although tribunals cannot make an order directly against a party's advisor or legal representative, they are able to take into account the behaviour of these third parties when assessing whether to make an award of costs (see *rule 14(1)* which specifically allows tribunals to award costs where '...a party's representative has, in conducting proceedings, acted vexatiously...'). The EAT in *Beynon* (see **24.4**)confirmed that a party to the proceedings can be held liable for the conduct of their representatives. In that case, the EAT upheld the decision to award costs against the applicants in circumstances where the union advising the applicants 'knew of or should have known that the claims had no reasonable prospects of success'.

Ability to pay [24.14]

The EAT in *Beynon* held that, although the rules did not specifically require an inquiry into a party's ability to pay, it was usually desirable to have regards to a party's means when ordering costs. The EAT went on to state that the mere fact that a party was unable to pay did not, of itself, prevent an award of costs against that party.

It is submitted, however, that where, due to lack of means, an award of costs would effectively prevent a party obtaining a determination of their claim, such an award may amount to a breach of Article 6 (1) of the European Convention of Human Rights in so far as it amounts to a denial of that party's right of access to a court (see *Ait-Mouhoub v France, Reports of Judgments and Decision 1998-VIII, p.3214 EctHR*, where the applicant's inability to pay the sums ordered was a key factor in the court finding that an order for security breached Article 6(1)).

When considering a party's ability to pay, a tribunal should not, as a general rule, take into account the means of a trade union that has supported the application. Examples of exceptions to this general rule include circumstances where a union ought to have known that a case had no reasonable prospects of success, or where a case was pursued as a 'test' case or where there was some imputed fault on the part of the union (see *Omar v Worldwide News Inc [1998] IRLR] 291* and *Beynon*; the latter case cautions against rigidly listing the exceptions where it is appropriate to have regard to the means of the union). In that case, the chairman gave a clear indication that he attributed significant fault to the trade union, and ordered the applicants to pay costs on an indemnity basis. Ability to pay is the one of the factors which may now be subsumed within the overriding objective.

Cost awards against employers [24.15]

Although tribunals may award costs against either party, as a general rule, awards are more likely to be made against an employee bringing the claim as opposed to the employer defending the application. This is because tribunals have long recognised that an employer 'must be entitled to defend proceedings brought against it' (*Cartiers Superfoods Ltd v. Laws [1978] 315 EAT*).

Clearly, however, an employer remains accountable for additional costs that arise due to its unreasonable/misconceived conduct in relation to the *proceedings*. Tribunals do not have the power to award costs with respect to conduct preceding the issuing of proceedings (*Davidson v John Calder (Publishers) Ltd and Calder Educational Trust Ltd [1985] IRLR 97* – where Bristow J held that 'it was the conduct in the course of the proceedings which alone is to be considered' and that the test was whether it was unreasonable for an employer 'to have defended this case as to liability once the application was launched and they had to consider the material available to the [employer]'). Having said this, obviously, the more flagrant the employer's behaviour in dismissing the applicant, the harder it will be for the former to justify a decision to defend proceedings as being 'reasonable'.

When can a costs application be made? [24.16]

Applications for costs can be made at any stage during employment proceedings. The EAT have given guidance that, in general, a costs application should be made *immediately* upon the tribunal giving an unreserved decision. Where the decision is reserved, the party seeking costs should indicate to the tribunal that, if successful, it wishes the tribunal to make a costs order (*Johnson v Baxter [1984] ICR 675*). In many cases tribunals will give guidance as to when they wish to be addressed on the issue of costs. So, for example, where a party applies for an adjournment, a tribunal may indicate that it wishes first to decide whether a postponement is necessary, before going on to consider who, if anyone, should bear the costs arising from the delay.

As a general rule, an application for costs should be made as soon as it becomes appropriate (see *Andrew Ladies Hairstylists v Baxter [1985] IRLR 96* where the EAT held that applications for costs should be made as soon as reasonably possible). Tribunals are keen to avoid the extra expense of additional hearings on costs alone. Moreover, any significant delay may weaken an application since it is likely to be viewed as prejudicial to the party against whom the order is sought.

If a party has strong objective grounds for asserting that a claim has no reasonable prospects for success, an application for a pre-hearing review should be made at the earliest opportunity. Similarly, where a tribunal gives an oral determination at the end of a hearing, the successful party should not delay in making any appropriate application for costs.

Against whom may costs be awarded? [24.17]

Costs may only be awarded against an actual party to the proceedings. Tribunals currently have no power to award costs directly against legal representatives or other third parties. If the costs are as a consequence of the representative's negligence, the tribunal is likely to indicate this fact.

Costs against representatives: changes under the new Employment Act 2002 (EA 2002) [24.18]

One of the first provisions in the new Act likely to come into force (probably before the end of 2002, see CHAPTER 29 – NEW DEVELOPMENTS: THE EMPLOYMENT ACT 2002) is the power to make costs award against representatives. The tribunal's powers in this respect will be extensive. They will not only be able to make an award against a representative personally where their conduct of the case has led to wasted costs being incurred by the other side, but they will also be able to *disallow* that representative's costs as between themselves and the other party. This latter provision will give the tribunal more extensive powers than those retained by the civil courts.

What costs/expenses are recoverable [24.19]

Under the old rules tribunals were only permitted to award a maximum of £500. If a party wished to recover a sum greater than £500, their costs had to be subjected to a detailed assessment. Recognising that this limitation severely restricted the tribunal's ability to compensate parties appropriately, the 2001 Regulations introduced a far higher ceiling. Tribunals can now order a party to pay:

- the other party costs not exceeding £10,000;

- the other party any sum that both parties have agreed represent the costs incurred;

- the whole or specified portion of the other party's costs to be assessed on a standard or indemnity basis if not otherwise agreed (this involves a party presenting a summary of legal costs to the civil courts where a district judge or costs judge will consider the amounts claimed in terms of proportionality and the overriding objective).

Parties can recover the legal costs spent on legal representation, whether that be an in-house lawyer, a solicitor, a barrister or other representative acting for a fee, such as an employment law consultant (*Wiggin Alloys Ltd v Jenkins [1981] IRLR 275*). What about where a company retains an HR manager to conduct its tribunal cases? Why should the company not be able to recover the daily rate of that person in respect of a wasted day at a tribunal? The situation is presently unclear, but there would appear to be no basis for differentiating them from in-house lawyers. Time spent by management in the preparation of a case and in attending a hearing is currently *not* recoverable. So a manager who attends a hearing cannot recover their daily rate. This, however, is due to change with the *EA*

2002 allowing regulations to be made specifying when such costs may be recoverable, and how they are to be assessed.

As indicated above, tribunals may only award costs to compensate parties for a loss that they have *actually suffered or are liable to incur*. Further, the loss must be limited to that flowing from the act in respect of which the costs award is made. So, if there is a postponement, it is only the costs in relation to the postponed hearing which are recoverable, not the entire costs of bringing or defending the proceedings. Where the entire claim is struck out, for example on the basis that it is misconceived, the tribunal will have a discretion as to what costs, if any, it awards. It is submitted that it is unlikely to award the respondent all of its costs arising from defending the proceedings and consideration will be limited to the hearing of the strike out application.

Making the application [24.20]

The starting point for any costs application is establishing that you will or have suffered costs *as a result* of the conduct you are complaining of. In most cases this can be best explained by drafting a costs schedule outlining a breakdown of the costs incurred.

In general, evidence put forward in support of an application for costs should focus solely on the conduct complained of. So, for example, where a party is applying for the costs arising from an adjournment, they should only put forward evidence as to how or why the need to adjourn has arisen. In this context, of particular importance will be any disclosable correspondence:

- notifying the other side that you intend to apply for costs and setting out the reasons why you are going to make the application;

- any reply from the other side.

Expenses [24.21]

Tribunals may order the Secretary of State to pay the expenses incurred by parties and witnesses in attending the hearing, whether or not the party on whose behalf the witnesses appeared was successful. These expenses, commonly relating to loss of wages and the cost of travel, are subject to statutory fixed scales provided for pursuant to *section 5(3)* of the *Employment Tribunals Act 1996*. Loss of earnings are recoverable under these provisions, currently at a maximum rate of £45 a day. Overnight expenses may be paid where there incurrence has been essential. Travel costs in excess of £5 are recoverable as are child and adult care costs up to a low maximum. Any person wishing to benefit from these provisions should collect the appropriate claim form from the tribunal office.

Under the provisions of *rule 14 (1)(b)* tribunals may also, when awarding costs against a party, direct that party to reimburse the Secretary of State for this outlay.

Do's and Don'ts

Do:

- Give written notice of intention and reasons for applying for costs.

- Give all parties (including the tribunal) as much written notice as possible of the reasons why an adjournment is needed.

- Seek guidance at an early stage from the tribunal as to when it wishes to be addressed on costs.

- Keep a schedule of costs identifying the hours worked on particular aspects of a case (i e for a particular hearing/application/aspect of the claim).

- Ask for a realistic figure of costs aimed at compensating you for the extra expense arising from the unreasonable/misconceived conduct.

- Provide documentary evidence of your costs.

- Try to avoid asking for hearings solely in relation to costs.

- Bear in mind the fact that the other party is unrepresented when considering whether to claim costs.

Don't:

- 'Ambush' parties with costs applications.

- Delay in making an application.

- Make unreasonable, oppressive or multiple applications for small amounts of costs.

- Ask for costs to 'punish' the other side for its conduct.

- Seek to over rely on previous case law.

25.

The Decision

Introduction [25.1]

A formal written decision must be given by the tribunal not merely after a full merits hearing but also when:

- determining under *rule 6* of the *Employment Tribunals (Constitution and Rules of Procedure) Regulations 2001 (SI 2001/1171)* a party's entitlement to bring or contest proceedings;

- striking out a claim or notice of appearance under rules *4(8)(b)* or *15(2)*;

- ordering the payment of a deposit after a pre-hearing review (it is not fully established whether this is a 'decision', but it is submitted that the courts would find it to be so);

- making a declaration as to a party's legal rights (for example a declaration that a person has been subjected to unlawful discrimination, or that there rights under the *Working Time Regulations 1998 (SI 1998/1833)* have been breached).

There is *no* requirement for the tribunal to give a formal written decision when making interlocutory orders, for example in relation to the provision of further particulars, disclosure, postponement or directions for full hearing. Indeed, its obligation to give reasons for such orders is extremely limited, making an appeal difficult to sustain (see CHAPTER 28 – STEPS AFTER THE DECISION II – APPEALS).

The characteristics of the formal written decision [25.2]

A formal written decision has certain characteristics:

- it contains the reasons for the tribunal's decision;

- it is either headed 'summary of reasons' or 'extended written reasons' (see **25.5** below);

- it is signed and dated;

- it is, when signed, placed upon the public register and is available for inspection to all.

The significance of the formal written decision [25.3]

The formal written decision:

- provides the basis for any appeal (although to do so extended written reasons must be obtained, see **25.5**);

- contains the reasons for the decision, whether in summary or extended form;

- constitutes the formal public record of what the tribunal has decided.

Decisions announced orally on the day [25.4]

Even where a decision is announced orally on the day, the tribunal has an absolute obligation to send to the parties a formal written decision (containing either summary or extended reasons), and it is the latter which constitutes the formal decision. Although there is no statutory deadline for how soon after the hearing parties should receive their written decision, the Employment Tribunals Service (ETS) sets a target of (currently) 85% of decisions being issued within four weeks, which is largely achieved.

At the conclusion of a case a tribunal may:

- reserve its decision entirely, indicating to the parties that a formal written decision will follow;

- announce its decision orally on the day, giving brief reasons or even no reasons at all and indicating that a formal written decision will follow;

- announce its decision with extended reasons on the day, with the chairman speaking into a dictaphone, in which case the formal written decision sent to the parties will be a word for word, subject to normal editing requirements, report of what was said.

The tribunal's written decision should not conflict with any decision which has been given orally. To that extent, an oral decision by the tribunal still has the character of a 'final decision.' A tribunal should not change its mind in relation to a decision announced orally without, at the very least, giving the parties a further opportunity to address it. Where, however, this involves revisiting issues of fact which it had already properly decided, the practice is likely to be frowned upon by the

Employment Appeal Tribunal (EAT) (*Lamont v Frys Metals Ltd [1985] ICR 566, Arthur Guinness Son and Co (GB) Ltd v Green [1989] ICR 581.* For cases emphasising the limited powers of recall, see *Spring Grove Services Group plc v Hickinbottom [1990] ICR 111* and *Casella London Ltd v Banai [1990] ICR 215*).

Extended written reasons   [25.5]

Parties should note that, in order to appeal, it is usually necessary to obtain extended written reasons, although the EAT do have a discretion, under *rule 39(2)* of the *Employment Appeal Tribunal Rules 1993 (SI 1993/2854)*, to waive this requirement if in the interests of justice. This power is exercised sparingly and a key factor is likely to be the completeness of the summary reasons (*Wolesley Centers Ltd v Simmons [1994] ICR 503, EAT*).

Caution: summary reasons can be surprisingly long, and have the appearance of extended written reasons. Always look at the heading of the decision, which will make the issue clear.

Extended written reasons may be requested either:

* at the conclusion of the hearing;

* or, at the latest, within 21 days of the summary reasons being sent to the parties (*rule 12(4)*).

Extended written reasons will be automatically sent to the parties in discrimination, equal pay and deduction of wages cases.

If the 21-day time period has expired, it is possible to make an application to a chairman for reasons to be provided out of time. A chairman has a discretion to do so, which must be exercised in accordance with the overriding objective. As with any decision involving the exercise of discretion, appealing against a refusal can be difficult. A useful case in this respect is *Weatherall v Haigh Investment Co Ltd EAT 304/88*.

What should the extended written reasons contain?   [25.6]

The obligation to give reasons for a decision is a fundamental principle of natural justice. What, in tribunal proceedings, is the extent of that obligation?

The tribunal must set out its conclusions on the issues of fact in the case. Unfortunately, there is some conflict in the case law as to the obligation to give reasons for those conclusions. The weight of case law suggests that there *is* an obligation to give basic reasons for important factual conclusions such that the parties can understand why that conclusion has been reached (*Meek v City of Birmingham DC [1987] IRLR 250, CA* suggests a slightly higher standard than the approach adopted in *British Gas PLC v Sharma [1991] ICR 19 [1991] IRLR 101, EAT*). The most helpful guidance to parties is contained in the case of *Meek* where the Court of Appeal stated that a decision must contain:

- an outline of the story (or factual background) which has given rise to the complaint;

- a summary of the tribunal's basic factual conclusions;

- a statement of the reasons for those conclusions;

- sufficient findings and reasons for the EAT to determine whether there has been an error of law and for the parties to understand why they have won or lost.

In discrimination cases, the tribunal must set out the primary facts upon which it bases its inferences.

Examples

Example one: The duty to give reasons in discrimination cases. The tribunal, in giving its reasons for finding in favour of the applicant, simply state that: 'we find that the employer discriminated against the applicant by not selecting her for promotion.' This, in itself, is insufficient. It probably would be sufficient, however, if it stated: 'We find, for the following reason, that that the applicant was the best qualified and most suitable candidate for the job [give reason]. We reject, for those reasons, the assertion of the respondent that the comparator relied upon by the applicant, who was promoted, had better qualifications. We draw an inference from those facts that the reason for the applicant's non-promotion was her ethnic background and not the reason relied upon by the respondent. We therefore conclude that she was treated less favourably on grounds of race.'

Example two: The duty to give reasons in unfair dismissal cases. The tribunal summarise the factual basis of the claim and then state as follows: 'We find that there was a potentially fair reason under *section 98* for dismissal, namely misconduct in the form of theft, that the employer entertained an honest belief in that reason, further that he had reasonable grounds for that belief and that he carried out a sufficient investigation. We are overwhelmingly of the view that the

cont'd

dismissal was fair and within the range of reasonable responses open to the employer'. Those reasons are inadequate, because the factual basis for the conclusions is not set out. Now compare those with the following reasons in an identical context: 'The applicant has not disputed that the employer held an honest belief in the reason for dismissal, namely misconduct in the form of theft, and that that reason falls within one of the potentially fair reasons for dismissal in *section 98* of the *Employment Rights Act 1996.*'

'Applying the test in *British Home Stores v Burchell [1978] IRLR 379,* there are two further issues for the tribunal to decide. First, did the respondent hold that belief on reasonable grounds. Having regard to the evidence before the employer at the time [brief explanation of evidence] we find that they did. Second, was there a sufficient investigation? Whilst we are of the view that failing to give the applicant sufficient notice of the disciplinary hearing rendered that hearing unfair, we find that this defect was cured upon appeal, when the applicant was given more than sufficient notice of the allegation he had to meet, ample opportunity to put his case and had all relevant aspects of his case considered. We further find that dismissal for this type of misconduct, namely theft, was clearly within the range of reasonable responses open to the respondent...'. Those reasons *probably* are sufficient because they set out basis upon which the tribunal has reached its conclusions.

In addition, parties should note the following:

- A tribunal is required to consider all relevant evidence, but there is no requirement, provided the duty to give sufficient reasons is complied with, for them to set out all of the evidence in their reasons. Where the tribunal has failed to record some evidence, the EAT will not assume that they have failed to consider it unless this is clear from the reasoning in the decision.

- The written reasons of a tribunal are not required to be akin to a judgement in a higher court of law.

- The tribunal should set out its conclusions separately in respect of each head of claim that it considers, e g unfair dismissal, sex discrimination etc.

- Codes of practice should be expressly referred to in disability discrimination cases.

- Award of compensation *must* be specified in a written decision, together with any award of interest, and the basis upon which interest is calculated.

The extent of the duty will differ widely depending upon the facts of the individual case.

It is not possible to give definitive advice in a handbook such as this as to when, in a given situation, reasons will and will not be adequate, but simply to point the reader in the right direction. When in genuine doubt as to the adequacy of reasons, parties should consider taking specialist advice (see CHAPTER 3 – GETTING ADVICE).

Do's and Don'ts

Do:

- Consider asking for extended reasons orally on the day in question, particularly if you have lost.

- Remember that extended reasons are normally required for an appeal.

Don't:

- Appeal minor clerical errors and slips – ask for these to be corrected under the slip rule.

26.

Remedies: Calculating Likely Awards

Introduction [26.1]

This chapter discusses the basic essentials of how tribunal awards are calculated, with reference to the areas of unfair dismissal and discrimination. In part, the intention is to assist the reader in considering the issue of settlement. For a comprehensive guide on remedies (including non-monetary awards such as reinstatement), the reader should consult a textbook on the substantive law of employment.

Early consideration of remedies is necessary:

- in order to judge what constitutes a reasonable settlement (see CHAPTER 18 – SETTLEMENT OF CLAIMS);

- to prepare effectively for the remedies hearing.

An award in an unfair dismissal case usually comprises a *basic award* and a *compensatory award*. The basic award, which tends to be the smaller of the two, is not calculated according to the applicant's financial loss, but simply their age, years of service and weekly pay. By contrast, the compensatory award compensates the applicant for the financial loss they have sustained as a consequence of the dismissal. This may be nil or it may be a substantial sum.

Unfair dismissal: the basic award [26.2]

The maximum amount of any such award is, at the time of writing, £7,500.

The basic award is calculated as follows:

(a) one week's pay for each year of employment (ending with the Effective Date of Termination (EDT)) in which the employee was between the ages of 22 and 40;

(b) one and a half weeks' pay for each year of employment in which the employee was not below the age of 41;

(c)   half a week's pay for any year of employment not falling into either of the above categories (i e when the employee was between the ages of 18 and 21).

A week's pay means (in contrast to the compensatory award – see **26.5**) the *gross* weekly pay of the employee, up to a limit of, at the time of writing of £250.

The best way to calculate the award is to find the correct multiplier and then apply it to the weekly pay figure. A necessary prerequisite for doing so is to note down the applicant's date of birth, date of commencement of employment and EDT.

Example one

Date of birth: 5.4.1970 (age 32)

Employment commenced:1.2.1996

EDT (effective date of termination): 9.5.2002

Gross weekly pay: £500 (i e above the maximum level)

Category (a) above applies and the *multiplier will therefore be 6.* TOTAL AWARD: 6 × 250 = £1,500

Example two

Date of Birth: 1.2.1958 (aged 44)

Employment commenced: 16.12.1989

EDT: 5.4.2002

Gross weekly pay: £600

Categories (a) and (b) above apply.

For three years of his employment (i e the final three), the applicant was not less than 41 years of age (category (b)), entitling him to a multiplier of 1.5 in respect of each of those years = 4.5.

For each of the remaining nine complete years he was not below the

cont'd

---

age of 22, entitling him to a multiplier of 1 in respect of each of those years = 9.

The total multiplier will therefore be 13.5 (9 + 4.5). TOTAL BASIC AWARD: 13.5 × 250 = £3,375.

Incomplete years [26.3]

An incomplete year of employment does not count. Where the applicant spans more than one age category, make sure you treat the incomplete year as being at the beginning of the employment rather than the end.

Reductions in the basic award [26.4]

There is not the same scope for reducing the basic award as exists with the compensatory award (see **26.5**). It may be reduced, however:

* under the just and equitable head (see **26.14**);

* where an ex gratia payment has been made by the employer sufficient to cover any basic and compensatory award which the tribunal might make; or

* where the employee has unreasonably refused an offer of reinstatement which would have restored them to the position as if they had never been dismissed.

Unfair dismissal: the compensatory award [26.5]

The maximum compensatory award available at the time of publication is £52,600. The compensatory award is calculated according to the loss sustained as a consequence of the dismissal. Such loss may be minimal, for example where the applicant immediately takes up a new job, or substantial, for example where the applicant is out of work for long periods. All applicants are under a duty to mitigate their loss (**26.10**). Further, such awards are frequently reduced by tribunals to reflect either contributory fault by the applicant or the fact that, if the unfairness had not arisen, the dismissal would still have occurred. The burden is on the applicant to prove the loss caused by the dismissal. In relation to failure to mitigate, the burden is on the respondent.

The compensatory award is typically made up of all or some of the following heads of loss:

* past loss of earnings to the date of tribunal decision, subject to the duty to mitigate (see **26.6**);

229

- future loss of earnings for such period (if any) as the tribunal thinks reasonable (**26.7**);

- loss of benefits such as company car, pension etc (see **26.8**);

- loss of statutory rights (usually a nominal figure of approximately £200).

Deductions from the compensatory award can then be made to reflect:

- a failure to mitigate loss;

- payments received by the employer since the dismissal;

- contributory conduct by the applicant;

- the fact that a dismissal might have occurred in any event;

- what is just and equitable.

All of the above deductions are discussed below.

Heads of loss under the compensatory award

Past loss of earnings [26.6]

Where the applicant has been out of work from dismissal to the tribunal hearing,they can claim for loss of earnings during that period, subject to the duty to mitigate. The reference point for calculating such loss is usually what the applicant earned prior to dismissal in the way of:

- net pay;

- overtime; and

- bonuses and other financial rewards.

There may, of course, be circumstances where this is not an accurate measure of the applicant's loss, for example if it can be shown that the applicant was about to receive a pay increase. With overtime the tribunal, in assessing any loss, will usually have regard to the overtime earned by the applicant over a particular period before dismissal (usually twelve weeks), unless for any reason this is not an accurate measure. Loss of bonus will, likewise, be assessed on the evidence before the tribunal.

Future loss of earnings [26.7]

Future loss will be calculated according to the length of time the tribunal consider it is reasonable for the applicant to be out of work or in work on lesser pay. Again, this is an area for the tribunal to make a finding of fact based on the evidence before it. Relevant factors are likely to include the availability of suitable alternative work on the job market.

Loss of benefits such as pension and company car [26.8]

Loss of a pension rights is a recoverable head. The size of any award will be dependent upon a number of factors, including the size of contributions, the type of pension and the extent of pension provision in new employment. With certain schemes, the loss can be calculated simply according to the total value of the lost contributions, although frequently this underestimates the loss, for example if there is a penalty for non-contribution in a given period.

Applicants who need assistance in this frequently complex area should consider:

- contacting the trustees of the pension fund/s in question (who have a duty to give them accurate information) to assist in any calculation; and

- using the guidance booklet on pensions written by tribunal chairman and the Government Actuary's Department *Compensation for Loss of Pension Rights*, published by HMSO and available from some tribunals.

Loss of a company car for which an applicant was allowed personal use is a recoverable head. Valuing a car for a given period is problematic and parties are advised to adopt one of the following two courses:

- obtain from the AA the list of annual estimates which they publish for this purpose; and

- rely upon the taxable value of the car.

Loss of statutory rights [26.9]

The tribunal usually makes a small award to reflect the fact that the applicant will lose protection from unfair dismissal in the first year of new employment and/or will lose the benefit of an accrued statutory notice period. The award is usually in the region of £200.

Recent law: Are injury to feelings awards recoverable in unfair dismissal cases? Until recently, the law has been clear that they are not (*Norton Tool Co Ltd v Tewson [1972] ICR 501 (NIRC)*). A recent case has, however, cast doubt on this proposition. Lord Hoffman commented in the case of

Johnson v Unisys [2001] ICR 480 that he could see no reason why, in an appropriate case unfair dismissal case, the tribunal should not award compensation for injury to feelings, which he defined as 'distress, humiliation, damage to reputation in the community or to family life'. The remarks of Lord Hoffman were 'obiter', that is to say they were not relevant to the issue which he had to decide. This means that a tribunal is not bound to follow them.

Further, none of the other four Law Lords hearing the case expressed a view on the subject, and Lord Steyn expressly indicated that it was not a on matter which they should be ruling. Nonetheless, some tribunals are relying upon the persuasive effect of Lord Hoffman's remarks to make awards, with one study indicating that they are forming part of the compensatory award in approximately 50% of successful cases, with awards ranging from £250 to £3,500 (White R, 'Hurt Feelings', *Solicitor's Journal*, 17 May 2002, p.460). This issue has not, at the time of publication, come before the Employment Appeal Tribunal (EAT). Readers should keep a careful eye out for a decision from the higher courts which clarifies this important issue. Given the fact that the law prohibiting the making of such awards was contained in a Court of Appeal judgment, it may be that only a House of Lords decision would suffice to overturn the traditional position.

Factors which go towards reducing the compensatory award

Failure to mitigate [26.10]

Applicants are under a duty to mitigate their loss by making reasonable efforts to obtain alternative employment. Where a tribunal find they have not done so, the compensatory award will be reduced to reflect the loss which would have occurred if reasonable efforts had been made. The extent to which, if at all, an applicant is expected to accept lesser paid work will depend upon what, in the circumstances, a tribunal consider is reasonable. Case law on this subject is limited, but the author submits that tribunals will not generally expect applicants to accept work which is in a different category of skill and status to that which they have enjoyed before. Where, however, the job is in the same bracket, they may be expected to accept the position if there is a minor decrease in pay.

What is reasonable will always depend upon the individual circumstances of the case including, for example, such matters as travel and working hours. It is submitted that where an employee unreasonably refuses an offer of reinstatement which would have restored them to a position as if they had never been dismissed, this could constitute a breach of the duty to mitigate loss. The burden is on the employer to prove that an applicant has not made reasonable efforts to mitigate their loss.

A fair dismissal might have occurred in any event [26.11]

An award can be reduced by up to 100% to reflect the fact that a fair dismissal might have occurred in any event. This is commonly known as a 'Polkey' reduction (named after the case in which the principle was first introduced, namely *Polkey v AE Dayton Services Ltd [1988] AC 344; [1987] IRLR 503, HL*) and, unlike contributory fault (see **26.12**), is not limited to misconduct cases. Note that, in these circumstances, a tribunal should also make a finding as to when dismissal would have occurred. Examples of where reductions under this head might be made are:

- where the dismissal is procedurally unfair, but a fair procedure might still have resulted in dismissal; and

- where the applicant would have lost his job at a certain point in any event, for example because the respondent went out of business or the branch in which he was employed closed down and no staff were relocated.

Example

A tribunal decides that a dismissal for redundancy is unfair because there has been insufficient consultation with the employee but that, even if there had been sufficient consultation, there is a 70% chance that dismissal would have occurred in any event. The compensatory award will therefore be reduced by 70%.

Contributory fault by the applicant [26.12]

Tribunals are entitled to reduce any award by up to 100% to reflect the fact that the applicant caused or contributed to their own dismissal. Such findings, which are relatively common, are usually only appropriate in misconduct cases. They tend to occur where there is evidence of blameworthy conduct on the part of the employee but the dismissal was unfair either because (a) the employer failed to carry out a fair procedure; or (b) dismissal was an excessively harsh sanction. Note that in the case of (a), the employer might additionally benefit from a reduction under the Polkey head above. When assessing contribution, tribunals are limited to examining evidence in existence prior to dismissal. The extent of any finding of contribution will always depend upon the circumstances of the case. The tribunal will usually make its finding on contribution when it gives its decision on whether the dismissal was fair or unfair.

Arguing 'Polkey' or 'contributory fault' [26.13]

In both cases, tribunals usually decide whether to make a reduction at the same time as considering whether the dismissal was fair or unfair, as opposed to during the remedies hearing. So, in a misconduct case, a tribunal might find that the dismissal was unfair, but that the applicant contributed to their dismissal by 50%. For this reason, parties should address both issues at the substantive hearing of the dispute, not at the remedies hearing, unless the tribunal indicates otherwise. Note that whilst the finding on the appropriate percentage reduction is usually made when giving the decision on the fairness of the dismissal, the reduction is not then *applied* until the tribunal has assessed the extent (without any reduction) of the applicant's financial loss.

Just and equitable [26.14]

This is a broad heading which, in practice, can overlap with others. It enables the tribunals to take into account a significant factor which makes it just and equitable to reduce the award (by up to 100%).

Examples

In deciding contribution, the tribunal is limited to assessing the evidence in existence prior to dismissal. If subsequent evidence comes to light (relating to events prior to dismissal), this could enable a just and equitable reduction to be made. So, if an employee, shortly after dismissal, is found to have stolen money from the employer, a total or partial reduction might be made.

Where, following a dismissal, an employee has chosen to retrain and carry out a completely different career for reasons of choice rather than economic necessity, they might not be entitled to an award which reflects the full extent of their financial loss. In other words, it could be said that part of the loss arises from a personal decision by the applicant.

Payments by the employer [26.15]

Where the employer has made payments to the employee, these will generally be taken into account and reduced from the award. So, if an employee is paid in lieu of notice, the loss will run from the end of the notice period. Similarly, an ex gratia payment may be taken into account. This can assist employers who have settled claims but failed to comply with the requirements of a compromise agreement (see CHAPTER 18), meaning that the applicant is not prevented from pursuing the claim in the employment tribunal. In such circumstances, the tribunal is likely to deduct the sum paid in settlement from any award which it makes (see **26.30**).

Checklist – compensatory awards

The tribunal will:

- Assess the loss of the applicant.

- Deduct amounts received from the employer or arising from a failure to mitigate.

- Make a Polkey reduction.

- Make a reduction for contributory fault.

- Apply the statutory maximum.

Compensation in discrimination cases [26.16]

There are four different remedies available in discrimination cases:

- compensation for financial loss;

- compensation for injury to feelings and personal injury;

- a declaration as to the rights of the applicant;

- a recommendation that the employer take, within a specified period, remedial steps in relation to the discrimination, with (in discrimination cases only) the power to increase compensation if there is, without justification, a failure to comply.

In addition, tribunals have the power to award interest in respect of awards of compensation.

Indirect discrimination [26.17]

In any case of indirect discrimination no award of compensation will be payable if the respondent proves that the requirement or condition in question was not applied with the intention of treating the claimant unfavourably on either racial grounds or grounds of sex (see the *Disability Discrimination Act 1995, s 8(2)–(6)*; *Sex Discrimination Act 1975, s 65* and *Race Relations Act 1976, s 56*).

Compensation for financial loss [26.18]

Compensation for financial loss in discrimination cases is assessed according to different principles from those that apply in unfair dismissal cases, but the outcome is often similar. The purpose of the compensation is to restore the applicant to the position they would have been in had the discrimination not occurred, subject to the applicant's duty to mitigate their loss (**26.10**). Due to the fact that this process involves predicting the likelihood of future events, the tribunal will frequently apply a percentage figure in deciding this issue (*Ministry of Defence v Cannock and Others [1994] ICR 918, EAT* and *Ministry of Defence v Hunt [1996] ICR 544, EAT*). Note that, with a discriminatory dismissal, the tribunal will elect whether to calculate loss according to unfair dismissal principles or on the tortious basis provided for in discrimination cases. Frequently, the outcome will be the same.

Example one: discriminatory dismissal [26.19]

The tribunal find that the applicant, who earned £400 a week net, was unfairly dismissed for reasons relating to her pregnancy. The tribunal must seek to restore her to the position she would have been in had the discriminatory act not occurred, subject to the duty on the applicant to mitigate her loss. They calculate her loss as follows:

- Loss of pay prior to the time when she would have gone on maternity leave – eight weeks pay: £3,200.

- Loss of statutory maternity pay (18 weeks): £2,906.40 (as of February 2002, statutory maternity pay is calculated as 90% of net wages for first six weeks and £62.20 for the remaining twelve weeks).

- The tribunal concludes that, on the evidence before it, there is a 60% chance that she would have returned to work at the conclusion of her maternity leave.

- It further finds that, applying the duty to mitigate her loss (**26.10**), she could be expected to find alternative work within four months of that date.

- In respect of the period after return to work, the applicant will therefore receive 60% of 14 week's pay: 14 × 400 × 60% = £3,360.

- TOTAL AWARD FOR FINANCIAL LOSS: £9,466.40 (Note the applicant will, in addition, be entitled to an award for injury to feelings).

cont'd

Note that it has been suggested by the EAT, in the case of a dismissal for a pregnancy related reason, that it will rarely be appropriate to award compensation for a period in excess of six months after the date when the applicant would have returned to work unless, as of that date, the applicant is actively engaged in looking for work (*Ministry of Defence v Cannock and Others*).

Example two: discriminatory non-selection   [26.20]

The tribunal finds, in a race discrimination case, that the applicant, who was not selected for a more senior post, was discriminated against on the basis of his race. The applicant is still employed by the respondent in his original post which pays £10,000 a year less than the more senior post he was applying for. The tribunal must assess the likelihood of the applicant, had the discriminatory act not occurred, being selected for the post. The tribunal concludes that there is a 50% chance that the applicant would have obtained the post. The tribunal hearing takes place six months after the date when the applicant would have commenced the new position.

The tribunal concludes that the applicant is entitled, in respect of past loss, to 50% of the additional pay which he would have received, namely £2,500 (£5,000 × 50%). Applying the principle of mitigation of loss (**26.10**), the tribunal conclude that the applicant could reasonably be expected to obtain a position of equivalent seniority to that for which he was not selected within three months of the hearing. It therefore awards a further £2,500 in respect of future loss.

TOTAL AWARD IN RESPECT OF FINANCIAL LOSS: £5,000. (The applicant will in, addition, be entitled to an award for injury to feelings).

Compensation for injury to feelings and personal injury (only available in cases of direct discrimination)   [26.21]

Injury to feelings is an increasingly important component of an award for unlawful direct discrimination. Whilst there is no statutory guidance on the size of these awards, they tend to range from £500 to a figure well in excess of £20,000 in exceptional cases. The EAT has issued general guidance on the principles to be applied in deciding the amount of such an award (see below), but there is relatively limited case law giving precise figures for different factual situations. Precise estimation of an award is hampered by two facts. First, the tribunal has a wide discretion in deciding what award to make, based upon the fact that it is in a position to hear the evidence and judge the extent of the injury first hand. Second, there is, as yet, no comprehensive and up to date reference source (similar to Kemp & Kemp) which parties can use in order to gain a flavour of the type of awards tribunals are making in cases comparable to their own. The Employment Tribunal Service (ETS) annual report 2001–2002 has indicated that the median award in sex discrimination cases was £5,000, in race discrimination £5,263, in disability discrimination £6,019, and in unfair dismissal cases £2,563. It must be emphasised, however, that there is a massive range in awards (and six figure awards, though rare, are not unknown in discrimination cases), and each case should be assessed on its own facts.

The principles upon which the award will be assessed [26.22]

The leading case on assessing awards for injury to feelings is that of Armitage (*(1) Armitage (2) Marsden and (3) HM Prison Service v Johnson [1997] IRLR 162, EAT*). It summarised the principles for deciding an award for hurt to feelings as follows:

- The aim of the award is to compensate the victim, not to punish the employer. It is hurt to the feelings of the victim, as opposed to indignation at the employer's conduct, which is the basis for assessing the award.

- The award should not be so low as to diminish respect for anti-discrimination legislation nor so high that it could be seen as a route to untaxed riches for the recipient.

- Awards should bear some broad similarity to the range of awards in personal injury cases.

- Tribunals should have regard to the value in everyday life of the sums they are awarding.

- Tribunals should have regard to the need for the public to have respect for the level of award which is made.

In addition, it is submitted that the following instances may serve to increase the injury which has been suffered, and hence the award:

- Where the employee has been subject to victimisation or harassment.

- Where the employer has not taken a complaint seriously and failed to investigate it properly and sensitively.

- Where, as a consequence of the dismissal, the employee has lost the chance to pursue congenial employment – an example of this would be a police officer who was dismissed from the force and thereby prevented from pursuing a career which he was committed to and vocational about.

•   Where the act of discrimination is intentional.

For a case where the EAT have given guidance on specific figures, parties should see *Ministry of Defence v O'Hare (No 2) and another [1997] ICR 306*. The circumstances under consideration were where a woman was compelled to choose between losing her job or aborting her child. The EAT suggested that £2,000 was a guideline figure in such cases. Where, however, the woman had opted to abort, this was capable of rising sharply. If the hurt to feelings from such a decision were transient, then the range of award would normally be £1,500 to £3,000. Where, however, the hurt was more long lasting, the right bracket was likely to be £3,000 to £7,500. Parties should take in to account inflation since the decision of the EAT in this case was made.

Personal injury [26.23]

Tribunals have jurisdiction to make an award for personal injury caused by the act of discrimination. Indeed, where such an injury is alleged, it is essential that the employee includes it in their employment tribunal claim as they are likely to be precluded from subsequently doing so in the civil courts. In the majority of cases were such an award is appropriate, the personal injury suffered will be psychiatric in nature. If possible, medical evidence should be adduced in support of the proposition that an injury has been sustained. In cases where there is the suggestion of a serious injury (psychiatric or otherwise), it is strongly advisable, both for employers and employees, to seek legal advice on the size of the likely award and any evidential steps which need to be taken to support or rebut the extent (or fact) of injury. Unlike 'pure' hurt to feelings awards, the personal injury element can usually be more precisely assessed and calculated with reference to existing tortious principles and case law. Tribunals are encouraged to include a personal injury award in any award for hurt to feelings.

Aggravated Damages [26.24]

The tribunal has the power to award aggravated damages where it considers that the employer, in committing an act of discrimination, has behaved in a high handed, malicious, oppressive or insulting manner. The employee must, in addition, have had some knowledge or suspicion of the conduct in question. In some instances, the award for aggravated damages will be included in the award for hurt to feelings, and in some instances expressed as an additional amount.

Interest on awards **[26.25]**

The provisions for interest on awards are dealt with in **26.29**.

Do's and Don'ts

Do:

- Remember that, in both unfair dismissal and discrimination cases, it is for the applicant to prove their loss, and for the employer to prove a failure to mitigate.

- The employer should request full details in advance of attempts which the employee has made to mitigate their loss and make it clear that you are putting the applicant to proof in respect of all aspects of their claimed loss, giving details of information you require.

- In unfair dismissal cases consider any reductions in the compensatory award which might be made under the Polkey heading and/or for contributory fault.

- In discrimination cases consider: financial loss, injury to feelings (including, where appropriate, personal injury and aggravated damages) and interest.

Don't:

- Leave consideration of remedy until the last minute.

- Forget that income support and jobseeker's allowance will be recouped from any award made by the tribunal, providing an incentive to settle (see CHAPTER 18).

Enforcement of awards and settlements [26.26]

Sometimes a party will fail to pay a sum which a tribunal has awarded. Or there may be some other default on their part, for example breaching an agreement for the provision of an agreed reference.

Enforcement of orders for the payment of money [26.27]

It is the County Court which is responsible for enforcement of orders by the tribunal for the payment of a sum of money. Provided there is an actual order for the payment of money in place, there is no need for the person seeking payment (the payee) to issue proceedings through a conventional claim form. The correct procedure is to lodge a completed

Form N322 (obtainable from the County Court) with the County Court together with:

- an affidavit setting out the amount owing and the decision under which it is owed; and

- a copy of the registered decision or award of the employment tribunal.

Subject to the application being in order, the County Court will then make an order for payment of the sum which is enforceable like any other order in the civil courts. The available enforcement options may include attachment of earnings orders, administration orders, bankruptcy orders, orders for execution against goods and garnishee proceedings. (the above does not apply to monetary orders accompanying an order for reinstatement, which are enforceable in the tribunal.)

Enforcement of out of court agreements and Tomlin orders [26.28]

What if there is an agreement to settle which is not incorporated in to a formal tribunal order, for example a COT3 or similar agreement?

Such agreements are again enforceable in the County Court, although not through the same means as above. The correct course is simply to issue proceedings in the County Court in the normal way. (Those in doubt as to how to proceed should contact their local county court or consult a book on civil procedure.) The claim is then treated like any other breach of contract case. If the court concludes that the other side have acted in breach, it will order them to pay the sum owed under the agreement. Frequently, it is possible in such circumstances to pursue summary judgement (i e judgement at an early stage in proceedings) because the defence has no real prospect of success.

Issuing proceedings in the County Court in the conventional way is also the correct means of enforcing parts of the schedule to a Tomlin Order which (because they are outside the jurisdiction of the tribunal to order) cannot be the subject of a direct order (see **CHAPTER 18**) So, for example, if the employer has breached a term in a Tomlin order relating to the provision of a reference, the correct method of enforcing the agreement is to issue proceedings for breach of contract in the County Court, where the claimant will have to prove loss resulting from the breach (for example loss of a job they would otherwise have been offered but for the breach). If, in the schedule to a Tomlin order, there is provision for payment of a sum of money, the payee has two choices. First, it can return to the tribunal, ask for the stay to be lifted and obtain a direct order for payment of the sum in question which is enforceable through the N322 procedure outlined above. Or it can, without returning to the tribunal, issue proceedings for breach of contract in the County Court. The former route is usually the most convenient.

Interest [26.29]

Interest starts to runs on most tribunal awards, including awards in unfair dismissal cases, 42 days from the date of decision. The rate payable is that defined in the *Judgements Act 1838*, currently standing at 7%. This occurs automatically, and should therefore be added by the claimant to any sum due when issuing county court proceedings.

With awards in discrimination cases, there is a particular incentive for the respondent to pay quickly. If payment is made within 14 days, no interest of any kind becomes available. If payment is not made within this period, interest will be awarded, in respect of a hurt to feelings or injuries award, from the date when the discriminatory act took place to the date of decision and, with other discrimination awards, from the 'midpoint date'. The midpoint date is the date half way between the commencement of the discriminatory act/s and the date of calculation by the tribunal of the award (see the *Employment Tribunals (Interest on Awards in Discrimination Cases) Regulations 1996 (SI 1996/2803)*). In addition, interest will accrue on the total award from the date of decision. The current rate of interest in discrimination cases is 7%.

Do's and Don'ts

Do:

- Pay promptly or risk paying more.
- Remember that interest is payable upon late payments.

Don't:

- Seek to enforce an order for the payment of money in the tribunal, the County Court is the correct place to do so.

Applicant's schedule of loss: unfair dismissal [26.30]

This example assumes a straightforward case of unfair dismissal. It assumes that the applicant is aged 45 (d.o.b. 01.07.57) at the date of dismissal and was employed by the respondent for seven and a half years between start date (14.01.95) and effective date of termination (13.07.02). It also assumes that the schedule is being prepared for a hearing that will take place nine months (39 weeks) after the effective date of termination (13.04.03) and that six months after the dismissal (14.01.03), the applicant has started a new job which pays less than her employment with the respondent. It is assumed that her salary with the respondent was £220 gross or £165 net per week.

IN THE EMPLOYMENT TRIBUNALS   **Case number XXX**
(ANYTOWN)

BETWEEN

MR AGGRIEVED

Applicant

– and –

THE DON'T BLAME US TRADING COMPANY

Respondent

APPLICANT'S SCHEDULE OF LOSS

1.)   **Basic Award**

The applicant earned £220 gross per week. The statutory maximum does not therefore apply.

He worked for 3 complete years aged not less than 22 (3 × 1 week).

He worked for 4 complete years aged not less than 41 (4 × 1 5 weeks).

Award is therefore 9 × £220 = £1,980.

Total   **£1,980**

2.)   **Compensatory Award**

a)   <u>Loss of earnings to date of hearing</u> (for the purposes of this schedule, accrued holiday pay has not been included. If at the time of dismissal the applicant has accrued holiday entitlement, most employers will resolve this issue by requiring the applicant to take the outstanding leave during the notice period. If the leave is in excess of the notice period, the employer does not adopt this course or the dismissal is without notice, advisors should be astute

243

to the need to claim outstanding accrued holiday pay. However, this is arguably better achieved by claiming for unlawful deduction from wages and/or under the *Working Time Regulations 1998 (SI 1998/1833))*.

(i)   14 July 2002 to 13 January 2003.

The applicant received no earnings during this period.

Net earnings prior to dismissal were £165 per week = £715 per month.

6 months × £715 = £4,290.

Total   **£4,290**

(ii)   14 January 2003 to 13 April 2003.

On 14 April 2003 the applicant commenced employment on a part-time basis at a net salary of £135 per week = £585 per month.

His loss of earnings during this period is therefore £130 per month.

3 months × £130 = £390.

Total   **£390**

b)   <u>Future loss of earnings</u>

The applicant has been informed that on 14 July 2003 his salary in his current employment will increase to £750 net per month, i e there will be no ongoing loss after that date.

His future loss of earnings will therefore be £130 per month for a further three months, i e £390.

Total   **£390**

c)   <u>Loss of bonus</u>

The applicant would have received a bonus on [date] and on [date]. The amount of each bonus would have been [£XXX].

Total   **£XXX**

d)   <u>Loss of pension</u>

[details]

Total   **£XXX**

e)   <u>Loss of use of company car</u>

The applicant had use of a company car which was used for personal use.

The net value of the car, petrol and running costs is estimated at [£XXX] (annual estimates published by, for example the AA or RAC may be of assistance in assessing the loss).

Total   **£XXX**

f)   Loss of private medical insurance policy

The respondent paid for a private health insurance policy for the applicant. He no longer has this benefit in his new job.

[details]

Total   **£XXX**

g)   Loss of other benefits in kind

[details]

Total   **£XXX**

h)   Cost of re-training

The applicant had to undertake a [e g computer] course prior to obtaining alternative employment. This course cost £XXX.

Total   **£XXX**

i)   Costs of seeking alternative employment (this head may also include the situation where, for example, the applicant has to move house in order to start a new job.)

The applicant incurred costs in applying for jobs and travelling to interviews. These are as follows:

[details]

Total   **£XXX**

j)   Loss of reputation (these 'stigma' damages are only available in limited circumstances to compensate for difficulties in finding alternative employment as a result of the poor reputation of the employer at the time of the dismissal.)

[details]

Total   **£XXX**

k)   Loss of statutory rights (there is no hard and fast rule as to the amount which will be awarded under this head. However, a figure of around £200 is often used.)

       Total   **£XXX**

l)   Injury to feelings (*Johnson v Unisys* award) (the practice of individual tribunals varies as to whether such awards will be made. It is not yet certain how they will be calculated but it seems likely to be along the lines of injury to feelings awards in discrimination cases.)

The applicant contends that the manner in which he was dismissed caused injury to his feelings.

[details]

       Total   **£XXX**

3.)   TOTAL   **£XXX**

27.

Steps after the Decision I: Review

Introduction [27.1]

A review is where the tribunal, upon application by one of the parties (or of its own motion), agrees to look again at its decision. It will only do so, however, where it decides that specific criteria are met which need to be addressed in any application for a review. The same tribunal whose original decision is under scrutiny will usually consider the application and conduct any review, frequently at the same hearing. At the conclusion of the review it may affirm, vary or revoke the original decision and order a complete re-hearing. In the latter circumstance, the parties should be ready to make representations as to whether the re-hearing should be before the same or a differently constituted tribunal. For guidance on whether to apply for a review or appeal to the Employment Appeal Tribunal (EAT), see **27.12**.

For a review to take place, there must be a 'decision' by the tribunal. Decision does not include interlocutory orders by the tribunal (for example in relation to further particulars or disclosure) but does include orders to strike out, decisions at preliminary hearings (and probably also pre-hearing reviews) as well, of course as any final determination of the tribunal in relation to liability or quantum. With interlocutory orders, if the party feels that there are grounds for a review and does not wish to pursue an appeal it should consider making an application to the tribunal for further directions.

The criteria for carrying out a review [27.2]

Under *rule 13(1)* of the *Employment Tribunals (Constitution and Rules of Procedure) Regulations 2001 (SI 2001/1171)* a party can apply for a review of a tribunal decision where:

- the decision was wrongly made as a result of an error on the part of the tribunal staff;

- a party did not receive notice of the proceedings leading to the decision;

- the decision was made in the absence of a party;

- new evidence has become available since the conclusion of the hearing to which the decision relates, provided that its existence could not have been reasonably known of or foreseen at the time of the hearing; or

- the interests of justice require such a review.

In addition, as with the exercise of all its procedural powers, the tribunal is required, in so far as it is practicable, to give effect to the overriding objective (see CHAPTER 9 – FAIRNESS: THE OVERRIDING OBJECTIVE) in deciding whether to conduct a review. In practice, this is likely to be most relevant in relation to ground E below.

Ground A: error by tribunal staff [27.3]

Staff does not include the tribunal chairman or lay members. Purely clerical errors can usually be more efficiently corrected under the slip rule (*rule 12(8)*). Note also that such an error will not, of itself, be sufficient to found a review unless it can be shown that the decision was 'wrongly made', i e the mistake is not purely technical in nature.

Ground B: no notice of proceedings [27.4]

A notice of hearing (or any other tribunal document) sent by post is deemed to have been received unless the person applying for the review proves otherwise. Note that if a relevant document is sent to the correct address of an organisation but lost internally, service is effective, emphasising the importance of efficient internal procedures for the processing of such information (*Interpretation Act 1978, s 7*. See also *Migwain Ltd (in liquidation) v TGWU [1979] ICR 597, EAT* and *T and D Transport (Portsmouth) Ltd v Linburn [1987] ICR 696, EAT*).

Further, where a document is sent to the registered office of a limited company (even if not the office dealing with the matter in question), service will usually be deemed to have taken place (see *Migwain* above).

Ground C: decision made in the absence of the party [27.5]

The party in question, when applying for the review, must show 'good cause' for their absence (*Morris v Griffiths [1977] ICR 153*). The tribunal will look both at the reason for non-attendance and whether the party asserting is telling the truth. The party seeking the review will be assisted by independent corroborative evidence in support of what they are saying. The opposing party is well advised, in these circumstances, to seek such evidence in advance of the hearing.

Ground D: new evidence [27.6]

The criteria for granting a review to hear new evidence are the same as the rules applicable on appeal to the EAT. In particular, it needs to be established:

- that the new evidence might have had an effect on the outcome of the case;

- that it is, on the face of it, credible, though it need not be undisputed;

- the evidence was unavailable at the time of the original hearing in the sense that its existence could not have been reasonably known or foreseen at that time.

Note that a review will not take place under this ground unless all three requirements are met, other than in the exceptional circumstances provided for under *rule 13(1)(e)*. The justification for this is the need for 'finality' in legal proceedings. Parties should note that there might be an overlap between the new evidence category, *rule 13(1)(d)*, and the interests of justice category, *rule 13(1)(e)* (see **27.7**).

Further, a review is not a substitute for applying for an adjournment at the original hearing if one is necessary in order to adduce evidence to reply to a new allegation by the other side.

An example of ground D where new evidence has been admitted upon review is:

- Subsequent to the hearing, the applicant obtained employment on higher pay than the tribunal anticipated when calculating future loss (note, however, that minor differences are unlikely to give rise to a review).

Ground E: interests of justice [27.7]

The courts have been keen to emphasise the restricted circumstances in which this ground can be relied upon. Tribunals are required to have regard to the public interest in ensuring that there is finality in legal proceedings, and also to the prejudice which the other party may suffer if the review is allowed to proceed. The overriding objective is also likely to be a relevant factor when considering this ground. Other than in special, or exceptional, circumstances, where a ground fails under *rule 13(1)(a)* to *(d)*, the interests of justice test cannot be used as a substitute. So where new evidence was available at the time of the original hearing, the party seeking to adduce it upon review will need to show that there were special mitigating circumstances why they failed to do so at the original hearing if they are to succeed under ground E.

A review under the interests of justice ground tends to fall into one of two categories. First, where there has been a procedural mishap, and second where the tribunal's decision has been undermined by recent events taking place after the original decision was made.

Procedural mishap [27.8]

'Procedural mishap' includes instances where:

(a) a party has not had a fair opportunity to respond to the other's case;

(b) there is an issue in relation to the jurisdiction of the tribunal to hear the case which was not raised at the original hearing;

(c) the originating application has been dismissed without a hearing in circumstances which amount to a miscarriage of justice;

(d) the originating application has been withdrawn after receiving erroneous legal guidance from the chairman and due to a failure on the part of the respondent to disclose relevant documents.

In relation to (a), a review will normally not be allowed where it was open to a party to apply for an adjournment at the original hearing in order to respond to a new allegation raised by the other side. The exception to this is where the party is unrepresented and the tribunal ought to have drawn their attention to the possibility of applying for an adjournment. An example of where a review might be justified is where the tribunal decide the case on a point which it has thought of independently after retiring to consider the decision and upon which the parties have not had an opportunity to address it. This would fit in to category (a) above.

Procedural mishaps (including issues of jurisdiction) constitute errors of law by the tribunal that can give rise to a review. In both instances, however, if the point has already been argued before the tribunal at the original hearing, it is normally not appropriate to apply for a review, but to pursue an appeal. Further, where a point of law (other than in relation to jurisdiction) has not been taken due to the error of a representative, this normally cannot give rise to a review.

Events after the decision [27.9]

Sometimes events occur after the tribunal's decision that undermine its conclusions. There is a considerable overlap between this category and the 'new evidence' category, meaning that it is often sensible for a party to rely upon both grounds where significant new evidence emerges. Note, however, that if the evidence was available at the original hearing, the party seeking to adduce it will need to demonstrate that there were exceptional or special circumstances, why it was not adduced at the original hearing.

An example of ground E, review in the interests of justice because of events after the decision is:

- The applicant was unfairly dismissed for possession of cannabis (the employer, without carrying out a sufficient investigation, relied upon the fact that they had been charged by the police). Subsequently, the applicant was convicted of the offence in court. Evidence of the conviction was permitted upon review in relation to the issue of contribution to dismissal, which was found to be 100%.

Applying for a review [27.10]

A review can be applied for orally on the day of the original hearing or, as is more common, in writing within 14 days of the date when the original decision was sent to the parties. The application should set out:

- the basis upon which the review is sought with reference to the grounds upon which one may take place; and

- the relevance of this in terms of the original decision.

Parties should ensure that the written application is thorough, setting out all the facts upon which they rely. So in the case of non-attendance the party should give the reason for the non-attendance and, where it is available, submit documentary evidence in support, which in any event should (wherever possible) be produced at the oral hearing. If a party is seeking to adduce new evidence, the application should:

- describe the new evidence and why it is credible;

- explain why it was not available at the original hearing and its existence not reasonably foreseen; and

- state why the original decision would or might have been different if the tribunal had seen the evidence in question.

At the oral hearing, the party in question should be ready to make submissions and give evidence in relation to all three contentions.

The application will normally be considered at first instance on the papers by the chairman of the tribunal who heard the case. It may also be considered by the regional chairman or the President of the employment tribunals. Unless the chairman considers that the application for a review has no reasonable prospects of success, the case will be listed for a hearing, in which the party seeking the review will need to persuade the tribunal that one or more of the grounds for carrying out a review have been met and address it upon what the outcome of any review should be. If the chairman concludes, upon considering the written application, that it has no reasonable prospects of success, he is obliged to invite the party concerned to present further written reasons why a review should take place.

The hearing [27.11]

Both parties may attend the hearing and address the tribunal on whether the grounds for review are met and, if so, the consequences in terms of the original decision. This may involve calling witnesses, using witness statements and preparing a bundle of documentary evidence. So if, for example, seeking to demonstrate that there was a good reason for non-attendance, the party in question may need to give evidence as to why they were unable to attend. In relation to new evidence (ground D), it may be necessary to call a witness not only to adduce the new evidence but also to explain why it was unavailable at the original hearing, a matter which the party in question will have to prove if ground C is to be fulfilled. Submissions alone are likely to be appropriate only where there is a matter, for example in relation to jurisdiction, where the giving of evidence is unnecessary.

Precisely how the review hearing is conducted is a matter for the tribunal and should always be clarified with the chairman from the outset. In particular, parties should clarify whether the tribunal wishes to deal with the application for review separately, or whether the tribunal should be addressed both on the application and the outcome of any review. Often the latter is the more practical option. For example, if the tribunal conclude there was, under ground B, a good reason for non–attendance, it will invariably list the case for a full merits hearing. It is normal for the party seeking the review to open with submissions as to why the review is sought (with reference to the grounds in *rule 13(1)* before proceeding to call relevant evidence. The opposing party will then have the opportunity to cross–examine and, if appropriate, call evidence of their own. Each party will then make closing submissions. The tribunal will then give its decision. Frequently, one decision will cover both: (a) whether the grounds for application for a review has been met; and (b) if so, the outcome of the review.

Review and appeal compared [27.12]

There are instances where one of either an appeal (to the EAT) or a review is the correct option and further instances where it is legitimate for the party to pursue both options simultaneously.

- Where a point of law has already been argued at the original hearing, an appeal is the most appropriate forum.

- Where the grounds for review are *rules 13(1)(a)*, *(b)* or *(c)*, a review, as opposed to an appeal, is the appropriate first avenue of recourse for the party concerned.

- Where the ground is seeking to adduce new evidence (whether under *rule 13(1)(d)* or *(e)*, a review is the appropriate first avenue of recourse.

- Where the ground is an error of law (either in relation to jurisdiction or a procedural mishap) under *rule 13(1)(e)*, the party normally has a choice whether to pursue an appeal or a review which may involve tactical considerations, such as the likely effect of going back in front of the same tribunal. If the application for a review is successful and the tribunal decide to revoke the original decision and order a re-hearing, it is possible to apply for the case to be heard by a differently constituted tribunal.

- If the tribunal decide the case on a point which the parties did not have an opportunity to address it on at the hearing, consideration should be given to an application for review.

- Points relating to jurisdiction which have not been argued at the original hearing are appropriate for dealing with by way of review, with a further appeal if necessary.

- Note that an appeal and a review are *not* mutually exclusive options. Parties should be aware that time limits for appeal still apply if a review has been applied for. It is possible, where appropriate, both to apply for a review and lodge an appeal. Both the tribunal and the EAT should be informed of this fact, and may stay of appeal pending hearing of the review.

- Note that a refusal to grant a review can itself be a ground for appeal.

- A party may be penalised in costs if it seeks to adduce new evidence on appeal as opposed to review, which is the most appropriate first avenue of recourse.

Review at the tribunal's own motion [27.13]

Under *rule 13(2)* the tribunal can, of its own motion, decide to review its decision, but it must give the parties notice of its intention in this respect, and an opportunity to respond to the issue of whether a review should take place. The grounds under which a tribunal may order a review are the same as that applicable to the parties.

Do's and Don'ts

Do:

- Ensure that an application for a review is effectively drafted with reference to the grounds upon which one may take place.

- Consider whether either a review and/or an appeal, is appropriate.

- Make any application for review within 14 days of the date the decision was sent to the parties.

- Prepare for the review hearing professionally, calling witnesses and preparing bundles as necessary.

Don't:

- Forget that applying for a review does not dispense with the need (where an appeal may be necessary) to comply with the time limits for the lodging of an appeal to the EAT.

- Apply for a review purely because you disagree with the decision of the tribunal – the ground/s need to be met.

- Apply for a review on issues which have already been properly argued before the tribunal – an appeal is the correct avenue in these circumstances.

28.

Steps after the Decision II: Appeal

Introduction [28.1]

This chapter gives a broad outline of the basis upon which an appeal can be made to the Employment Appeal Tribunal (EAT) and the procedures which exist in that tribunal. Since the book is concerned primarily with employment tribunals, this chapter does not attempt to provide a comprehensive guide to practice and procedure in the EAT. In addition to reading the chapter, parties should have careful regard to the EAT's procedural rules, relevant practice direction and guidance notes (see 28.2). They should also be careful to read very carefully the guidance sent to parties by the EAT, for which this chapter is not intended as a substitute.

Contacting the EAT [28.2]

On the EAT website (www.employmentappeals.gov.uk) it is possible to access and download forms for appealing (e g Form 1 Notice of Appeal) and the procedural rules and practice direction. It also offers basic guidance on the procedure for appealing (note that this guidance is not a substitute for reading thoroughly any other information sent to the parties). In addition, the EAT can be contacted by telephone on 020 7273 1040. The EAT staff may (at their discretion) be prepared to give advice on uncontentious procedural matters, but will not be able to advise on the merits of any appeal or application. The address of the EAT is Audit House, 58 Victoria Embankment, London EC4Y 0DS.

Appealing to the EAT [28.3]

Parties sometimes feel a deep sense of grievance when they lose a case and are determined to appeal. They should be aware, however, that avenues of appeal to the EAT are limited. It is only possible to appeal where the tribunal has erred in law. In practice, this encompasses six different scenarios:

- The tribunal has misapplied the law (i e case law, other than merely guideline authorities) or statute.

- The tribunal has improperly exercised the discretion derived from its procedural powers (including a breach of natural justice).

- The tribunal has reached a conclusion or made a finding of fact unsupported by any evidence.

- The tribunal has failed to make a finding of fact which it was required, on a proper application of the law, to make or has failed to give sufficient reasons.

- The tribunal has been guilty of bias in its decision making.

- The tribunal has reached a decision which is perverse – namely one which no reasonable tribunal could, on the evidence before it, have made.

All of these scenarios are deemed to be errors of law by the tribunal. Note that the same ground may engage one or more of them. Most grounds of appeal will, for example, involve a misapplication of case law or statute. The most common ground of appeal, perversity, is also generally one of the hardest to succeed upon. The higher courts are strong defenders of the rights of individual employment tribunals to decide issues of fact, something borne out by the 'industrial jury' label which both the EAT and the Court of Appeal have applied to them (*Williams v Compair Maxam Ltd [1982] ICR 156*).

New points of law or fact [28.4]

All parties should note that, generally, they may not take on appeal a point of law which was not raised at the tribunal unless:

- the point goes to the jurisdiction (or right) of the tribunal to hear the case; or

- the error of law is so basic that the tribunal ought to have considered it as a matter of course (*Langston v Cranfield University [1998] IRLR 172, EAT*).

In relation to issues of fact, a party may not adduce evidence at the EAT which was not before the employment tribunal unless:

- the evidence could not have been obtained with reasonable diligence before the employment tribunal;

- it is apparently credible; and

- they can demonstrate that it would have had an important (though not necessarily decisive) influence on the tribunal's decision.

Parties should note that, in relation to new evidence, it is usually best to pursue a review (see CHAPTER **17** – POSTPONEMENTS AND ADJOURNMENTS) and they may be penalised in costs if they fail to do so.

Appealing interlocutory orders [28.5]

An interlocutory order (e g as to disclosure further particulars etc) can be appealed in the same way as a final decision. Time starts to run from the date of the order, not the date of the final decision in the case. Usually, appealing an interlocutory order will involve demonstrating that the tribunal has improperly exercised its discretion (see **28.8**). In practice, such appeals are rare and difficult to sustain. Parties should be aware that where an interlocutory appeal is pursued without merit (and its only purpose is to delay proceedings), a costs award may be made.

Doctrine of precedent [28.6]

As tribunals are bound by authorities in the EAT (provided they have not been overturned by a higher court), so the EAT is bound by authorities in the Court of Appeal, House of Lords and European Court of Justice.

Possible grounds of appeal

Misapplying the law [28.7]

On occasions, a tribunal will:

- fail to give any consideration to an authority or statute which is binding upon it;

- misconstrue (i e misinterpret) that case or statute; or

- fail to properly apply that statute – for example by omitting to make a finding of fact which, on a proper construction of the law, it was required to make.

In these circumstances, a party will need to demonstrate:

(a) the authority or statute which the tribunal misconstrued or failed to consider;

(b) that as a consequence of the omission or misconstruction it applied the law wrongly in making its decision; and

(c) that this may have affected the outcome – often called the 'would it have made any difference?' hurdle.

Note that (b) by no means follows as a consequence of (a), or (c) as a consequence of either. If a tribunal has omitted from or misdescribed in its reasons the applicable principle of case or statute law, it by no means follows that an appeal is bound to succeed. The decision will be upheld if it can be demonstrated that despite this error the tribunal followed the right approach in law to the evidence. It will even be upheld in a case where the tribunal has followed the wrong approach if the circumstances disclosed by its findings of fact make it obvious that application of the right approach would have been virtually certain to lead to the same conclusion.

Failure properly to exercise discretion [28.8]

'Discretion' means any area where the law gives the tribunal a choice, according to the facts and nature of the dispute that is before it, as to how to proceed. The tribunal, within the confines of statute and case law, has a discretion in operating a wide range of its procedural powers. Examples include the conduct of the hearing (including rulings on evidence, permissible questions to witnesses and the identification of issues), postponements, adjournments, striking out claims in default of an order, payments of a deposit under *rule 7(4)* (*Employment Tribunals (Constitution and Rules of Procedure) Regulations 2001 (SI 2001/1171)*), and rulings on disclosure and the provision of further particulars. Where a party seeks to appeal an interlocutory order by the tribunal then, more often that not, this will involve an exercise of the tribunal's discretion (see **28.5**).

To found an appeal on the improper exercise of discretion it is necessary to show either:

- that the tribunal has taken into account an improper consideration;

- that it has failed to take into account a proper consideration; or

- that it has exercised its discretion in a manner which is perverse (*Carter v Credit Change Ltd [1980] 1 All ER 252*).

'Improper' consideration includes an irrelevant consideration. There can be an overlap between this category and the first (misapplying the law). For example, there are a number of cases governing how the tribunal should exercise its discretion with regard to such matters as the admissibility of evidence and postponements and orders for disclosure. Where the tribunal has failed to apply these cases, an appeal could lie both under improper exercise of discretion and, in the alternative, the first category of failing to apply a principle contained in statute or case law. Where the tribunal has failed to conduct proceedings in accordance with the principles of natural justice, this will frequently engage both categories.

Finding of fact unsupported by any evidence [28.9]

To succeed on this ground, a party will need to demonstrate that there was no evidence at all for a particular conclusion reached by the tribunal, and that this might have had an effect on the outcome of the case. Usually, the chairman's notes of evidence will be required in order to prove this ground (see **28.16**).

For example, in the decision the chairman records that the employee had been warned for misconduct in 2001. There was no evidence at all before the tribunal that this had occurred.

Note that where there has been some evidence, however weak, upon which a finding is based, the only avenue of appeal is perversity (see **28.12**).

There will be occasions when a tribunal has committed a simple, factual misunderstanding of the evidence. It is submitted that, in these circumstances, there should be an appeal both under the 'no evidence' heading and (phrased in the alternative) the perversity heading.

Failure to make a relevant finding of fact and/or give reasons for its decision [28.10]

The tribunal is required to make a finding of fact on all the relevant issues which are before it. It if fails to do so, this may found an appeal. Sometimes it is necessary for a tribunal to disclose the secondary findings of fact upon which its primary findings are based. So, for example, where a tribunal finds that an employee has contributed to their dismissal, it must set out the factual findings upon which this conclusion is based. For the extent to which the tribunal is obliged to give reasons for its decision, see CHAPTER 25 – THE DECISION.

Bias [28.11]

Bias means that one or more of the tribunal members might unfairly regard the case of a party with favour or disfavour. Both actual bias and the appearance of bias to a hypothetical reasonable person not involved in the case can give rise to an appeal, since an unbiased tribunal is a fundamental feature of a fair hearing. Bias can range from situations where a tribunal member has a direct interest in or association with one of the parties (or a third party with a direct interest in the outcome), to more mundane concerns such as a member failing to pay attention or falling asleep to the extent that one party may have been prejudiced (*Greenaway Harrison Ltd v Wiles [1994] IRLR 380, R v Gough [1993] 2All ER 724* and *R v Bow Street Metropolitan Stipendiary Magistrate ex parte Pinochet Ugarte (No2) [1999] 2 WLR 272 (HL)*). In respect of cases in the latter category, where the prejudice is of a transient nature, parties are generally expected to raise the matter before the tribunal at first instance either, for example, to ask that certain evidence be reheard or, in more extreme cases, that the case be listed for a rehearing.

The appearance of bias may also be given where the chairman makes remarks which would cause an impartial onlooker to perceive that he had formed a hostile view of one party's case before even hearing the evidence (*Peter Simpler and Co Ltd v Cooke [1986] IRLR 19, EAT*). A further example of the appearance of bias is where the tribunal fail to use moderate or temperate language in its questioning of the parties or the witnesses although, in practice, the higher courts have been resistant to find an appearance of bias in these circumstances (*Kennedy v Metropolitan Police Commissioner (1990) Times, 8 November, EAT*, see also *Docherty v Strathhelm 1994 SLT*). Other, if very rare, examples have included a chairman putting undue pressure on the parties, refusing to allow a party to cross-examine a witness and refusing to permit a party to make closing submissions. Generally, however, parties should not confuse the asking of difficult questions by a tribunal with bias. Many tribunals adopt the practice of expressing to a party during the course of proceedings particular concerns it has about their case in order to give them the opportunity to answer them. Provided the tribunal does not state it has already made up its mind about the issue, such questioning can enhance rather than detract from the fairness of the hearing.

The tribunal has reached a perverse decision   **[28.12]**

The meaning of perverse is essentially that the tribunal has reached a decision which no reasonable tribunal could have made. The test is emphatically not whether the EAT agree with the decision or whether they would, on the facts, have reached a different one. It has been held that the decision must be so plainly wrong as not to have been a permissible option open to the tribunal, although this may be placing the test too highly (*Piggott Bros and Co Ltd v Jackson [1991] IRLR 309*).

Examples of where a decision has been held to be perverse are:

- A decision that an employee was unfairly dismissed for a second instance of dishonesty shortly after a previous incident for which they received a warning (*United Distillers v Conlin [1992] IRLR 503*).

- A decision that a nurse was unfairly dismissed for making nuisance calls to other staff (*East Berkshire Health Authority v Matadeen [1992] IRLR 336*).

Examples are far more numerous of cases where the EAT has declined to interfere in decisions which are arguably perverse. Notable amongst them is a case where the EAT refused to interfere with a finding that displaying pictures of nude women in a male dominated work environment did not constitute less favourable treatment of women employees on grounds of their sex (*Stewart v Cleveland Guest (Engineering) Ltd [1994] IRLR 440*). In that case, the EAT was at pains to point out that individual tribunals will take a different view of such situations according to the factual context, and that this was an area where there was room for legitimate variation in decision making.

Common pitfalls when appealing

Appealing because of a failure to mention evidence in a decision   [28.13]

Whilst a tribunal is obliged, in the exercise of its discretion, to apply its mind to all the relevant evidence in a case, the EAT will not assume that, because a tribunal has failed to mention a piece of evidence in its decision, it has not considered it. The basic requirement (in terms of the written reasons) is simply that the tribunal should make findings of fact on all relevant issues before it and correctly apply the law. Whilst it is desirable that a tribunal give reasons for the findings of fact this, in most cases, is not obligatory. In practice, it is often difficult, other than in the most glaring circumstances, for a party to prove that a tribunal has not addressed its mind to evidence. For the requirement to give sufficient reasons, see CHAPTER 25.

Weight   [28.14]

Often, a party will read a decision by a tribunal and conclude that it attached insufficient weight (i e importance) to one piece of evidence and too much weight to another aspect. This, of itself, cannot form the basis of an appeal, unless it can be shown that decision was perverse (see 28.12). Perversity apart, the weight to be attached to evidence is considered to be a matter for the tribunal, which is able to observe witnesses at first hand.

Useful guidance when appealing findings of fact [28.15]

In *Ellot v Welsh Products Ltd [1982] EAT*, Browne-Wilkinson J commented that:

> 'an error of law can be shown if a tribunal has failed to make a finding of fact where there was uncontrovertible evidence, or has made a finding of fact contrary to all the evidence. It is equally clear that there is no error where there is some evidence pointing in one direction and some evidence in the other direction and the employment tribunal has preferred one lot of evidence to the other'.

Appealing findings of fact: the chairman's note of evidence [28.16]

Where it is alleged that there was no evidence upon which the tribunal could base its finding, or that the tribunal misunderstood a piece of evidence, or that the decision was perverse, it is usually necessary to obtain the chairman's notes of evidence (*Ministry of Defence v Hunt [1996] ICR 554*). Tribunal proceedings are not tape recorded. The only official record of proceedings is the note taken by the chairman. It is necessary to obtain an order from the EAT for the production of the chairman's notes. This should be done at the preliminary hearing directions (PHD) (see **28.25**), and full reasons set out on the PHD form. A party will need to set out in the form why the notes are necessary to argue the point of appeal. The party seeking the notes should be clear in its mind about precisely why the notes are necessary in order to prove one or more of its grounds of appeal, or the application is unlikely to succeed. Specifically, the EAT Guidance Notes (Preliminary Hearing/Directions) [1997], IRLR 618 require it, in respect of the evidence for which the notes are required:

- to identify the issues in the appeal or cross appeal to which that evidence is relevant;

- to give the names of the witnesses; and

- to state the relevant parts of their evidence (EAT Guidance Notes, para 7(5)).

Orders which the EAT can make [28.17]

The possible order which the EAT might make in the event of an appeal succeeding is an important consideration in deciding whether to appeal. For example, where the tribunal has misdirected itself in law but has made findings on the evidence which demonstrate the case to be a weak one, an appeal might not be regarded as worthwhile if the most likely outcome in the EAT would be an order remitting the case back to a tribunal for a rehearing.

The EAT can:

(a) dismiss an appeal;

(b) allow an appeal and replace the tribunal's decision with one of its own (thereby finally resolving the issue in favour of the party who is appealing); or

(c) remit the case to a same or different tribunal either for a complete rehearing or for consideration to be given to a particular point.

A broad summary of the criteria the EAT use for deciding which course to adopt is as follows. Where the tribunal has not erred in law (including not making a perverse decision) course (a) will be adopted. Where the decision of the tribunal is found to be perverse, course (b) will normally be adopted. Where the tribunal has misdirected itself as to the law (i e misconstrued or failed to apply the law), the EAT will remit for a rehearing if, on a correct application of the law, it is still uncertain (or open to question) as to how the tribunal would, in the exercise of its fact finding function, have determined the matter. The above powers should be seen in the context of the rule that that it is not for the EAT to usurp the fact finding function of the tribunal (*O'Kelly v Trusthouse Forte plc [1983] IRLR 369, [1983] ICR 728, [1983] 3 All ER 456.* See also *Wilson v Post Office [2000] IRLR 834*).

Procedure for appealing

Step one: time limits [28.18]

An appeal must be lodged with the EAT within 42 days of the date when the *extended written reasons* were sent to the parties. Time starts to run from the day after the date (recorded on the reasons) upon which it was sent to the parties. It is a common mistake for those not experienced in tribunal proceedings to confuse the extended written reasons with the written decision of the tribunal, which can often appear to be in extended form but which is headed 'summary reasons'. The extended written reasons are not usually produced by the tribunal unless specifically requested, except in discrimination cases. They usually must be requested within 21 days of receipt of the date of the written summary of reasons. Alternatively, it is perfectly permissible to request extended written reasons on the day on which the decision is orally announced by the tribunal. The EAT does have a discretion to allow an appeal to proceed on the basis of the summary of reasons, but only if it considers that it can do so without causing unfairness to the respondent.

An appeal out of time will not be allowed unless there are exceptional circumstances (Practice Direction (EAT Procedure) [1996] IRLR 430, para 3(5) and *United Arab Emirates v Abdelghafar [1995] ICR 65*). An application for an extension of time must be lodged with the notice of appeal. It will be considered at first instance by the registrar, with a right of appeal to the EAT itself.

Documents to be lodged [28.19]

When appealing, an appellant must, within the time limit, lodge the following documentation at the EAT:

- the notice of appeal (Form 1);

- a copy of the decision which is the subject of the appeal;

- a copy of the extended written reasons for the decision.

Notice of appeal [28.20]

The notice of appeal provides space for inserting the grounds of appeal. It is often best other than in straightforward cases, to attach a separate sheet containing the grounds of appeal.

Drafting grounds of appeal [28.21]

The importance of drafting effective grounds of appeal is underlined by the fact that all cases go to a preliminary hearing where it must be demonstrated that there is an arguable point of law. If this is not apparent from the face of the grounds, a party may face an uphill battle to persuade the EAT to proceed. Each ground of appeal must disclose a point of law, as defined above. This handbook (with its concentration on tribunals) is not intended to provide comprehensive guidance on the drafting of such grounds. Parties may wish, however, to bear in mind the following:

- Consider starting each ground with the words: 'The tribunal erred in law by...'.

- Reference should then be made to one of the criteria outlined above: e g 'The tribunal erred in law by misconstruing the provisions of *section 98(4)(a)* of the *Employment Rights Act, 1996*'.

- The reasons for this assertion should then be given:

'In paragraph 19 of its determination, the tribunal asserted that "it did not consider the respondent behaved reasonably in dismissing the applicant". In so doing the tribunal substituted its own view for that of the hypothetical, reasonable employer. The test the tribunal ought to have applied (as confirmed in the recent Court of Appeal case of *Foley v Post Office [2000] IRLR 827*) was whether dismissal was within the range of reasonable responses open to the respondent.'

- Where there is an appeal on grounds of perversity, it is unacceptable to simply state 'the decision was one which no reasonable tribunal could have reached'. You must go on to give particulars of why this was the case.

Step two: action by the respondent [28.22]

Upon the appeal being lodged, the registrar will first consider whether the EAT has jurisdiction (i e the right or power) to hear the appeal. Provided they so conclude, they will usually send to the respondent: (a) a respondent's answer (Form 3); and (b) a PHD form. The PHD needs to be completed and returned to the EAT within 14 days.

The position with the answer is more complicated. Where there is to be no cross appeal (see **28.25**), the respondent need not complete and return the answer until 14 days after any order at a PHD permitting the appeal to proceed. Where the respondent wants to cross appeal the decision of the tribunal, then the respondent must complete and send the answer disclosing the grounds with the PHD form. The exception to this is in the relatively common situation where the respondent only intends to cross appeal if the appellant is successful at the PHD, in which case it can serve its answer within 14 days of the relevant order at the PHD.

The answer [28.23]

The answer is where the respondent sets out the basis upon which they resists the appeal of the appellant, together with any cross appeal of their own. A form is sent by the EAT for this purpose, but if there is insufficient space on that form then, as with the notice of appeal, a separate sheet can be attached. Where the respondent simply wishes to rely upon the reasons given by the tribunal below, this should be stated in the answer. Generally, it is sensible to give fuller grounds.

Step three: completing the form [28.24]

Upon the appeal being lodged, the appellant will also be sent a PHD form, which they need to complete within 14 days, or whatever time limit is specified.

All instructions accompanying that form relating to the lodging of skeleton arguments and authorities should be followed.

Meaning of cross appeal [28.25]

This is where the respondent also wishes to appeal the decision of the tribunal. Whilst this does not occur in the majority of cases, one example of where it might arise is where the employee brings a claim for constructive dismissal and race discrimination. The employment tribunal dismiss the claim for race discrimination but find that the applicant was constructively dismissed for reasons unrelated to race. The employee appeals the decision on race discrimination and the employer decides to cross appeal the decision on constructive dismissal. A further instance is where the tribunal could have found in a party's favour on an additional ground, but failed to do so due to an error in law.

The PHD serves two functions. First, to determine whether there is a reasonably arguable ground of appeal upon which to proceed to a full appeal hearing, and second, if so, whether there are any directions which need to be given for the hearing of the appeal. It usually takes the form of a hearing before the presiding judge and two lay members. Ordinarily, it is the appellant only who has the right to address the EAT at a PHD, although the respondent may attend to take notes of what has occurred or address the tribunal on directions they seek.

This is not the case, however, where the respondent lodges a cross appeal, in which case they too will be required to demonstrate an arguable point of law. It is essential, however, that (regardless of whether they are appearing) both parties fill in the PHD form which is sent, since the EAT will make directions for the future conduct of the case at this hearing. Particular thought should be given (in an appeal relating to the evidence the employment tribunal heard) as to whether it is necessary to request the chairman's notes of evidence (see **28.16**). Note that a skeleton argument should be served by the party appearing not less than seven days prior to the PHD. A list of any authorities sent or faxed to the EAT's librarian at least 24 hours before the hearing, but should be kept to that which is strictly necessary to demonstrate a reasonably arguable appeal.

Preparation: steps prior to the full hearing [28.26]

As with employment tribunals, the EAT has the power to give directions in relation to the conduct of any future hearing. In addition, the parties should follow the practice direction in relation to preparatory steps for that hearing.

Directions and interlocutory applications [28.27]

The EAT has the power, either of its own motion or upon the application of one of the parties, to make directions relating to:

- the amendment of any notice (i e notice of appeal or answer);
- the admission of facts or documents;
- the mode in which evidence is given at the hearing;
- the consolidation of proceedings;
- and the date of hearing (*rule 24(5)*).

Such directions may be given either pursuant to a directions hearing or be made on the papers. Any interlocutory application, whether for directions or otherwise (provided there is sufficient time before a hearing), should be made in writing to the registrar, who will usually determine the application on the papers but may list the case for a directions meeting. Parties should note that one of the central purposes of the PHD is to make directions for the appeal hearing and the PHD form provides for this. They should, therefore, be prepared at the PHD to make all necessary applications. If, due to an error, they fail to do so thus necessitating a further directions meeting, there may be costs implications (EAT Guidance Notes, para 6).

Preparation for the hearing

Documents [28.28]

It is incumbent upon the parties to send to the EAT all *relevant* documents upon which they wish to rely as soon as possible after service of the notice of appeal, and no later than six weeks before the date when the appeal is due to be heard. The EAT's staff will then prepare, from the documents submitted by the parties, an indexed bundle (the EAT will make copies for the tribunal members). The EAT will send to the parties a copy of the index so that the parties can prepare their own bundle in the same order. If the index is incomplete, the parties should notify the EAT of this as soon as possible, with any additional documentation.

Skeleton arguments [28.29]

Skeleton arguments are required in all hearings unless the EAT otherwise directs. (EAT Practice Direction, para 8.)

These should be served no less than two weeks before the hearing or, in the case of the preliminary hearing, not less than seven days before the hearing. Paragraph 8 of the Practice Direction deals with the contents of the skeleton argument.

Chronologies [28.30]

The appellant's skeleton argument should be accompanied by a chronology, which if possible should be agreed between the parties. The contents of the chronology are covered in paragraph 8 of the practice direction.

Legal authorities [28.31]

A list of all authorities upon which a party proposes to rely should be sent or faxed to the EAT's librarian not less than 24 hours before the hearing is due to be heard. Where the authority is reported, there is no need to enclose a copy. (EAT Practice Direction, para 15.) The EAT has stated that, where authorities are central to a case, it is useful for a photocopy to be attached to the skeleton argument. It has also published guidance on restricting use of authorities to those which are necessary to argue the case (EAT Practice Direction, para 15) – remember that it is quality, as opposed to quantity, which will impress the tribunal.

The hearing [28.32]

The hearing involves legal arguments from both parties or their representatives. The appellant presents their case first. The old practice of addressing the presiding judge by their formal legal title (i e 'My Lord' or 'Your Honour') has been abandoned in the interests of accessibility. They should be addressed as sir or madam. In contrast to tribunal hearings, parties stand when they address the EAT.

Composition of the EAT [28.33]

The composition of the EAT is very similar to that of employment tribunals. It consists of a lawyer sitting with two lay members (from employers' and employees' organisations). The principle difference is that the lawyer is either a high court judge or a senior circuit judge, and is described as the 'presiding judge' as opposed to the chairman. The presiding judge will possess considerable legal experience. The extent of their experience of employment law will vary according to whether the judge sits permanently in the EAT, or is doing a temporary stint there. The president of the EAT (a high court judge) sits permanently in addition to one other judge.

Relevant materials governing jurisdiction and procedure [28.34]

The EAT's jurisdiction is derived from statute (*Employment Tribunals Act 1996, s 21*). As with tribunals, the EAT has the power (within the confines of its own procedural rules) to regulate its own procedure. Parties should have regard to the following: *Employment Appeal Tribunal Rules 1993 (SI 1993/2854)* and *Employment Appeal Tribunal (Amendment) Rules 2001 (SI 2001/1128)*. Further, parties should consider the relevant practice direction in force, currently the EAT Practice Direction. In respect of PHDs, parties should have regard to the EAT Guidance Notes. All of the above can be downloaded from the EAT's website: www.employmentappeals.gov.uk.

Costs [28.35]

The EAT has the power to award costs where it considers that proceedings were 'unnecessary, improper or vexatious' or where there has been unreasonable delay or other unreasonable conduct in bringing or defending proceedings (*rule 34*).

Representation at the EAT [28.36]

As with tribunals, any person may appear in the EAT, and there is no requirement for that person to possess a legal qualification. Despite this, it is not surprising that, given the requirement to appeal on a point of law (and the somewhat daunting requirements relating to submission of skeleton arguments), parties do commonly instruct professional advocates to appear for them.

Where a party does not have the resources to do so, they might consider the following alternatives (see also **CHAPTER 3 – GETTING ADVICE**):

- Applying for legal aid – a solicitor should be instructed to make the application. Legal aid will normally be granted where a case gets past the PHD stage.

- The free service offered by members of the bar to represent parties at a preliminary hearing, details of which can be obtained from the EAT.

- The Bar Pro Bono Unit (consisting of barristers in independent practice who provide their services free).

- The Free Representation Unit (consisting of barristers and solicitors and those undergoing training).

- Citizens Advice Bureau or Law centre.

Where a party chooses to represent themselves, they should not feel daunted by the process. The tribunal will strive to assist them to understand the proceedings and is likely to be more lenient in respect of non-compliance with certain procedural requirements.

Do's and Don'ts

Do:

- If you are thinking of appealing, request extended written reasons either at the conclusion of the full hearing or, at the latest, within 21 days of receipt of the summary of reasons.

- Consider taking specialist legal advice on the prospects of a successful appeal.

- Lodge your appeal within 42 days of the date upon which it is recorded that the extended written reasons were sent to the parties.

- Consider whether it is necessary to apply for the chairman's note of evidence.

- Consider what directions you require before the PHD.

Don't:

- Forget to read carefully the guidance notes sent to appellants and respondents by the EAT.

- Allow frustration with a tribunal's decision to cloud your judgement on the prospects of a successful appeal.

29.

New Developments: the Employment Act 2002

Introduction [29.1]

After a period of relative inertia, last year witnessed an explosion of activity in the field of employment law reform. Major changes included the introduction of the ACAS voluntary arbitration scheme in May 2001 (see **CHAPTER 4 – OPTIONS FOR AVOIDING TRIBUNALS**), and the long awaited implementation of the *Employment Tribunals (Constitution and Rules of Procedure) Regulations 2001 (SI 2001/1170)*, which came into effect on 16 July 2001. The ACAS arbitration scheme provides an alternative mechanism for resolution of certain types of unfair dismissal claims. All parties must consent to having the dispute determined by arbitration. The scheme has enjoyed limited initial success, with only five cases being referred to arbitration in 2001. Potential advantages of arbitration include relatively low costs, speed of resolution and confidentiality of the proceedings.

It is clear, however, that these changes, although undoubtedly significant, are only the first steps in what looks set to be a wide-ranging overhaul of the entire approach to employment law. The need to 'modernise' the approach to employment disputes was identified in two Government commissioned reports published in the summer of last year.

The first, a report written by Sir Andrew Leggatt, assessed the practice and procedure of tribunals generally. Although this report was not concerned exclusively with employment tribunals, it made a number of practical recommendations aimed at improving employment dispute resolution and the manner in which employment tribunals operated.

The second, a consultation paper issued by the Department of Trade and Industry (DTI), proposed a range of measures aimed at promoting the resolution of disputes in the workplace as well as improving the performance of employment tribunals.

Although the two reports do not reach identical conclusions with respect to employment tribunals, there is a considerable overlap between many of the recommendations put forward. The central theme of both reports is, in fact, remarkably similar, and focuses on shifting the obligation of dispute resolution away from the tribunals back to the employers and the work place. A notable divergence can be seen in Leggatt's recommendation that all claims ought to be referred to ACAS before proceeding to the tribunal, and the DTI's proposal that claims limited to breach of contract, deduction of wages and redundancy pay ought to be 'fast-tracked' without any ACAS involvement.

Following the publication of these reports, the Government unveiled the Employment Act in November 2001. The Act received Royal Assent in July 2002 (*Employment Act 2002 (EA 2002)*), but it remains difficult to say precisely when the various statutory changes are likely to come into force. The current view is that it is *unlikely* that substantial parts of the Act will commence before early to mid 2003. This view is supported by the fact that the Government intends to ensure that there is a consultation process, involving a variety of interested groups (ACAS, the Law Society, bodies representing employers and employees etc), prior to most of the provisions coming into force. For an up to date view on when relevant provisions of the Act are due to come into force, readers should contact the Department of Trade and Industry (see CHAPTER 2 – TROUBLE AHEAD? (**2.3**)).

The Act contains a number of provisions concerning dispute resolution in the workplace, together with some significant proposed changes to tribunal practice and procedure. There are also a number of provisions relating to maternity and paternity rights. The major relevant proposals contained in the Act are outlined below.

Dispute resolution: statutory disciplinary and grievance procedures [29.2]

The general thrust of the Act focuses on resolving disputes before they reach the tribunal. The legislators look to employers to help achieve this goal by requiring them, irrespective of the size of the business (*section 36* of the Act removes the existing exemption for small businesses (i e businesses with less than 20 employees), to include statutory dismissal and disciplinary procedures (DDP) and grievance procedures (GP) into every employee's contract of employment).

The fact that it is intended for both the DDP and the GP to be incorporated into all contracts of employment (*section 30* of the Act – this effectively amounts to a reversal – *Johnson v. Unisys Ltd [2001] ICR 480 (HL)*) means that a failure by an employer to respect these procedures will give rise to a claim for wrongful dismissal. Consequently, even where an employee lacks sufficient time in employment to bring a claim for unfair dismissal, they can still challenge any failure to follow and/or implement the procedures.

A copy of both the DDP and the GP, as set out in *Schedule 2* of the *EA 2002* can be found at **29.12**.

These statutory procedures will amount to a *minimum* standard that employers will be required to adhere to when dealing with their employees. Consequently, for employers who already have effective procedures in place (i e procedures that are consistent with the ACAS code or good practice), introducing the new statutory procedures is unlikely to require any significant change to the existing system.

That said, it is likely that most existing procedures will have to be amended to reflect the fact that, under the new procedures, both the disciplinary and the grievance process need to be initiated in writing. Oral warnings or complaints will no longer suffice. Instead, both employee and employers will be required to set our their grounds of complaint in written statements; employers will need to draft a statement of grounds for action and an invitation to meeting, and employees will have to complete a statement of grievance.

It is important to note that the requirement to use the procedures applies equally to employers and employees alike. Indeed, under the new proposals, an employee who fails to use their employer's GP, within the required time limits, is likely to find themselves prevented from issuing a claim before an employment tribunal.

Failure to comply with procedures – automatically unfair dismissal [29.3]

Any failure by an employer, either to implement the statutory procedures or to comply with the procedures, will render a dismissal 'automatically' unfair – *section 34* of the *EA 2002* inserts into *section 98A* of the *Employment Rights Act 1996 (ERA 1996)* provisions to this effect. So, for example, where an employer refuses to allow an employee to appeal an initial disciplinary decision, this will render a dismissal automatically unfair. In these circumstances, whether or not the dismissal is unfair for any other reason, an employee will be entitled to a minimum award equivalent to four weeks' pay; save if this would result in injustice to the employer.

It is further intended that the introduction of the notion of automatically unfair dismissals will be accompanied by a reversal of the rule established in *Polkey v A E Dayton Services Ltd [1988] ICR 142*. In practice, this will mean that an employee will not be regarded as unfairly dismissed, on account of a failure to follow a procedure not required by the DDP, where it can be established that the employee would have been dismissed even if the procedure in question had been followed.

Employee's right to bring a claim [29.4]

Under *section 33(2)* of the Act, where an employee fails to comply with the requirements of the GP they will be unable to bring a claim before an employment tribunal. In addition, an employee will be unable to present a complaint to an employment tribunal where:

- less than 28 days have elapsed since the date on which the requirement was complied with; and

- the requirement was complied with more than one month after the end of the original time limit for making the complaint. So, for example, where an employee completed their statement of grievance, alleging an unlawful deduction of wages, four and half months after the date of the deduction they would be time barred from presenting a complaint before a tribunal. The time limit for bringing a claim for unlawful deduction from wages is three months from date of deduction (*ERA 1996, s 23*).

The notion that a failure to use an in-house GP may deny an employee access to the tribunals is undoubtedly controversial and it is submitted that, in practice, any restriction on an employee's right to issue proceedings is likely to be accompanied by a statutory term giving tribunals a wide discretion as to whether to allow an employee to present a claim directly to the tribunal (perhaps along the lines of the 'just and equitable' test).

Adjustment of awards [29.5]

The Act also envisages a change in the approach to awards of compensation (*EA 2002, s 31*). In order to further encourage parties to comply with and to use the statutory procedures, tribunals will have the power to increase or decrease awards by between 10%–50%, depending on which party has failed to comply with the procedures and the extent of any non-compliance. Tribunals will determine which party is 'wholly or mainly' to blame for the failure to comply with a requirement of the procedure and reduce or increase an award accordingly.

A finding of procedural non-compliance will normally result in a 10% increase or decrease of the award. In appropriate cases, where a tribunal considers that it is 'just and equitable' to do so, the award may be further reduced or increased up to a maximum of 50%. In exceptional circumstances, a tribunal has the discretion not to adjust the award or to order such lesser percentage as it considers just and equitable.

Written terms and conditions [29.6]

The Act also includes measures designed to ensure greater consistency of written statements of terms and conditions of employment. In the future, it is proposed that employers will be compelled to provide employees with a written copy of the statement of terms and conditions (which must set out the DDP and GP) within two months of the employee starting work. This will apply to all employers irrespective of their size. The current exemption enjoyed by employers with less than 20 employees will be removed.

Any term in an employment contract that purports to limit the operation of the DDP or GP will be null and void. However, existing in-house grievance procedures, in so far as they are not inconsistent with the requirements of the statutory procedures, will remain lawful and unaffected by the implementation of either the DDP or GP (*EA 2002, s 30(3)*). This reflects the fact that the DDP and GP are merely designed to provide the minimum procedural safeguards.

Where, in proceedings relating to some other complaint are issued, it transpires that an employer has failed to provide written particulars of employment or particulars of changes of employment, a tribunal must make an award. It is important to stress that this is not intended to create a separate,'stand alone' right to bring a claim. Indeed, a tribunal can only consider making an award, under this section where, in relation to *other* proceedings, it has:

- found in favour of the employee but makes no award with respect to those proceedings; or

- found in favour of the employee and makes an award with respect to those proceedings.

Under the first limb, a tribunal must make an award of two weeks' pay where an employer has failed to provide written particulars of employment, and one week's pay where the employer has failed to provide particulars of change of employment.

Where, on the other hand, an award has been made, a tribunal must increase the award by a minimum of 5% of the award (or two weeks'/one week's pay, whichever is greater). There is also a discretionary power to increase the award up to a maximum of 25% where it is considered 'just and equitable.'

Time limits [29.7]

The obligation on parties to first try and resolve the dispute using in-house procedures is likely to lead to an extension to the time limits within which claims must be presented to a tribunal (*EA 2002, s 32*). Although not specifically dealt with in the Act, it would appear that the Government intends to allow parties an extra three months to bring a claim, in circumstances where the statutory procedures have not yet been completed. There is also a suggestion that parties may be allowed to agree to extend the time for presenting a claim in circumstances where the internal appeal has not run it's course for up to a further three months.

Section 32 of the Act specifically provides for the creation of secondary legislation to implement the necessary changes to time limits for bringing proceedings.

Costs [29.8]

The Act introduces two significant changes to the rules on costs. First, *section 22(1)* creates a power to award costs directly against the representatives of a party where it is considered that the manner in which the proceedings were conducted was unsatisfactory. In addition, a tribunal can disallow part or all of the representatives' costs (as between themselves and their client) on similar grounds. Consequently, in circumstances where in the past a tribunal would have refrained from punishing a party for the faults of their representatives, the new rules will enable it to penalise directly those who are at fault.

The second major change is the widening of the ambit of recoverable costs so as to allow recovery of a sum reflecting the time spent in preparing for a case.

The President of the employment tribunal: practice directions [29.9]

Section 27 of the Act empowers the President to issue practice directions determining the procedure of employment tribunals. This will enable the President to give guidance as to the correct approach in areas where the law is uncertain and in relation to a wide range of procedural matters, for example the preparation of bundles and format of witness statements.

Maternity and paternity leave [29.10]

Broadly speaking the Act contains provisions aimed at improving the existing arrangements for statutory maternity leave. It is intended that these improvements will be in force in 2003. The main provisions in the Act include measures aimed at ensuring that:

- working mothers to have the right to six months' paid and an additional six months' unpaid maternity leave;

- working fathers to have the right to two weeks' paid paternity leave;

- adoptive parents to have the right to six months' paid and an additional six months' unpaid leave;

- there is an increase in Statutory Maternity Pay from £62 to £100 per week to be implemented in 2003;

- employers are reimbursed some of the maternity, paternity and adoption payments they make, with small employees (not yet defined) eligible to recover all payments and potentially being entitled to additional payments over and above those made to their employees.

Miscellaneous provisions [29.11]

Lastly, there are a number of rather technical changes to employment tribunal procedure. In brief, the major proposals include:

- broadening the power of employment tribunals to determine proceedings without a hearing by removing the need for consent of the parties (*EA 2002, s 26*);

- the possibilities for ACAS conciliation being made available whenever the employment tribunal adjourns a case so as to give the parties an opportunity to settle (*EA 2002, s 24*).

Schedule 2, section 29: statutory dispute resolution procedure [29.12]

Part 1 – dismissal and disciplinary procedures

Chapter 1: standard procedure

Step 1: statement of grounds for action and invitation to meeting

1.

(1)   The employer must set out in writing the employee's alleged conduct or characteristics, or other circumstances, which lead it

to contemplate dismissing or taking disciplinary action against the employee.

(2) The employer must send a copy of the statement to the employee and invite the employee to attend a meeting to discuss the matter.

Step 2: meeting

2.

(1) The meeting must take place before action is taken, except in the case where the disciplinary action consists of suspension.

(2) The meeting must not take place unless:

(a) the employer has informed the employee what the basis was for including in the statement under paragraph 1(1) the ground or grounds given in it; and

(b) the employee has had a reasonable opportunity to consider his response to that information.

(3) The employee must take all reasonable steps to attend the meeting.

(4) After the meeting, the employer must inform the employee of its decision and notify them of the right to appeal against the decision if they are not satisfied with it.

Step 3: appeal

3.

(1) If the employee does wish to appeal, they must inform the employer.

(2) If the employee informs the employer of their wish to appeal, the employer must invite them to attend a further meeting.

(3) The employee must take all reasonable steps to attend the meeting.

(4) The appeal meeting need not take place before the dismissal or disciplinary action takes effect.

(5) After the appeal meeting, the employer must inform the employee of its final decision.

Chapter 2: modified procedure

Step 1: statement of grounds for action

4.   The employer must:

(a) set out in writing:

(i) the employee's alleged misconduct which has led to the dismissal;

(ii) what the basis was for thinking at the time of the dismissal that the employee was guilty of the alleged misconduct; and

(iii) the employee's right to appeal against dismissal.

(b) send a copy of the statement to the employee.

Step 2: appeal

5.

(1)   If the employee does wish to appeal, they must inform the employer.

(2)   If the employee informs the employer of their wish to appeal, the employer must invite them to attend a meeting.

(3)   The employee must take all reasonable steps to attend the meeting.

(4)   After the appeal meeting, the employer must inform the employee of its final decision.

Part 2 – grievance procedures

Chapter 1: standard procedure

Step 1: statement of grievance

6.   The employee must set out the grievance in writing and send the statement or a copy of it to the employer.

Step 2: meeting

7.

(1)   The employer must invite the employee to attend a meeting to discuss the grievance.

(2)   The meeting must not take place unless:

    (a) the employee has informed the employer what the basis for the grievance was when they made the statement under paragraph 6; and

    (b) the employer has had a reasonable opportunity to consider its response to that information.

(3)   The employee must take all reasonable steps to attend the meeting.

(4)   After the meeting, the employer must inform the employee of its decision as to its response to the grievance and notify them of the right to appeal against the decision if they are not satisfied with it.

Step 3: appeal

8.

(1)   If the employee does wish to appeal, they must inform the employer.

(2)   If the employee informs the employer of their wish to appeal, the employer must invite them to attend a further meeting.

(3)   The employee must take all reasonable steps to attend the meeting.

(4)   After the appeal meeting, the employer must inform the employee of its final decision.

Chapter 2: modified procedure

Step 1: statement of grievance

9.   The employee must:

    (a) set out in writing:

        (i) the grievance in writing; and

        (ii) the basis for it; and

    (b) send the statement or a copy of it to the employer.

Step 2: response

10.   The employer must set out his response in writing and send a copy to the employee.

Part 3 – general requirements

Introductory

11.   The following requirements apply to each of the procedures set out above (so far as applicable).

Timetable

12.   Each step and action under the procedure must be taken without unreasonable delay.

Meetings

13.

(1)   Timing and location of meetings must be reasonable.

(2)   Meetings must be conducted in a manner that enables both employer and employee to explain their cases.

(3)   In the case of appeal meetings which are not the first meeting, the employer should, as far as is reasonably practicable, be represented by a more senior manager than attended the first meeting (unless the most senior manager attended that meeting).

Appendix I: Claims a Tribunal Can Hear

Unfair Dismissal

STATUTE	COMPLAINT	QUALIFYING EMPLOYMENT	TIME LIMIT
Transfer of Undertaking (Protection of Employment) Regulations 1981			
Regulation 8	Unfair dismissal arising from business transfer.	1 year	3 months from Effective Date of Termination (EDT)[a]
Trade Union and Labour Relations (Consolidation) Act 1992	*Unfair dismissal for:*		
s 152	reasons relating to union membership.	None	3 months from EDT[a]
s 153	reasons underlying selection for redundancy relating to union membership.	None	3 months from EDT[a]

STATUTE	COMPLAINT	QUALIFYING EMPLOYMENT	TIME LIMIT
s 238(a)	participating in official industrial action.	None	6 months from date of dismissal – this is either: i) date of employer's notice or ii) where no notice the EDT[a]
sch A1 s 161	reasons arising from a claim for union recognition.	None	3 months from EDT[a]
s 161	request for interim relief in s 152 application (see above).	None	7 days from EDT[c]
Employment Rights Act 1996 (ERA 1996)			
s 92(1)/s 93/s 97	Written statement of reasons for dismissal.	1 year	3 months from EDT[a]
s 94/s 95	Unfair dismissal.	1 year	3 months from EDT[a]
	Unfair dismissal for:		
s 99	reasons relating to maternity, pregnancy/childbirth, or parental/ dependant care leave.	None	3 months from EDT[a]
s 100	health and safety reasons.	None	3 months from EDT[a]
s 101	refusing to work on Sunday (applies to protected shop/betting workers).	None	3 months from EDT[a]

STATUTE	COMPLAINT	QUALIFYING EMPLOYMENT	TIME LIMIT
s 101(a)	reasons arising from *Working Time Regulations 1998*.	None	3 months from EDT[a]
s 102	carrying out the functions of occupational pension trustee.	None	3 months from EDT[a]
s 103	carrying out the functions of an employee representative.	None	3 months from EDT[a]
s 103(a)	whistle blowing (protected disclosures) asserting a statutory right.	None	3 months from EDT[a]
s 104	asserting a statutory right.	None	3 months from EDT[a]
s 104(a)	securing right to national minimum wage.	None	3 months from EDT[a]
s 104(b)	securing benefit of tax credits.	None	3 months from EDT[a]
s 108(2)/s 64(2)	reasons relating to treatment whilst on medical suspension.	1 month	3 months from EDT[a]
s 128	provides for *interim* relief in dismissal cases relating to specific health and safety issues.	None	7 days from EDT[c]

STATUTE	COMPLAINT	QUALIFYING EMPLOYMENT	TIME LIMIT
Consultation of Employees Regulations 1999			
Regulation 28	Unfair dismissal connected to establishment of/participation in European Works Council, or information/consultation procedure.	None	3 months from EDT[a]
Part-time Workers (Prevention of Less Favourable Treatment) Regulations 2000			
Regulation 7	Unfair dismissal relating to status as part-time worker.	None	3 months form EDT[a]
Wrongful Dismissal/Contract Claims			
Contract claims	Employee complaint to employment tribunal.	None	3 months from EDT/or last day that employee worked[a]
Contract claims	Employer counterclaim to employment tribunal.	None	6 weeks from receipt of employee's claim[a]

STATUTE	COMPLAINT	QUALIFYING EMPLOYMENT	TIME LIMIT
Employment Rights Act 1996 (ERA 1996)	*Unlawful Deduction from Wages*		
s 23	Unlawful deduction from wages.	None	3 months from date of deduction/final one in series[a]
Equal Pay Act 1970 (EPA 1970)	*Discrimination Claims*		
s 2	Breach of male/female implied equality clause – equal pay claim.	None	6 months from end of employment[1]
Sex Discrimination Act 1975 (SDA 1975)			
s 63	Sex discrimination on the basis of gender or against married persons.	None	3 months from date of act complained of. In limited circumstances to the end of period over which the act extends[b]
s 68	Right to appeal against a non-discrimination notice.	None	6 weeks from service of the notice
s 72	Proceedings brought by Equal Opportunities Commission against persons who instruct / pressure others to discriminate or against discriminatory advertising.	None	6 months from date of act complained of[b]
s 77	Assertion that term of contract is void because contravenes *SDA 1975 /EPA 1970.*	None	None[2]

STATUTE	COMPLAINT	QUALIFYING EMPLOYMENT	TIME LIMIT
Race Relations Act 1976 (RRA 1996)			
s 54	Discrimination on the basis of race.	None	3 months from date of act complained of[b]
s 59	Right to appeal against a non-discrimination notice.	None	6 weeks from service of the notice
s 63	Proceedings brought by Commission for Racial Equality (CRE) against persons who instruct/pressure others to discriminate or against discriminatory advertising.	None	6 months from date of act complained of[b]
s 64	Preliminary proceedings by CRE as above.	None	6 months from date of accomplained of[b]
Disability Discrimination Act 1995 (DDA 1995)			
s 8	Discrimination on the basis of disability.	None	3 months from date of act complained of[b]
Equal Treatment Directive 76/207			
Art 5	Sex discrimination claim under EC law.	None	3 months from date of act complained of[3]

STATUTE	COMPLAINT	QUALIFYING EMPLOYMENT	TIME LIMIT
EC Treaty and Equal Pay Directive 75/117			
Art 141 and Art 1	Equal pay/value claim under EC law.	None	3/6 months respectively from date of act complained of[3]
Maternity/Parental Rights Claims			
Employment Rights Act 1996 (ERA 1996)			
s 48	Detriment sustained as a result of pregnancy, maternity leave/parental leave.	1 month to act[a]	3 months from date of act /failure to act[a].
s 57/57(b)	Failure to allow paid time off for ante-natal care.	None	3 months from date of refusal/failure to act[a].
s 70	Failure to offer alternative work/pay remuneration during maternity suspension[4].	1 month	3 months from date of act /failure to act[a]
s 71	Failure to allow ordinary maternity leave (18 weeks)/to allow employee to return to same job etc.	None	not applicable
s 73	Failure to allow additional maternity leave (29 weeks from the week of childbirth).	1 year	not applicable

STATUTE	COMPLAINT	QUALIFYING EMPLOYMENT	TIME LIMIT
s 80	Failure to allow/unreasonable postponement of parental leave.	1 year	3 months from date of refusal/ failure to act[a]
Maternity and Parental Leave etc Regulations 1999			
Regulation 13/14	Failure to allow 13 weeks unpaid parental leave (per child).	1 year	3 months from date of refusal/ failure to act[a]
Regulation 18	Failure to allow: i) employee after maternity leave/parental leave of more than 4 weeks to return to same/suitable alternative job if not practicable, or ii) employee after less than 4 weeks parental leave to return to same job.	None	Not applicable
Time off Work			
Safety Representatives and Safety Committees Regulations 1977			
s 11	Failure to allow safety representative paid time off to perform his functions.	None	3 months from date of refusal/ failure to act[a]

STATUTE	COMPLAINT	QUALIFYING EMPLOYMENT	TIME LIMIT
Trade Union and Labour Relations (Consolidation) Act 1992			
s 168/169	Failure to allow paid time off for union duties.	None	3 months from date of refusal/failure to act[a]
s 170	Failure to allow unpaid time off for union activities.		None 3 months from date of refusal/failure to act[a]
Employment Rights Act 1996 (ERA 1996)			
s 48	Detriment sustained as a result of i) health and safety, ii) refusal to work Sunday, iii) pension trustee, iv) employee representative v) time off for study, vi) dependant care leave.	None	3 months from date of act/failure to act[a]
s 51	Failure to allow unpaid time off for public duties.	None	3 months from date of refusal/failure to act[a]
s 54	Failure to allow paid time off to look for work to an employee who has been given notice of redundancy.	2 years	3 months from date of refusal/failure to act[a]
s 57(b)	Failure to allow unpaid time off for dependant care.	None	3 months from date of refusal/failure to act[a]

STATUTE	COMPLAINT	QUALIFYING EMPLOYMENT	TIME LIMIT
s 60	Failure to allow trustee of pension scheme paid time off to perform their functions.	None	3 months from date of refusal/failure to act[a]
s 63	Failure to allow an employee representative paid time off to perform their functions.	None	3 months from date of refusal/failure to act[a]
s 63(c)	Failure to allow 16/17 year old employee paid time off to undertake training that will lead to a prescribed qualification.	None	3 months from date of act/date when time off should have been allowed[a]
Health and Safety (Consultation with Employees) Regulations 1996			
s 11	Failure to allow safety representative paid time off to perform their functions/stand for election.	None	3 months from date of refusal/failure to act[a]
Trade Union and Labour Relations (Consolidation) Act 1992			
s 170	Failure to allow unpaid time off for union activities time off to perform their functions.	None	3 months from date of refusal/failure to act[a]

STATUTE	COMPLAINT	QUALIFYING EMPLOYMENT	TIME LIMIT
Employment Rights Act 1996 (ERA 1996)			
s 45(a)	Detriment sustained as a result of Working Time Regulations 1998.	None	3 months from date of act/failure to act[a]
Working Time Regulations 1998[5]			
Regulation 10	Failure to allow statutory daily rest.	None	3 months from date right should have been allowed[a]
Regulation 11	Failure to allow statutory weekly rest.	None	3 months from date rest should have been allowed to begin[a]
Regulation 12	Failure to allow statutory rest break.	None	3 months from date right should have been allowed[a]
Regulation 13	Failure to allow annual leave to be taken.	None[6]	3 months from date leave should have been allowed to begin[a]
Regulation 14	Failure to be paid in lieu of untaken holiday on termination of employment.	None	3 months from date payment should have been made[a]
Regulation 16	Failure to be paid for annual leave.	None	3 months from date payment should have been made[a]

STATUTE	COMPLAINT	QUALIFYING EMPLOYMENT	TIME LIMIT
Regulation 24	Failure to allow compensatory rest where collective agreement to work during rest period.	None	3 months from date right should have been allowed[a]
	Other Trade Union Related Claims		
Trade Union and Labour Relations (Consolidation) Act 1992			
s 66	Unjustifiable disciplining by the union.	None	3 months from date of union determination[d]
s 67	Compensation for unjustifiable disciplining and failure by union to revoke determination (EAT).	None	after 4 weeks and before 6 months after tribunal decision[c]
s 68	Unauthorised deduction of union subscription.	None	3 months from date payment from which deduction made[a]
s 137	Refusal of employment on grounds relating to union membership.	None	3 months from date of refusal/act complained of[a]
s 138	Refusal of service employment agency on grounds relating to union membership.		None 3 months from date of refusal/act complained of[a]
s 146	Detriment sustained due to union membership/activities.	None	3 months from date of act/failure to act[a]

Appendix I: Claims a Tribunal Can Hear

STATUTE	COMPLAINT	QUALIFYING EMPLOYMENT	TIME LIMIT
s 174	Unlawful exclusion/expulsion from/by union.	None	6 months from date of expulsion[a]
s 176	Compensation for unlawful exclusion/expulsion from/by union (EAT).	None	after 4 weeks and before 6 months after tribunal decision[c]
TUPE/Redundancy Claims			
Transfer of Undertaking (Protection of Employment) Regulations 1981 (TUPE)			
Regulation 10	Failure to consult with employees representatives in relation to business transfer.	None	3 months from completion of transfer[a]
Regulation 11	Employer's failure to comply with compensation order made by tribunal under *Regulation 11*.	None	3 months from date of tribunal's order[a]
Trade Union and Labour Relations (Consolidation) Act 1992			
s 189.	Failure to consult with employees representatives in relation to redundancy.	None	prior to dismissal/3 months from date dismissal takes effect[a]
s 192	Failure to pay remuneration due under protective award.	None	3 months from date of last day of failure to act[a]

STATUTE	COMPLAINT	QUALIFYING EMPLOYMENT	TIME LIMIT
Employment Rights Act 1996 (ERA 1996)			
s 163	Right to pay the whole/part of redundancy pay.	2 years	6 months from 'relevant date'[7]-d
	Other Claims		
Employment Rights Act 1996 (ERA 1996)			
s 34	Failure to pay the whole or part of guarantee payment.	1 month	3 months from date for which payment claimed[a]
s 11	Failure to provide written particulars of employment.	2 months	3 months from date on which employment ended[a]
s 11	Failure to provide itemised pay statement employment.	None	3 months from date on which employment ended[a]
s 70	Failure to offer alternative work/pay remuneration during medical suspension.	1 month	3 months from date refusal/ failure to act[a]

STATUTE	COMPLAINT	QUALIFYING EMPLOYMENT	TIME LIMIT
National Minimum Wage Act 1998 (NMW)			
s 11	Failure of employer to produce relevant records/allow employee to inspect them where employee suspects that they are/have been paid less than NMW.	None	3 months 14 days from date employer receives production notice from employee
s 24	Detriment sustained where employer attempts to avoid provisions of NMW/penalty imposed.	None	3 months from date of act/failure to act[a]
Human Rights Act 1998			
s 7	Public authority acts in a way that is incompatible with a Convention right.	None	1 year from date of act complained of – time limit may be extended for such period as is equitable having regard to all circumstances
Employment Relations Act 1999			
s 11	Refusal/threatened refusal to allow employee to be accompanied at disciplinary hearing/postpone hearing to allow employee to be represented.	None	3 months from date of refusal/threat of refusal[a]

STATUTE	COMPLAINT	QUALIFYING EMPLOYMENT	TIME LIMIT
Tax Credits Act 1999			
s 2	Detriment sustained where employer attempts to prevent employee securing tax credit/on the basis that employee entitled to tax credit.	None	3 months from date of act/ failure to act[a]
Part-time Workers (Prevention of Less Favourable Treatment) Regulations 2000			
Regulation 5	Less favourable treatment arising due to status as part-time worker.	None	3 months from act/ failure to act complained of[b]
Regulation 6	Failure to provide part-time worker with written statement of reasons for less favourable treatment.	None	None

a. The tribunal can extend the time limit where they consider that it was 'not reasonably practicable' to present the complaint in time.

b. The tribunal can extend time limit where they consider it 'just and equitable' to do so.

c. Time limit cannot be extended – save perhaps where there is evidence of fraud by the employer causing employee to miss time limit and giving rise to real injustice – see *Grimes v Sutton London Brought Council [1973] ICR 240.*

d. The time limit may be extended if it was 'not reasonably practicable' to present the complaint in time *or* where the delay arose due to reasonable attempt to pursue internal appeal etc.

1. The Court of Appeal indicated this time limit in *Preston and & ors v (1) Wolverhampton Healthcare NHS Trust, (2) SoS for Health and ors [1997] IRLR 233.*

2. See *SDA 1986, s 6 4(A)*.

3. There are no expressly stated time limits prescribed by EU law, however, it has repeatedly been held that time limits will be analogous to those under national law – see for example *Biggs v Somerset County Council [1996] ICR 364*.

4. There is a similar right to remuneration if suspended on medical grounds.

5. All these claims are brought under *regulation 30 of the Working Time Regulations 1998 (SI 1998/1833)*.

6. *Working Time (Amendment) Regulations 2001 (SI 2001/3256)* abolished 13-week qualifying period of employment from the 25 October 2001.

7. The 'relevant date' is defined in *s 164 of ERA 1996* as the date when:

   i) when the payment has been agreed and paid; or

   ii) an employee made a written claim for payment; or

   iii) a question as to the right/unfair dismissal referred to the tribunal.

   In certain restricted circumstances the time limit can be extended for a further six months.

Appendix II: Questionnaire and Response (SD 74)

Issued by The Department for Education and Employment

1046/1

Sex Discrimination Act 1975: The Questions Procedure

This booklet is in four parts:

Part 1: Introduction *(SD 74)*.

Part 2: Questionnaire of the person aggrieved: The Complainant *(SD 74(1)(a))*.

Part 3: Reply: The Respondent *(SD74(1)(b))*.

Appendix: Notes on the scope of the Sex Discrimination Act 1975.

Part 1: Introduction

General

*   The purpose of this introduction is to explain the questions procedure under Section 74 of the Sex Discrimination Act 1975 *(the prescribed forms, time limits for serving questions and manner of service of questions and replies under section 74 are specified in the Sex Discrimination (Questions and Replies) Order 1975 No. 2048)*.

*   The procedure is intended to help a person *(referred to in this booklet as the complainant)* who thinks he/she has been discriminated against by another *(the respondent)* to obtain information from that person about the treatment in question in order to:

    *   decide whether or not to bring legal proceedings; and
    *   if proceedings are brought, to present his/her complaint in the most effective way.

*   We have devised a questionnaire which the complainant can send to the respondent. There is also a matching reply form for use by the respondent - both are included in this booklet. The questionnaire and reply form are designed to assist both the complainant and respondent to identify information which is relevant to the complaint. It is not obligatory for the questionnaire and reply form to be used: the exchange of questions and replies may be conducted, for example by letter.

*   The complainant and respondent should read this booklet thoroughly before completion and retain a copy of the information supplied.

*   Guidance for the complainant on the preparation of the questionnaire is set out in Part 2.

*   Guidance for the respondent on the use of the reply form is set out in Part 3.

*   The Appendix explains the main provisions of the Sex Discrimination Act 1975.

*   If you require further information about the Act it can be found in the various leaflets published by the Equal Opportunities Commission (EOC) and also in the detailed Guide to the Sex Discrimination Act 1975. You can obtain copies of the leaflets and the Guide, as well as further copies of this booklet *(by quoting "Form SD74")* free of charge from:

The Equal Opportunities Commission
Overseas House
Quay Street
MANCHESTER
M3 3HN
Telephone: 0161 833 9244

DfEE Publications
PO Box 5050
Sudbury
SUFFOLK
CO10 6QZ
Telephone   0845 6022260
Fax: 0845 6033360
Text 'phone   0845 6055560
e-mail DfEE@PrologCS.Demon.co.uk

and Employment Service Jobcentres or Citizens Advice Bureaux.

Part 1: Introduction *(continued)*

How the questions procedure can benefit both parties

- The procedure can benefit both the complainant and the respondent in the following ways:
  - if the respondent's answers satisfy the complainant and the treatment was not unlawful discrimination, there will be no need for legal proceedings.
  - If the respondent's answers do not satisfy the complainant, they should help to identify what is agreed and what is in dispute between the parties. For example, the answers, should reveal whether the parties disagree on the facts of the case, or, if they agree on the facts whether they disagree on how the Act applies. In some cases, this may lead to a settlement of the grievance, making legal proceedings unnecessary.
  - If it turns out that the complainant institutes proceedings against the respondent, the proceedings should be that much simpler because the matters in dispute will have been identified in advance.

What happens if the respondent does not reply or replies evasively

- The respondent cannot be compelled to reply to the complainant's questions. However, if the respondent deliberately, and without reasonable excuse, does not reply within a reasonable period, or replies in an evasive or ambiguous way, the respondent's position may be adversely affected should the complainant bring proceedings against him/her. The respondent's attention is drawn to these possible consequences in the note at the end of the questionnaire.

Period within which the questionnaire must be served on the respondent

- There are different time limits within which a questionnaire must be served in order to be admissible under the questions procedure in any ensuing legal proceedings. Which time limit applies depends on whether the complaint would be under the employment, training and related provisions of the Act *(in which case the proceedings would be before an industrial tribunal)* or whether it would be under the education, goods, facilities and services or premises provisions *(in which case proceedings would be before a county court or, in Scotland, sheriff court)*.

Industrial tribunal proceedings

- In order to be admissible under the questions procedure in any ensuing industrial tribunal proceedings, the complainant's questionnaire must be served on the respondent either:
  - before a complaint about the treatment concerned is made to an industrial tribunal, but not more than 3 months after the treatment in question; or
  - if a complaint has already been made to a tribunal, within 21 days beginning when the complaint was received by the tribunal.

  However, where the complainant has made a complaint to the tribunal and the period of 21 days has expired, a questionnaire may still be served provided the leave of the tribunal is obtained. This may be done by sending a written application to the Secretary of the Tribunal, stating the names of the complainant and the respondent and setting out the grounds of the application. However, every effort should be made to serve the questionnaire within the period of 21 days as the leave of the tribunal to serve the questionnaire after the expiry of the period will not necessarily be obtained.

Use of the questions and replies in industrial tribunal proceedings

- If you decide to make (or have *already made*) a complaint to an industrial tribunal about the treatment concerned and if you intend to use your questions and the reply *(if any)* as evidence in the proceedings, you are advised to send copies of your questions and any reply to the Secretary of the Tribunals before the date of the hearing. This should be done as soon as the documents are available. If they are available at the time you submit your complaint to a tribunal, send the copies with your complaint to the Secretary of the Tribunal.

County or sheriff court proceedings

- In order to be admissible under the questions procedure in any ensuing county or sheriff court proceedings, the complainant's questionnaire must be served on the respondent before proceedings in respect of the treatment concerned is brought, but not more than 6 months after the treatment'- However, where proceedings have been brought, a questionnaire may still be served provided the leave of the court has been obtained. In the case of county court proceedings, this may be done by obtaining form Ex23 from the county court office, completing it and sending it to the Registrar and the respondent, or, by applying to the Registrar at the pre-trial review. In the case of sheriff court proceedings, this may be done by making an application to a sheriff.

¹ *Where the respondent is a body in charge of a public sector educational establishment, the 6 month period begins when the complaint has been referred to the appropriate Education Minister and 2 months have elapsed or, if this is earlier, the Minister has informed the complainant that he/she requires no more time to consider the matter.*

Part 2

Questionnaire of person aggrieved: The Complainant

Note: • Before filling in this questionnaire, we advise you to prepare what you want to say on a separate piece of paper.
        • If you have insufficient room on the questionnaire for what you want to say, continue on an additional piece of
          paper, which should be sent with the questionnaire to the respondent.

Enter the name of the person to be questioned (the respondent)	To	
Enter the respondent's address	of	

Enter your name (you are the complainant)	1. I	
Enter your address	of	

Please give as much relevant information as you can about the treatment you think may have been unlawful discrimination. Tell us about the circumstances leading up to that treatment and if possible give the date, place and approximate time it happened. You should bear in mind that in question 4 of this questionnaire you will be asking the respondent whether he/she agrees with what you say here.

2.   consider that you may have discriminated against me contrary to the Sex Discrimination Act 1975.

In 3 you are telling the respondent that you think the treatment you have described in 2 may have been unlawful discrimination by them against you. It will help to identify whether there are any legal issues between you and the respondent if you explain why you think the treatment may have been unlawful discrimination.

3.   I consider that this treatment may have been unlawful because:

• You do not have to complete 3. **If you do not wish or are unable to do so, you should delete the word 'because'. If you wish** *to complete 3, but feel you need more information about the Sex Discrimination Act before doing so, see the appendix attached.*

• *If you do decide to complete 3, you may find it useful to indicate what kind of discrimination you think the treatment may have been ie. whether it was:*
  • *direct sex discrimination;*
  • *indirect sex discrimination;*
  • *direct discrimination against a married person;*
  • *indirect discrimination against a married person; or*
  • *victimisation;*
  and which provision of the Act you think may make unlawful the kind of discrimination you think you may have suffered.

Appendix II: Questionnaire and Response (SD 74)

4. Do you agree that the statement in 2 is an accurate description of what happened? It not, in what respect do you disagree or what is your version of what happened?

5. Do you accept that your treatment of me was unlawful discrimination by you against me?
If not:

a) why not?
b) for what reason did I receive the treatment accorded to me?
c) how far did my sex or marital status affect your treatment of me?

6. Other questions *(if appropriate)*:

7. My address for any reply you may wish to give to the questions I have raised is:

on page 3, at question 1 ☐   below ☐   *(Please tick the appropriate box.)*

Signed

Date

Address *(if appropriate)*

How to serve the papers
· We strongly advise that you retain and keep in a safe place, a copy of the completed questionnaire.
· Send the person to be questioned the **whole** of this document either to their usual last known residence or place of business or if you know they are acting through a solicitor, to that address. If your questions *(ie the introduction, the questionnaire as completed by you and the reply form)* are directed at a limited company or other corporate body or a trade union or employer's association, you should send the papers to the secretary or clerk at the registered or principal office. You should be able to find out where this is by enquiring at your public library. However, if you are unable to do so you will have to send the papers to the place where you think it is most likely they will reach the secretary or clerk. It is your responsibility to see that they receive them.
· You can deliver the papers in person or send them by post.
· If you send them by post, we advise you to use the recorded delivery service *(this will provide you with evidence of delivery).*

*By virtue of **section 74** of the Act, this questionnaire and any reply are (subject to the provisions of the section) admissible in proceedings under the Act and a court or tribunal may draw any such inference as is just and equitable from a failure without reasonable excuse to reply within a reasonable period, or from an evasive or equivocal reply, including an inference that the person questioned has discriminated unlawfully.*

— 4 —

Part 3   **The Sex Discrimination Act 1975 Section 74(1)(b)**

Reply: The Respondent

Note: • Before completing this reply form, we advise you to prepare what you want to say on a separate piece of paper.
        • If you have insufficient room on the reply form for what you want to say, continue on an additional piece of paper, which should be attached to the reply form and sent to the complainant.

Enter the name of the person you are replying to (the complainant)   To

Enter the complainant's address   of

Enter your name (you are the respondent)   1. I

Enter your address   of

Complete as appropriate   hereby acknowledge receipt of the questionnaire signed by you and dated

which was served on me on *(date)*

*Please tick relevant box: you are answering question 4 of the complainants questionnaire here. If you **disagree** with the complainant's statement of events, you should explain in what respects you disagree, or your version of what happened, or both.*

2. I agree ☐ that the statement in 2 of the questionnaire is an accurate description of what happened.

I disagree ☐ with the statement in 2 of the questionnaire in that:

Please tick relevant box: you are answering question 5 of the complainant's questionnaire here. If, in answer to paragraph 4 of the questionnaire you have agreed that the statement is an accurate description of what happened but dispute that it is an unlawful description, you should state your reasons. If you have **disagreed** with the facts in the complainant's statement of events, you should answer the question on the basis of your version of the facts. We advise you to look at the attached Appendix and also the relevant parts of the 'Guide to the Sex Discrimination Act 1975'. You will need to know:

- how the Act defines discrimination - see paragraph 1 of the Appendix;
- in what situations the Act makes discrimination unlawful - see paragraph 2 of the Appendix; and
- what exceptions the Act provides - see paragraph 3 of the Appendix.

If you think that an exception (eg. the exception for employment where a person's sex is a genuine occupational qualification) applies to the treatment described in 2 of the complainant's questionnaire, you should mention this in paragraph 3a, with an explanation about why you think the exception applies.

3a. I accept ☐ that my treatment of you was unlawful discrimination by me against you.

I dispute ☐ that my treatment of you was unlawful discrimination by me against you. My reasons for so disputing are:

3b. The reason you received the treatment accorded to you is:

3c Your sex or marital status affected my treatment of you to the following extent:

Replies to the questions in paragraph 6 of the complainant's questionnaire can be entered here.

4.

Delete the whole of this sentence if you have answered all the questions asked in the complainant's questionnaire. If you are unable or unwilling to answer the questions please tick the appropriate box and give your reasons for not answering them.

5. I have deleted *(in whole or in part)* the paragraphs numbered [ ] above

since I am unable [ ]

since I am unwilling [ ] ▶ *to reply to the relevant questions in the complainant's questionnaire for the reasons given in the box below.*

The reply form must be signed and dated. If it is to be signed on behalf of (rather than by) the respondent the person signing should:
· *describe himself / herself eg. 'solicitor acting for (name of respondent)' or 'personnel manager of (name of firm)'; and*
· *give business address (or home address if appropriate)*

Signed [ ]

Address *(if appropriate)*

Date [ ]

How to serve the reply form on the complainant
· If you wish to reply to the questionnaire we strongly advise that you do so without delay.
· You should retain, and keep in a safe place, the questionnaire sent to you and a copy of your reply.
· You can serve the reply either by delivering it in person to the complainant or by sending it by post.
· If you send it by post, we advise you to use the recorded delivery service *(this will provide you with evidence of delivery)*.
· You should send the reply form to the address indicated in paragraph 7 of the complainant's questionnaire.

——————— 8 ———————

Appendix

Notes on the scope of the Sex Discrimination Act 1975

Definitions of discrimination

1. The different kinds of discrimination covered by the Act are summarized below *(the reference numbers in the margin refer to the relevant paragraphs in the Guide to the Sex Discrimination Act 1975)*. Some of the explanations have been written in terms of discrimination against a woman, but the Act applies equally to discrimination against men.

2.4 **Direct sex discrimination** arises where a woman is treated less favorably than a man is *(or would be)* treated
to
2.7 because of her sex.

    Indirect sex discrimination arises where a woman is treated unfavorably because she cannot comply with a condition or requirement which:
- is *(or would be)* applied to men and women equally; and
- is such that the proportion of women who can comply with it is considerably smaller than the proportion of men who can comply with it; and
- is to the detriment of the woman in question because she cannot comply with it; and
- is such that the person applying it cannot show that it is justifiable regardless of the sex of the person to whom it is applied.

2.8 **Direct discrimination against married persons in the employment field** arises where a married person is
to
2.11 treated, in a situation covered by the employment provisions of the Act *(ie- those summarised under Group A in the table on page 10)*, less favourably than an unmarried person of the same sex is *(or would be)* treated **because she or he is married.**

    Indirect discrimination against married persons in the employment field arises where a married person is treated, in a situation covered by the employment provisions of the Act, unfavourably because she or he cannot comply with a condition or requirement which:
- is *(or would be)* applied to married and unmarried persons equally; and
- is such that the proportion of married persons who can comply with it is considerably smaller than the proportion of unmarried persons of the same sex who comply with it; and
- is to the detriment of tile married person in question because she or he cannot comply with it; and
- is such that the person applying it cannot show it to be justifiable irrespective of the marital status of the person to whom it is applied.

2.12 **Victimisation** arises where a person is treated less favourably than other persons *(of either sex)* are *(or would be)* treated because the person has done *(or intends to do or is suspected of having done or intending to do)* any of the following:
- brought proceedings under the Act or the Equal Pay Act; or
- given evidence or information in connection with proceedings brought under either Act; or
- done anything else by reference to either Act (eg. given information to the Equal Opportunities Commission); or
- made an allegation that someone acted unlawfully under either Act.
Victimisation does not, however, occur where the reason for the less favourable treatment is an allegation which was false and not made in good faith.

Unlawful discrimination

2. The provisions of the Act which make discrimination unlawful are indicated in the table over the page. Those in Group A are the employment provisions, for the purposes of which discrimination means direct sex discrimination, indirect sex discrimination, direct discrimination against married persons, indirect discrimination against married persons, and victimisation. Complaints about discrimination which is unlawful under these provisions must be made to an industrial tribunal. For detailed information about these provisions see chapter 3 of the **Guide to the Sex Discrimination Act 1975**. For the purposes of the provisions in Group B, discrimination means direct sex discrimination, indirect sex discrimination and victimisation, but not direct or indirect discrimination against married persons. Complaints about discrimination which is unlawful under these provisions must be made to a county court or, in Scotland, a sheriff court. For detailed information about these provisions see chapters 4 and 5 of the **Guide.**

Exceptions

3. Details of exceptions to the requirements of the Act not to discriminate maybe found in the **Guide.** The exceptions applying to the employment field are described in chapter 3; those applying to the educational field, in chapter 4; and those applying to the provision of goods, facilities and services and premises, in chapter 5. General exceptions are described in chapter 7.

Provisions of the Sex Discrimination Act 1975 which make discrimination unlawful	Section of Act	Paragraphs of Guide to the Act
Group A		
Discrimination by employers in recruitment and treatment of employees.	6	3.1-3.17
Discrimination against contract workers	9	3.21
Discrimination against partners	11	3.22
Discrimination by trade unions, employers' associations etc	12	3.23, 3.24
Discriminiation by qualifying bodies.	13	3.25-3.28
Discrimmation in vocational training.	14	3.29-3.30
Discrimination by employment agencies	15	3.31-3.34
Group B		
Discrimination by bodies in charge of educational establishments	22	4.2-4.6,4.11-4.15
Other discrimination in education	23	4.7-4.8,4.14-4.15
Discrimination in the provision of goods, facilities or services	29	5.2-5.9,5.13-5.16
Discrimination in the disposal or management of premises.	30	5.10-5.16
Discrimination by landlords against prospective assignees or sublessees	31	5.17
Discrimination by; or in relation to, barristers.	35A	5.18-5.20

Appendix III:
Application to an
Employment Tribunal (IT1)

Application to an
Employment Tribunal

For office use

Received at ET	
Case number	
Code	
Initials	

1 Please give the type of complaint you want the tribunal to decide (for example, unfair dismissal, equal pay). A full list is available from the tribunal office. If you have more than one complaint list them all.

2 Please give your details

Mr ☐ Mrs ☐ Miss ☐ Ms ☐ Other _____

First names
Surname
Date of birth
Address
Postcode
Phone number
Daytime phone number
Please give an address to which we should send documents if different from above
Postcode

3 If a representative is acting for you please give details
(all correspondence will be sent to your representative)

Name	
Address	
Postcode	
Phone	Fax
Reference	

4 Please give the dates of your employment

From _____ to _____

5 Please give the name and address of the employer, other organisation or person against whom this complaint is being brought

Name
Address
Postcode
Phone number

Please give the place where you worked or applied to work if different from above

Address
Postcode

6 Please say what job you did for the employer (or what job you applied for). If this does not apply, please say what your connection was with the employer

309

Appendix III: Application to an Employment Tribunal (IT1)

7 Please give the number of normal basic hours worked each week Hours per week	**9** If your complaint is not about dismissal, please give the date when the matter you are complaining about took place

8 Please give your earning details Basic wage or salary £ : per Average take home pay £ : per Other bonuses or benefits £ : per	**10** Unfair dismissal applicants only Please indicate what you are seeking at this stage, if you win your case ☐ Reinstatement: to carry on working in your old job as before (an order for reinstatement normally includes an award of compensation for loss of earnings). ☐ Re-engagement: to start another job or new contract with your old employer (an order for re-engagement normally includes an award of compensation for loss of earnings) ☐ Compensation only: to get an award of money

11 Please give details of your complaint

If there is not enough space for your answer, please continue on a separate sheet and attach it to this form/

12 Please sign and date this form, then send it to the address on the back page of this booklet.

Signed

Date

Appendix IV:
Notice of Appearance (IT3)

EMPLOYMENT TRIBUNALS

NOTICE OF APPEARANCE BY RESPONDENT

In the application of

Case Number
(please quote in all correspondence)

* This form has to be photocopied, if possible please use Black Ink and Capital letters
* If there is not enough space for your answer, please continue on a separate sheet and attach it to this form

1. Full name and address of the Respondent:	3. Do you intend to resist the application? (Tick appropriate box)

YES　　NO
☐　　☐

4. Was the applicant dismissed? (Tick appropriate box)

YES　　NO
☐　　☐

Please give
reason below

Reason for dismissal:

5. Are the dates of employment given by the applicant correct? (Tick appropriate box)

Post Code:

Telephone number:

YES　　NO
☐　　☐

please give correct dates below

2. If you require documents and notices to be sent to a representative or any other address in the United Kingdom please give details:

Began on

Ended on

6. Are the details given by the applicant about wages/salary, take home or other bonuses correct? (Tick appropriate box)

YES　　NO
☐　　☐

Please give correct details
below

Basic Wages/Salary	£	per
Average Take Home Pay £		per
Other Bonuses/Benefits £		per

PLEASE TURN OVER

for office use only
Date of receipt　　　　　　　　　Initials

Post Code:

Reference:

Telephone number:

Form IT3 E&W - 9/98

*Published by **everyform***

311

7. Give particulars of the grounds on which you intend to resist the application.

8. Please sign and date the form.

Signed   Dated

DATA PROTECTION ACT 1984
We may put some of the information you give on this form on to a computer. This helps us to monitor progress and produce statistics. We may also give information to:
* the other party in the case
* other parts of the DTI and organisations such as ACAS (Advisory Conciliation and Arbitration Service), the Equal Opportunities Commission or the Commission for Racial Equality.

Please post or fax this form to:

* IF YOU FAX THE FORM, DO NOT POST A COPY AS WELL
* IF YOU POST THE FORM, TAKE A COPY FOR YOUR RECORDS

Form IT3 E&W - 9/98

Appendix V: Case Study

Fearless v The 'Trouble Likes Us' Trading Company

This case study provides examples of a number of documents in the context of a fictional case. A female employee has been dismissed for an episode of fighting at work and is claiming unfair dismissal and sex discrimination.

The examples are intended to give the reader a broad idea of how to draft documents of this nature by placing them in a specific context.

Taken together, they are *not* intended to constitute a comprehensive survey of a case from beginning to end. Readers will notice, for example, that there is no pre-claim correspondence or questionnaire and many steps which might arise in a case like this, such as applications for a witness order, are also not included. Further, witness statements have only been produced for two witnesses, rather than the total number that would be needed in this kind of scenario.

On the respondent's side, witnesses would normally include at least the dismissing manager and the appeals manager. With the applicant, you would expect her to adduce corroborative evidence, if possible, in relation to the assertions she has made about the respondent.

Readers might also note that the grounds of complaint (originating application) and resistance (notice of appearance) are fairly comprehensive. It may not always be possible or desirable to provide this much information. Care should be taken not to create hostages to fortune, or make assertions at such an early stage which are abandoned later on.

In the mythical employment tribunal

CASE NO:

BE T W E E N:

Felicity Fearless

<u>Applicant</u>

And

The 'Trouble Likes Us' Trading Company

<u>Respondent</u>

GROUNDS OF COMPLAINT

---

1.   The applicant's claim is for unfair dismissal and sex discrimination. On 25 May 2002, the applicant was engaged in an altercation with her supervisor, Anne Beattie, in which the applicant is alleged to have pushed Ms Beattie and been threatening towards her. The respondent dismissed the applicant on 17 June 2002. The reason given for dismissal was gross misconduct.

UNFAIR DISMISSAL:

2.   The applicant will contend that the respondent acted unreasonably in treating the applicant's conduct as a reason for dismissal (Author's note – on the facts of this particular case the reason for dismissal is not in dispute). The applicant contends that there was both an insufficient investigation by the respondent and that the decision to dismiss fell outside the range of reasonable responses open to the respondent.

3.   Sufficiency of investigation: The respondent failed to carry out a sufficient investigation into the issue of whether the applicant was the first to make physical contact or whether, as the applicant alleges, she pushed Ms Beattie away in self-defence after the latter grabbed the applicant by her collar. There were four eyewitnesses to the altercation which took place between herself and Ms Beattie. The respondent only interviewed three of them stating that the fourth, Peter Sleep, was away sick during the course of the investigation and could not be interviewed. The applicant will contend that the respondent made no effort to contact Peter Sleep to obtain his account despite an express request from the

applicant. The applicant will rely upon the fact that, of the three witnesses they interviewed, only one, Marjorie Gossforth, stated that she saw the applicant make physical contact first. The applicant will further contend that the respondent failed to investigate her claim during the disciplinary hearing that she had been victimized by Ms Beattie over a period of two years.

4. Reasonableness of the sanction of dismissal: The applicant will contend that, as she acted in self-defence, the decision to dismiss must have been outside the range of reasonable responses open to the employer. She will further contend that, even on the version of events which the respondent acted upon, dismissal was not within the range of reasonable responses. In this respect the applicant will rely, amongst other things, upon: (a) her immaculate conduct record during the twelve years of her employment; (b) the fact that the altercation between herself and Ms Beattie was provoked by the unreasonable behaviour of the latter; (c) Ms Beattie had victimized her over a period of time, a matter which had been the subject of a number of informal complaints; and (d) that the respondent treated her differently (and less favourably) than two male employees who, the previous month, were involved in a serious incident of fighting at work, but who merely received a formal warning (see sex discrimination below).

SEX DISCRIMINATION:

5. The applicant will allege that, in deciding to dismiss the applicant, the respondent treated the applicant less favourably on grounds of her sex. The applicant alleges that, if a male employee had been involved in a similar incident, he would not have been dismissed. In or about May 2002, John Striker and Michael Ram, two male employees of the respondent, were involved in a serious incident of fighting at work in which both sustained injuries. Despite this, each escaped dismissal and received a written warning. Further, the applicant knows of numerous other incidents in which fights have resulted in nothing more severe than a warning.

6. The applicant will contend that there was a culture in place in the respondent's organisation in which fighting was tolerated amongst men but not amongst women.

7. The applicant will claim compensation for unfair dismissal and sex discrimination including, in the case of the latter, an award for hurt to feelings.

In the mythical employment tribunal

CASE NO:

B E T W E E N:

Felicity Fearless

<u>Applicant</u>

And

The 'Trouble Likes Us' Trading Company

<u>Respondent</u>

GROUNDS OF RESISTANCE

---

1. The respondent denies that it unfairly dismissed the applicant or treated her less favourably on grounds of her sex.

2. The applicant was summarily dismissed for gross misconduct on 17 June 2002. The conduct in question was violent and threatening behaviour, constituting gross misconduct under the respondent's disciplinary procedure.

3. The respondent will assert that it had reasonable grounds for believing that the applicant was guilty of the misconduct in question, that it carried out a sufficient investigation and that dismissal was within the range of reasonable responses open to it.

4. Sufficiency of investigation: On 25 May 2002 the respondent's level one supervisor, Anne Beattie, reported to her line manager, John Weary, that she had been the victim of an assault by the applicant, a member of the team of whom Ms Beattie had charge. Mr Weary decided that, in view of the seriousness of the allegation, he would suspend the applicant on full pay pending further investigation, in accordance with provisions in the respondent's disciplinary procedure.

5. After enquires, John Weary established that there were four eyewitnesses to the incident. Three of those were interviewed. The fourth, Peter Sleep, could not be interviewed because he was unwell at the time when the interviews were carried out. The respondent will contend that it had sufficient information to proceed without his evidence.

6. Of the three witnesses interviewed, Marjorie Gossforth (a worker at the same grade as the applicant) stated that she saw the entire incident and that the applicant pushed Mrs Beattie in the face aggressively. She also stated that she never observed Ms Beattie make physical contact with the applicant. The other two eyewitnesses, Bettie Chatter and Sharon Stonewall, did not observe the assault itself, but turned around after hearing Ms Beattie shout out in pain and further heard Ms Beattie say 'she's just hit me'. Finally, Ms Beattie herself was interviewed. She stated that the applicant, after being told to carry out a reasonable instruction, had become rude and aggressive and had hit her in the face. The applicant was asked to attend a disciplinary hearing on 15 June 2002. She was informed of the allegations against her, and maintained that she had pushed Ms Beattie away in self-defence after being grabbed by her collar. On this particular occasion, the applicant was angry because Ms Beattie had asked her to clear up a spillage on the floor.

7. The respondent's manager reached the conclusion, on the evidence before him, that the applicant had physically pushed away Ms Beattie in a violent and threatening manner. He did not believe the applicant when she stated that she was assaulted first by Ms Beattie. Whilst he accepted that the applicant was, at the time of the assault, angry about the instruction she had received, he did not believe that she was subjected to any provocation. If, which he did not accept, there was any problem with the behaviour of Ms Beattie towards the applicant, he considered the correct course was for the applicant to make a formal complaint through the grievance procedure. He also considered the applicant's clean conduct record. Having come to the conclusion, however, that the applicant had carried out an unprovoked assault upon a supervisor who was simply carrying out her duties, he considered that the right sanction was dismissal.

8. The applicant exercised a right of appeal and a full rehearing was conducted by John Judge, the respondent's chief line manager, on 2 July 2002. The decision to dismiss was confirmed.

9. The reasonableness of the sanction of dismissal: The respondent will rely upon the fact that fighting is a serious offence of gross misconduct. It will further rely upon the fact that the assault was carried out upon a senior member of staff who was simply trying to carry out her duties. Further, the applicant showed no remorse for what had taken place. The respondent denies, for the reasons set out below, that there was any disparate treatment between the applicant and two male colleagues.

317

10.   Sex discrimination: The allegation of sex discrimination has taken the respondent completely by surprise. At no stage, prior to the application being made, were they given any intimation of it or served with a questionnaire by the applicant. The respondent denies that it views fighting amongst female employees more seriously than amongst men, or that there is any culture in place in the workplace to that effect. It denies that there was less favourable treatment of the applicant on account of her sex.

      The respondent accepts that two male employees, John Striker and Michael Ram, were involved in an incident of fighting at work during the week prior to the applicant's dismissal, and received a formal warning. The circumstances of that case were different, and the decision not to dismiss was unrelated to the sex of those involved. The respondent will rely upon the fact that, in relation to that incident: (a) both employees admitted their involvement in the fight from the outset and expressed remorse for what had occurred; (b) the fight was not related to the giving of a work instruction by a manager; and (c) both employees had since resolved their difficulties and were prepared to work together as part of a team. If, which is denied, any employee of the respondent is found to have acted unreasonably, the respondent will assert that it carried out all reasonable steps to prevent such an act taking place, including thorough equal opportunities training.

In the mythical employment tribunal

CASE NO:

B E T W E E N:

Felicity Fearless

Applicant

And

The 'Trouble Likes Us' Trading Company

Respondent

APPLICANT'S REQUEST FOR FURTHER PARTICULARS OF THE GROUNDS OF RESISTANCE

---

1. Of 'The fourth, Peter Sleep, could not be interviewed because he was unwell at the time…'.

   Request:

   Please state: (a) the date when Peter Sleep went sick; (b) the date when he returned; (c) all attempts that were made to communicate with Peter Sleep about the incident which led to the applicant's dismissal giving. In relation to each such attempt: (i) the date when the communication took place; (ii) whether the communication was oral or in writing; and (iii) the contents of the communication in question.

2. Of 'If, which he did not accept, there was any problem with the behaviour of Ms Beattie towards the applicant, he considered the correct course was for the applicant to make a formal complaint through the grievance procedure.'

   Request:

   Please state whether it is the respondent's case that the applicant was aware of the respondent's grievance procedure. If it is so claimed, please state the basis upon which it is so claimed, including the date, place and means by which she was informed about the procedure.

3. Of 'The respondent will assert that it carried out all reasonable steps to prevent such an act taking place, including thorough equal opportunities training.'

<u>Request</u>:

Please give full details of the training which was carried out, including dates and the nature of the training in question.

In the mythical employment tribunal

CASE NO:

B E T W E E N:

Felicity Fearless

<u>Applicant</u>

And

The 'Trouble Likes Us' Trading Company

<u>Respondent</u>

RESPONDENT'S REQUEST FOR FURTHER PARTICULARS OF THE GROUNDS OF COMPLAINT

---

1. Of 'Ms Beattie had victimized her over a period of time, a matter which had been the subject of a number of informal complaints…'.

   <u>Request:</u>

   Please state the date (or approximate date) when the alleged complaints were made and the person/s to whom the complaint/s were made.

2. Of 'Further, the applicant knows of numerous other incidents in which fights have resulted in nothing more severe than a warning.'

   <u>Request:</u>

   Please give details of each such incident, including the date when it occurred and who was involved.

Application for disclosure

Case: Felicity Fearless v The 'Trouble Likes Us' Trading Co.

Case no:

The order sought:

The applicant requests an order for disclosure of all documents in the possession of the respondent relating to the incident between John Striker and Michael Ram, including, but not limited to:

- the notes of any formal investigation that took place, including interview notes;

- the notes of any disciplinary hearing which took place;

- any letters sent out informing the parties of the outcome of the investigation and/or the sanction which was to be imposed upon them.

The reasons for the application:

The respondent has refused a voluntary request for the provision of the information, stating that it is irrelevant, and that disclosure of the information would be disproportionate to the complexity of the issues the tribunal has to decide.

The information sought is of fundamental importance to the applicant's case both in relation to unfair dismissal and sex discrimination. The applicant has alleged from the outset of the claim that two other male employees were treated more favourably than her in comparable circumstances. The respondent has denied this, stating that the circumstances are different. The applicant has no means of proving her case except by reference to the documents sought. It is not accepted that disclosure would be disproportionate to the complexity of the issues before the tribunal. The documentation sought is limited in nature.

In the mythical employment tribunal

CASE NO:

B E T W E E N:

Felicity Fearless

<u>Applicant</u>

And

The 'Trouble Likes Us' Trading Company

<u>Respondent</u>

WITNESS STATEMENT OF JOHN WEARY

I.   I, John Weary, am the respondent's senior shift manager. The respondent is an organisation which manufactures furniture. I have worked for the respondent for a total of 15 years and have held the post of senior shift manager since 1999. In that capacity, I have responsibility for approximately 100 staff, including the applicant. I have attended, in my position as manager, a number of seminars relating to equal opportunities. I have also given equal opportunities briefings to the staff under my supervision, including the applicant. I am the manager responsible for taking decisions in relation to formal warnings and dismissals under the disciplinary procedure. A copy of the procedure currently in place can be found at page 20 in the bundle. I would refer the tribunal in particular to page 24, the section entitled 'Gross Misconduct.'

2.   I have known the applicant since I started my current post in 1999. Prior to that date, I was engaged in a different part of the factory. I have not, since 1999, had a great deal of contact with the applicant. We did, however, exchange pleasantries from time to time and I like to think that, had there been any difficulty, the applicant could have approached me.

3.   On 25 May 2002, Ms Anne Beattie, the applicant's supervisor, walked into my office on the first floor. She was in tears and said to me: 'I have just been assaulted by Felicity'. I told her to sit down and confirmed that this is a matter that I would take seriously. I did not ask her in detail about the incident as I knew I would be carrying out a formal interview with her at a later

stage. I did ask her for the names of other people who witnessed the incident. I was given the names of four individuals.

4. I decided that the matter was potentially one of gross misconduct. As such, it fell to be dealt with under the respondent's disciplinary procedure. I further concluded that the matter was sufficiently serious to warrant suspension of the applicant on full pay pending the outcome of the investigation. The right to suspend in these circumstances is referred to both in the disciplinary procedure at page 23 and also the applicant's contract of employment (page 18). I called the applicant in to my office and informed her of her suspension, also giving her a letter to that effect (page 35)].

5. I next began the process of interviewing the witnesses to the incident. I planned the questions that I would ask to each witness. They were as follows: (a) were you present at the altercation between Felicity Fearless and Anne Beattie on 25 May 2002; and (b) describe what you saw. Depending upon the answers, I would then ask a number of follow up questions. During each interview, my secretary made a contemporaneous note of what was said. Notes of all of the interviews can be found at pages 36–39 in the bundle.

6. The first witness to be interviewed, Marjorie Gossforth, said she saw the entire incident. She was an employee at the same level as the applicant. She stated that she was standing about ten yards away. Anne Beattie had asked the applicant to clear up a spillage on the floor. The applicant had become extremely annoyed and refused to do so. The applicant 'squared up' to Ms Beattie and then pushed her away aggressively.

7. No other third parties witnessed the incident from beginning to end although two, Bettie Chatter and Sharon Stonewall, said they turned around at the point when they heard Ms Beattie cry out and heard her say of the applicant: 'she hit me'.

8. I next interviewed Ms Beattie, the complainant. She informed me that she had asked the applicant to clean a spillage on the floor. The applicant became very angry, claiming that she had not caused the spillage. Ms Beattie was attempting to explain the reason for the request when the applicant aggressively squared up to her as if about to start fighting. The applicant then put her hand on Ms Beattie's face and pushed her away so that Ms Beattie almost fell to the floor.

9. There was a fourth eyewitness to the incident, Peter Sleep, who was off sick on the day when the interviews were being carried out. I considered that I had sufficient information to call the applicant to attend a disciplinary hearing without interviewing

Mr Sleep. I should add that I am an extremely busy manager with many other duties. I had set aside a specific time to carry out interviews in relation to this matter during which Mr Sleep was not available. I concluded, on the information before me, that I had sufficient information upon which to proceed to a disciplinary hearing.

10. On 5 June 2002 I wrote to the applicant requesting that she attend a disciplinary hearing on 14 June 2002. The notes of that hearing, typed up from a contemporaneous note made by my secretary, are contained at pages 43–48 in the bundle. At the hearing, I informed the applicant that there was evidence before me that she had assaulted a manager, but that I certainly had not made up my mind on the issue and that this was her opportunity to tell me her side of the story. I asked the applicant whether she had assaulted Anne Beattie. The applicant replied that she had not. She admitted pushing Ms Beattie but only after Ms Beattie grabbed her by the collar. The applicant stated that she was very upset and that Ms Beattie had been victimising her for the entire year they had been working together. On this occasion, the applicant was asked to clear up a mess on the floor she had not created. At the conclusion of the hearing, which lasted approximately 40 minutes, I told the applicant that I would consider all of the evidence in the case, including what she had told me, and reach my decision. I also, at the conclusion of the hearing, summarised her case as she had told it to me, and asked her to confirm that this was an accurate summary, which she duly did.

11. Prior to making my decision, there was one matter that I decided required further investigation. I asked Marjorie Gossforth whether she saw Anne Beattie make physical contact with the applicant at any stage. Ms Gossforth replied that she did not. I recorded this conversation in a written memorandum, which is at page 41 in the bundle.

12. I next came to consider my decision. I formed the view that the applicant had committed an assault and should be dismissed. My reasons for so concluding are set out in a memorandum written at the time, to be found at page 49. It can be seen from the memorandum that I did not believe the applicant's account of what had taken place. It was contradicted by that of Anne Beattie, a supervisor whose judgement and integrity I had come to respect, and by Marjorie Gossforth, an independent witness. I also considered that the other witnesses' accounts were consistent with the version given by Ms Beattie. I had little doubt that the applicant had assaulted Ms Beattie. I next considered the issue of the appropriate sanction. I took in to account the applicant's

previous good conduct, but concluded that unprovoked assaults on managers in the workplace could not be tolerated. I formed the view that the Ms Beattie was simply trying to do her job and needed to be protected in doing so. If, which I was doubtful of, there was any truth in the suggestion that the applicant had been victimized, I consider that the correct course would have been for the applicant to pursue a complaint through the grievance procedure, or to at least mention her concerns to me. The first mention of it was at her disciplinary hearing. I further considered that the applicant had shown no remorse for what took place.

13. I informed the applicant of the outcome of her hearing by letter, which can be found at page 50 in the bundle. I also informed her that she had the right to appeal against the decision, a right which the applicant chose to exercise. I enclosed the typed notes of the disciplinary hearing and asked the applicant to sign in the space at the bottom to confirm their accuracy and return the notes to me. This she duly did. I had no further involvement with the case. The outcome of the appeal, which I understand took the form of a complete rehearing, is for the respondent's chief line manager to give evidence upon.

14. I have been informed of the allegation by the applicant that I treated her differently from two male employees involved in fighting the week before. I further understand that the applicant is claiming that this constituted sex discrimination. I can confirm that two male employees, John Striker and Michael Ram, had been involved in a fight the previous week for which both had received a formal warning from myself. The circumstances were, however, different. Both informed me that they had fallen out over a personal matter unrelated to work. They were both sorry for what had occurred and had since made up. In those circumstances, I considered that a formal warning was merited. The circumstances of the applicant's case was different. She carried out an unprovoked assault on a manager who was simply trying to carry out her duties. I refute the suggestion that there is any 'culture' in place in our workplace whereby violence is tolerated amongst men and not women. Any violence at work is treated extremely seriously, regardless of the sex of those involved. On a personal level, I find the allegation of sex discrimination to be grossly unfair.

15. I confirm that the contents of this statement are true.

Signed:

Dated:

In the mythical employment tribunal

CASE NO:

B E T W E E N:

Felicity Fearless

<u>Applicant</u>

And

The 'Trouble Likes Us' Trading Company

<u>Respondent</u>

WITNESS STATEMENT OF FELICITY FEARLESS

---

1. I, Felicity Fearless, am the applicant in these proceedings. I was employed by the respondent from 24 April 1990 until my dismissal on 17 June 2002. I had an immaculate conduct record and was an extremely hard working employee. I had carried out the same job on the production line, that of production assistant, for all of the twelve years I had been at the company. Approximately one year before my dismissal, Anne Beattie became my supervisor. I had previously enjoyed a good relationship with all of the supervisors with whom I had worked.

2. For some reason, Anne Beattie took a strong dislike to me from the moment she started in the job. On one occasion, shortly after she started, she told me that I was too 'stuck in my ways' and that I would need to change. I got the strong impression that she felt insecure about the fact that I was older than her. Whenever there was an unpleasant task that needed doing, she would always pick me out to do it. This was very upsetting, as I considered I was being bullied. I never made a formal complaint, but I did mention to Mr Weary on a number of occasions that I was not happy in my team and that I wanted to move. He asked me why this was and I stated that I did not get on with my supervisor.

3. On 25 May 2002, I was asked by Anne Beattie to clean up a spillage on the floor which a member of another team had caused. I could not believe it. There was a special cleaning unit in the factory who could have been asked to come down. Ms Beattie said that it needed cleaning immediately. I said: 'in that case, why don't you do it'. At this point, Ms Beattie grabbed me by my

327

collar. I panicked and pushed her away, whereupon she cried out 'she hit me'. I don't think that more than two people saw the incident. One of those was Marjorie Gossforth and the other was Peter Sleep. Each was standing to my left about ten yards away. I am very surprised that Marjorie Gossforth states that she did not see Anne Beattie grab me by the collar. That said, the whole thing happened very quickly and she could easily have missed it. Peter Sleep also witnessed the incident. He is not part of my team and works in a different part of the factory. I am amazed that the respondent has not interviewed him. I told John Weary at the disciplinary hearing that he also saw the incident and that they should ask him for his account. The whole incident happened very quickly and it is perfectly possible that Marjorie Gossforth simply got it wrong.

4.   I now understand that the respondent is saying that Peter Sleep was off sick on the day that interviews were being held. I cannot understand why he was not interviewed after his return. I notice that, after my disciplinary hearing, John Weary carried out another interview with Marjorie Gossforth. It would have been easy for him to do the same thing with Mr Sleep. I also cannot understand why Mr Judge, the chief line manager who conducted the appeal hearing, relied solely upon Mr Weary's interview records and did not, at the very least, interview Mr Sleep. Given the importance of the matter, and the draconian nature of the penalty they were considering, I think this was both necessary and fair.

5.   I am both angry and upset that Mr Weary and Mr Judge did not investigate my complaint that I had been victimized by Ms Beattie over a period of twelve months. This was obviously a relevant factor. I was never, during the course of my employment, made aware that there was a grievance procedure which I could use. Mr Weary must have known that I had been a loyal and hardworking employee, and that there might be more to the incident that Anne Beattie had led him to believe. I really believe that, had he taken the trouble to look in to the issue, other members of the team would have told him about the unfair treatment I had received. I am also surprised that he did not speak to my previous supervisors, who would have told him that I was a calm and hardworking employee.

6.   I worked in a section of the factory where the majority of employees were women. In the warehouse section, however, the vast majority of employees were men. It is a well-known fact that fights break out in that section of the factory on a fairly frequent basis. The fights are usually overlooked completely. The week

before the incident that led to my dismissal, a serious fight broke out between two men in that section. It is my understanding that one of them suffered from a broken jaw. Despite this, both received a written warning and were not dismissed. It is quite obvious that this was a much more serious incident than the one I was involved in. I do not believe that anything can justify the different way in which I was treated. I firmly believe that the respondent had a different attitude towards fights amongst women than amongst men, and that I was treated less favourably as a result.

Signed:

Dated:

In the mythical employment tribunal

CASE NO:

B E T W E E N:

Felicity Fearless

<u>Applicant</u>

And

The 'Trouble Likes Us' Trading Company

<u>Respondent</u>

INDEX TO BUNDLE OF DOCUMENTS

DIVIDER D – Incident between John Striker and Michael Ram

In the mythical employment tribunal

Felicity Fearless v The 'Trouble Likes Us' Trading Company

CAST LIST

Felicity Fearless (applicant)	Production Assistant
Anne Beattie	Supervisor
Bettie Chatter	Production Assistant
Marjorie Gossforth	Production Assistant
John Judge	Chief Line Manager
Michael Ram	Warehouse Assistant
Peter Sleep	General Assistant
Sharon Stonewall	Production Assistant
John Striker	Warehouse Assistant
John Weary	Senior Shift Manager

In the mythical employment tribunal

CASE NO:

B E T W E E N:

Felicity Fearless

<u>Applicant</u>

And

The 'Trouble Likes Us' Trading Company

<u>Respondent</u>

APPLICANT'S SKELETON ARGUMENT

---

1. THE LAW

1.1 <u>Unfair dismissal</u>

1.2 <u>Statute</u>.

1.3 The relevant statutory provisions are *s 98(1), (2) (4)* of the *Employment Rights Act 1996 (ERA 1996))*.

1.4 <u>Relevant case law</u>

1.5 *British Home Stores v Burchell [1978] IRLR 379* :

1.6 In a case where misconduct is relied upon as the reason for dismissal, the tribunal should address itself to the following questions:

- Did the employer have a genuine belief in the reason for dismissal?

- Was that belief held on reasonable grounds?

- At the final stage when the belief was held, had the employer carried out such investigation as was reasonable in the circumstances?

1.7 In addition to applying the test in *Burchell* cited above, the tribunal should have regard to the global issue of whether the decision of the employer fell within the range of reasonable responses available to it (*Iceland Frozen Foods v Jones [1983] ICR 17*).

2.   Sex discrimination

2.1   A person discriminates against a woman if, on the ground of her sex, they treat her less favourably than they would treat a man (*Sex Discrimination Act 1975 (SDA 1975), s 1*).

2.2   The applicant relies, as comparators, upon John Striker and Michael Ram, whom it is alleged were treated more favourably in comparable circumstances.

2.3   In the alternative if, which is denied, those circumstances are held not to be comparable, the applicant relies upon the case of a hypothetical male comparator whom she alleges would have been treated more favourably than herself.

2.4   THE LAW APPLIED TO THE FACTS OF THIS CASE

3.   Unfair dismissal

3.1   Applying the three-fold test set out in *Burchell*.

3.2   Did the employer have a genuine belief in the reason for dismissal?

3.3   This is not disputed by the applicant (Author's note – this limb is commonly conceded, since to do otherwise necessitates an allegation of bad faith against the employer something, which, on the facts of this case, is not part of the applicant's case).

3.4   Was this belief held on reasonable grounds?

3.5   It is asserted, for the following reasons that, this was not so:

(a) There was no interview by either the dismissing manager or the appeals manager with a crucial witness to the incident, Peter Sleep, who might have corroborated the applicant's account that she has been assaulted by Ms Beattie.

(b) There was no investigation by either the dismissing manager or the appeals manager of the applicant's claim that she had been victimized for a year by the alleged the victim, Anne Beattie. This was central to the issue of whose account was credible and to the issue of provocation.

3.6   Did the employer carry out an investigation which was reasonable in the circumstances?

3.7   For the reasons given in 3.5(a) and (b) above, the applicant contends that this was not so, particularly in view of the size and resources of the respondent's organisation.

3.8   Was the decision within the range of reasonable responses?

3.9   The applicant will contend that the decision was outside the range of reasonable responses open to the respondent because:

- the applicant had worked for the respondent for twelve years with an immaculate conduct record;

- even on the version accepted by the respondent, the incident was relatively minor;

- there was disparate treatment between the applicant and two male employees who had received a formal warning the week before for a more severe incident.

4.   SEX DISCRIMINATION

4.1   The applicant will contend that, in being dismissed by the respondent, she was treated less favourably by them on grounds of her sex, and that a male employee would have received a lesser sanction.

4.2   The applicant relies, as comparators, upon two male employees – John Striker and Michael Ram – who were treated more favourably in comparable circumstances. In that case, the only material difference was that the altercation was much more serious, resulting in injuries, yet both escaped with formal warnings.

4.3   If, which is denied, the above case is held not to be comparable, the applicant relies, in the alternative, upon a hypothetical comparator as proof of less favourable treatment. In support of the proposition that such a comparator would be treated more favourably the applicant relies upon: (a) the fact that fights between men at the factory were, in general, tolerated, but not amongst women; and (b) the incident between John Striker and Michael Ram cited above.

In the mythical employment tribunal

CASE NO:

B E T W E E N:

Felicity Fearless

<u>Applicant</u>

And

The 'Trouble Likes Us' Trading Company

<u>Respondent</u>

RESPONDENT'S SKELETON ARGUMENT

---

1. THE LAW

1.1 <u>Unfair dismissal</u>

1.2 <u>Statute</u>.

1.3 The relevant statutory provisions are *s 98(1), (2), (4) of the ERA 1996*.

1.4 <u>Relevant case law.</u>

1.5 *British Home Stores v Burchell [1978] IRLR 379.*

1.6 In a case where misconduct is relied upon as the reason for dismissal, the tribunal should address itself to the following questions:

- Did the employer have a genuine belief in the reason for dismissal?

- Was that belief held on reasonable grounds?

- At the final stage when the belief was held, had the employer carried out such investigation as was reasonable in the circumstances?

1.7 In addition to applying the test in *Burchell*, the tribunal should have regard to the global issue of whether the decision of the employer fell within the range of reasonable responses available to it (*Iceland Frozen Foods v Jones [1983] ICR 17*).

1.8   Sex discrimination

1.9   A person discriminates against a woman if, on the ground of her sex, they treats her less favourably than they would treat a man (*SDA, s 1*).

1.10   *Section 5(2)* states: ' A comparison of the cases of persons of different sex…must be such that the relevant circumstances in the one case are the same, or not materially different, in the other.'

1.11   The burden of proving less favourable treatment than a comparator, either actual or hypothetical, lies on the applicant. Only if less favourable treatment is proved does the burden then shift to the respondent to prove that this was not on grounds of sex (*SDA 1975, s 63(a)*).

2.   THE LAW APPLIED TO THE FACTS OF THIS CASE

2.1   Unfair Dismissal

2.2   Applying the three fold test set out in *Burchell*

2.3   Did the employer have a genuine belief in the reason for dismissal?

2.4   This is not disputed by the applicant (Author's note – this should be clear from the grounds of complaint but, if not, then established before the start of the case).

2.5   Was this belief held on reasonable grounds?

2.6   The respondent relies on the following:

(a)   the evidence of the victim as to what had occurred;

(b)   the evidence of Marjorie Gossforth that the applicant assaulted Ms Beattie and was not assaulted first;

(c)   the accounts of Bettie Chatter and Sharon Stonewall which did nothing to contradict the victim's account;

(d)   the fact that the applicant was given a full opportunity to give her account of what took place, both at her disciplinary hearing and at the appeal hearing;

(e)   the fact that Ms Beattie was a respected senior employee who was thought to be unlikely to fabricate her account.

3.   Did the employer carry out an investigation which was reasonable in the circumstances?

3.1   The respondent relies on 2.6(a) to (e) in support of the fact that it carried out a reasonable investigation. Interviews were carried out with all of the eyewitnesses to the event, except for one witness who was away sick. Given the information gathered from those interviews, the respondent could not reasonably be expected to delay its investigation pending the return to work of Peter Sleep.

3.2 The respondent denies that it was under a duty, as part of a reasonable investigation, to investigate the allegation of victimization levelled against Ms Beattie by the applicant. The applicant had the right to pursue a formal grievance in relation to this but at no time did so. The applicant's main 'defence' was, in any event, that she was not the aggressor in the incident and acted in self defence. It was this that the respondent was under a duty to investigate, a duty it fulfilled.

3.3 <u>Was dismissal within the range of reasonable responses?</u>

3.4 The assault committed by the applicant constituted gross misconduct under the respondent's disciplinary procedure, rendering the applicant liable to dismissal.

3.5 Full consideration was given to applying another sanction but, for the following reasons, the respondent's managers, both at first instance and at appeal, considered that dismissal was the appropriate response:

- this was an assault on a manager who was simply attempting to carry out her duties;

- the respondent had a duty to protect its staff in such circumstances;

- the applicant had shown no remorse for what had taken place;

- The respondent further contends that, as the incident constituted gross misconduct under the disciplinary procedure, the issue of what sanction to apply was a matter for the discretion of the respondent's managers, a discretion which should only be interfered with on the basis that the choice they made was not open to them.

4. SEX DISCRIMINATION

4.1 The respondent denies that it treated the applicant less seriously on grounds of her sex. Each episode of fighting at the work place is considered separately on its own merits. The manager with responsibility for taking the decision has a discretion whether to dismiss or not.

4.2 The respondent denies that the applicant is entitled to rely upon

John Striker and Michael Ram as comparators. The circumstances in relation to that case were materially different:

- the cause of their dispute was unrelated to work and, in particular, did not relate to the giving of a reasonable instruction by a manager to an employee;

- both had shown genuine remorse and regret for the incident, and expressed a determination that it would not happen again;

- the respondent contends that it was plainly open to their management to take the different views they did of the two incidents and that the views which they did hold were unrelated to sex. The issue of sanction was a matter within their discretion, a discretion which was exercised reasonably. It is denied that the applicant was treated less favourably than a male comparator, either actual or hypothetical.

- the respondent disputes that fights break out on a regular basis amongst men at its factory. The applicant has been unable to single out specific incidents to support this assertion. The respondent denies that there is a culture in place where fighting is tolerated amongst men. Fighting amongst both men and women is deemed to constitute gross misconduct and treated equally seriously in both cases.

In the mythical employment tribunal

CASE NO:

B E T W E E N:

Felicity Fearless

<u>Applicant</u>

And

The 'Trouble Likes Us' Trading Company

<u>Respondent</u>

CHRONOLOGY

---

24 April 1990	Applicant commences employment with the respondent as a production assistant.
18 May 2002	An incident takes place of fighting at work between two other employees, John Striker and Michael Ram.
25 May 2002	Incident of alleged fighting between the applicant and Ms Beattie.
25 May 2002	Applicant suspended at work by John Weary.
27 May 2002	John Weary, the production manager, carries out interviews with witnesses to the event.
5 June 2002	Applicant invited to attend a disciplinary hearing.
14 June 2002	Disciplinary hearing takes place.
17 June 2002	Applicant told of her dismissal.
2 July 2002	Appeal hearing takes place.
25 July 2002	Decision to dismiss confirmed.
24 August 2002	Application to employment tribunal.

Appendix VI: Sample Compromise Agreement

The following compromise agreement is reproduced from *Harvey's Industrial Relations and Employment Law*, Division U, 2.I.

Compromise Agreement[1]

[Agreement to refrain from instituting or continuing with proceedings before an employment tribunal]

This Agreement is made between [AB (hereafter referred to as 'the Employee' [*or* 'Applicant', *or as the case may be*])] and [XYZ & Co Ltd (hereafter referred to as 'the Company' [*or* 'Respondent', *or as the case may be*])]

It is agreed between the parties as follows:

1. The Company will pay to the Employee the sum of [£3,000] within [seven days hereof *or* forthwith *or as the case may be*].[2]

2. The Employee will refrain from [instituting a complaint against the Company before an employment tribunal] [*or* continuing his complaint against the Company before the employment tribunal under Case No [*specify*]] in respect of his allegation that on [*date*] the Company:

    dismissed him unfairly; and/*or*

    discriminated against him/her on the grounds of sex or race by (*give sufficient details to identify the particular complaint*); and/*or*

    made an unlawful deduction from his wages by (*give sufficient details to identify the particular complaint*); and/*or*

    took action short of dismissal against him relating to his trade union membership or activities by (*give sufficient details to identify the particular complaint*);

    (*or as the case may be*).[3]

3. The Employee accepts the payment made by the Company in full and final settlement of all other claims which he has or may

have against the Company arising out of his employment or the termination thereof, being claims in respect of which an employment tribunal has no jurisdiction [except any claims for damages for personal injury *or as the case may be*].][4]

4. The Employee acknowledges that, before signing this Agreement, he received independent legal advice from (*name of advisor*), [a qualified lawyer *or* certified union official *or* certified advice centre worker, *as the case may be*][5], as to the terms and effect of this Agreement and in particular its effect on his ability to pursue his rights before an employment tribunal.

5. The conditions regulating compromise agreements under the [Employment Rights Act 1996 *and/or* Sex Discrimination Act 1975 *and/or* Race Relations Act 1976 *and/or* Trade Union and Labour Relations (Consolidation) Act 1992 *and/or* Disability Discrimination Act 1995] are satisfied in relation to this Agreement.[6]

(Signed)

(Employee/Applicant):   Date:

(Employer/Respondent):   Date:

---

[1]   See ERA s 203(3)–(4); SDA s 77(4A)–(4C); RRA s 72(4A)–(4C); DDA s 9(3)–(4C); and TULRA s 288(2A)–(5), all as amended by ERDRA ss 9–10 and Sch 1. Although these statutes refer variously to both compromise *agreements* and compromise *contracts*, the difference in nomenclature is immaterial.

[2]   The agreement need not necessarily involve the payment of money, but may involve any other form of consideration, such as an undertaking to remove the cause of the employee's complaint.

[3]   It is to be noted that a compromise agreement must relate to 'the particular complaint' or 'the particular proceedings'. The Government's intention when introducing these provisions (originally enacted in TURERA was to ensure that the wide exclusionary words which it is possible to include in a conciliated settlement (e g 'all other claims which the employee has or may have arising out of the termination of his employment etc') should not be used in a compromise agreement so as to exclude other possible tribunal claims (see Hansard [HL] 6 May 1993, col 904). This has in fact been held to be the legal effect of the statutory provisions: *Lunt v Merseyside TEC Ltd* [1999] IRLR 458, [1999] ICR 17, EAT. However, as the same act by an employer may give rise to more than one complaint (eg unfair dismissal, race/sex discrimination), there is no reason why all such complaints, provided they have been raised by the employee, should not be disposed of in the one compromise agreement (see *Lunt*).

[4]   Such a paragraph is likely only to be appropriate where the employee has been dismissed. It is important to note that its value will be limited to the exclusion of claims over which a tribunal has *no* jurisdiction (see note 3 above); it will, therefore, only be relevant to exclude contractual claims which are capable of being brought in the civil courts. Contract claims, which may be

brought in employment tribunals under ETA s 3 and the Employment Tribunals Extension of Jurisdiction (England and Wales) Order 1994 SI 1994/1623 are *not* covered by compromise agreements (see ERA s 203(2)(*f*), ETA s 18(1)(*d*)).

5   Changes made by ERDRA enlarged the categories of person who could give independent legal advice in relation to compromise agreements. Originally it was limited to qualified lawyers, but this was extended by ERDRA to cover, in addition to barristers and solicitors, authorised advocates and litigators, and also officials of independent trade unions, and advice centre workers, who have been certified as competent to give advice and are authorised to do so on behalf of the union or centre respectively; all of these are 'relevant independent advisers' for the purpose of giving advice (see ERA s 203(3)–(4); SDA s 77(4B)–(4C); RRA s 72(4B)–(4C); DDA s 9(4)–(5); TULRA s 288(4)–(5). It is a requirement that the lawyer be identified in the agreement (see, for example, ERA s 203(3)(*e*)).

6   Such a statement must be made in the agreement (ERA s 203(3)(*f*); SDA s 77(4A)(*f*); RRA s 72(4A)(*f*); TULRA s 288(2B)(*f*); DDA s 9(3)(*c*)). Where complaints are made under more than one statute, it is important to state in the agreement that the conditions regulating compromise agreements have been satisfied in relation to each such statute (see *Lunt v Merseyside TEC Ltd* [1999] IRLR 458, [1999] ICR 17, EAT).

Index